"Even today Lady Idina Sackville could get tongues wagging. . . . A lively portrait of the UK-born troublemaker, a woman who took countless lovers, raised hell in England and Africa, inspired novels by Nancy Mitford and carried around a dog she named Satan. . . . Through [Idina's] story, we not only get a sexy and difficult-to-put-down read, we also get a good look at the shadow side of this prim and proper era and the real women who defied convention to live in it."

—Jessa Crispin, "Books We Like," NPR

"A racy romp underpinned by some impressive research."

—*The Sunday Telegraph* (London)

"Passionate and headstrong, Lady Idina was determined to be free even if the cost was scandal and ruin. Frances Osborne has brilliantly captured not only one woman's life but an entire lost society."

—Amanda Foreman, author of *Georgiana: Duchess of Devonshire*

"Told very much like a novel, *The Bolter* introduces readers to a world where every rule is broken and creating a scene is the latest fashion accessory."

—*The Daily Texan*

"Not only is it a beautifully written, intriguing chronicle of a frenetic, privileged, and profoundly sad life, it catches a social group and the madcap lives they led—so luxurious, so wasted. . . . Superb."

—Barbara Goldsmith, author of *Obsessive Genius* and *Little Gloria . . . Happy at Last*

"Drawing on family letters, Osborne's portrait creates sympathy not for Idina's reckless behavior but for the emotional emptiness that provoked her far-flung, self-defeating yet undeniably glamorous search for love."

—*More*

"Fascinating. . . . Beautifully written. . . . Frances Osborne brings the decadence of Britain's dying aristocracy vividly to life in this story of scandal and heartbreak."   —Simon Sebag Montefiore, author of *Young Stalin* and *Stalin: The Court of the Red Tsar*

"Sex, money, glamour, and scandal make Idina Sackville's story hard to put down. What brings that story to life is the courage of an incorrigibly stylish survivor. Searching for the woman behind the legend, Osborne [gives us] a heroine impossible to resist."

—Frances Kiernan, author of *The Last Mrs. Astor* and *Seeing Mary Plain: A Life of Mary McCarthy*

FRANCES OSBORNE

THE BOLTER

Frances Osborne was born in London and studied philosophy and modern languages at Oxford University. She is the author of *Lilla's Feast*. Her articles have appeared in *The Daily Telegraph*, *The Times*, *The Independent*, the *Daily Mail*, and *Vogue*. She lives in London with her husband, a Member of Parliament, and their two children.

www.francesosborne.com

ALSO BY FRANCES OSBORNE

Lilla's Feast

THE BOLTER

The
BOLTER

FRANCES OSBORNE

VINTAGE BOOKS

A DIVISION OF RANDOM HOUSE, INC. • NEW YORK

FIRST VINTAGE BOOKS EDITION, MAY 2010

Copyright © 2008 by Frances Osborne

All rights reserved. Published in the United States by Vintage Books,
a division of Random House, Inc., New York, and in Canada by
Random House of Canada Limited, Toronto. Originally published in
slightly different form in Great Britain as *The Bolter: Idina Sackville—
The Woman Who Scandalised 1920s Society and Became* White Mischief*'s
Infamous Seductress* by Virago Press, an imprint of Little, Brown Book
Group, London, in 2008, and subsequently published in hardcover
in the United States by Alfred A. Knopf, a division of
Random House, Inc., New York, in 2009.

A portion of this work originally appeared in *Vogue*.

The Library of Congress has cataloged the Knopf edition as follows:
Osborne, Frances.
The bolter / by Frances Osborne.—1st ed.
p. cm.
Originally published: London: Virago, 2008.
Includes bibliographical references.
1. Sackville, Idina. 2. Women—England—Biography. 3. Women—Sexual
behavior—England—History—20th century. 4. Colonists—Kenya—
Biography. 5. Women colonists—Kenya—Biography. I. Title.
CT788.S118083 2009
942.082092—dc22   {B} 2009003090

Vintage ISBN: 978-0-307-47642-5

Author photograph © Tony Buckingham
Book design by Iris Weinstein

www.vintagebooks.com

146975530

To my mother

Contents

The Marriages of Idina Sackville *viii*

List of Illustrations *ix*

Claridge's Hotel, Mayfair, 1934 *3*

BOOK ONE
Edwardian London *5*

BOOK TWO
Kenya—Happy Valley *131*

Notes *303*

Select Bibliography *319*

Acknowledgments *323*

Index *327*

THE MARRIAGES OF IDINA SACKVILLE

Gilbert Sackville
8th Earl De La Warr
b.1869 d.1915
m.1891 div.1902
m — Muriel Brassey
b.1872 d.1930

Herbrand "Buck"
9th Earl De La Warr
b.1900 d.1976
m1 — Diana Gerard Leigh
3 children
m2 — Sylvia
Viscountess Kilmuir

Avice "Avie"
b.1897 d.1985
m1 — Stewart Menzies
m2 — Frank Spicer

(MYRA) IDINA
b.26 Feb 1893
d.5 Nov 1955

m1 — (David) Euan Wallace
m.1913 div.1919

m2 — Charles Gordon
m.1919 div.1923

m3 — Josslyn Hay
22nd Earl of Erroll
m.1923 div.1929

m4 — Donald Haldeman
m.1930 div.1938

m5 — Vincent Soltau "Lynx"
m.1939 div.1945

Gerard Euan "Gee"
b.1915 d.1943
m — Elizabeth Koch
de Gooreynd

David John
b.1914 d.1944
m — Joan Prudence Magor
"Pru"

Diana Denyse Hay
"Dinan"
23rd Countess of Erroll
b.1926 d.1978
m1 — Sir (Rupert)
Iain Moncreiffe
of that Ilk
m2 — Raymond
Carnegie

Laura
b.1941
m1 — Dominic
Morland
m2 — Keith Fitchett

(Cary) Davina
b.1942
m — David Howell
later
Lord Howell
of Guildford

Merlin
24th Earl of Erroll
b.1948
m — Isabelle Hobler
4 children

Peregrine David Euan
b.1951
m — Miranda Fox-Pitt
6 children
(including a Euan
and an Idina)

Alexandra
b.1955
m — John Connell
3 children

Jocelyn
b.1966

Susie Butler
6 children

Sophy
b.1964
m — Mark Skeet
3 children

Daniel
b.1967
m — Kate Trinder
3 children

Frances
(the author)
b.1969
m — George Osborne
2 children

Kate
b.1970
m — Paul Bain
2 children

Toby
b.1975

---

m = marriages

Illustrations

ii (Frontispiece) Idina Sackville in the 1920s (author's photograph)

9 Idina Sackville standing between a pair of elephant tusks (courtesy of the 24th Earl of Erroll)

10 Idina as painted by Sir William Orpen in 1915

12 Nancy Mitford (Topfoto)

18 Idina and Euan's sons, Gerard ("Gee"), left, and David (author's photograph)

22 Idina's great-grandfather Thomas Brassey (Getty Images)

23 Idina's grandparents Annie and Tom Brassey Jr. (courtesy of Bexhill Museum)

25 Annie and children pulling specimens out of the South Seas (courtesy of Bexhill Museum)

27 Gilbert Sackville (courtesy of Bexhill Museum)

27 Muriel (née Brassey) (courtesy of Bexhill Museum)

34 Idina, her sister, and her brother in their pony cart, drawn by miniature Shetland ponies bred by their mother (courtesy of the 11th Earl and Countess De La Warr)

35 Idina; her sister, Avie; and their brother, Buck (courtesy of the 11th Earl and Countess De La Warr)

42 Idina the debutante, February 1913

48 Euan Wallace (author's photograph)

49 Idina's engagement photo

53 *Spy* cartoon of Idina's father, Earl De La Warr, the motoring enthusiast (author's photograph)

56 Kildonan House, Ayrshire (*The Builder* 124, 15 June 1923)

69 Idina and Euan's sons, David and Gerard ("Gee") Wallace

75 The *salon d'essayage* at Lanvin in Paris (courtesy of Lanvin)

85 Stewart Menzies, the best man at Idina and Euan's wedding (courtesy of the 24th Earl of Erroll)

88 Idina's gas-bag-powered Calcott car (*Illustrated London News*)

100–101 Euan Wallace and friends at Dunkeld, 1918 (all courtesy of the 24th Earl of Erroll)

119 Idina's friend the travel writer Rosita Forbes (*Appointment in the Sun*)

128 Euan and his sons after Idina's departure (courtesy of the 24th Earl of Erroll)

136 Idina's second husband, Charles Gordon (courtesy of the de Trafford family)

145 Euan Wallace and Barbie Lutyens on their wedding day (author's photograph)

149 Idina in the newspapers with the serval cat

154 Tallulah Bankhead (Getty Images)

160 Idina and her third husband, Joss Hay (courtesy of the 24th Earl of Erroll)

162 Idina and Joss on their wedding day (Topfoto)

166 Idina and Joss clearing ground (courtesy of the 24th Earl of Erroll)

169 Idina and Joss's house, Slains (courtesy of the 24th Earl of Erroll)

171 Idina with her Hispano-Suiza in Kenya

174 A Happy Valley picnic (courtesy of the 24th Earl of Erroll)

177 Idina and Joss (courtesy of the 24th Earl of Erroll)

183 Idina, Raymond de Trafford, Alice de Janzé, Joss (courtesy of the de Trafford family)

191 Oserian (courtesy of the de Trafford family)

192 Molly Ramsay-Hill (courtesy of the *East African Standard*)

193 Joss at Gilgil with Gerry and Kiki Preston and friend (courtesy of the 24th Earl of Erroll)

197 Idina and Alice in Idina's garden at Slains (author's photograph)

201 Raymond de Trafford and Alice de Janzé (courtesy of the de Trafford family)

217 Newspaper report of Idina's fourth marriage, to American
    Donald Haldeman (*Nevada State Journal*)
218 Donald and Idina's wedding (Planet News)
220 Clouds, the house Idina built when married to her fourth
    husband, Donald
222 Idina, dressed for a Rift Valley picnic with her friend Paula
    Gellibrand (courtesy of the late Robin Long)
224 Idina and her eight-year-old daughter, Diana Hay (courtesy
    Errol Trzebinski)
236 Idina's son David Wallace (author's photograph)
237 David Wallace (author's photograph)
240 The foyer of Claridge's Hotel, Mayfair (courtesy of Claridge's)
247 Kildonan House, Ayrshire, from the southwest (*The Builder*
    124, 15 June 1923)
248 Kildonan House (*The Builder* 124, 15 June 1923)
255 David traveling in Greece (author's photograph)
260 Idina's son David at his wedding to Pru Magor (author's
    photograph)
261 Idina at her fifth wedding, to Vincent Soltau ("Lynx") (author's
    photograph)
268 Joss's body in his Buick (courtesy of the 24th Earl of Erroll)
270 Dinan in her early teens (courtesy of the 24th Earl of Erroll)
273 David at home in England (author's photograph)
278 David Wallace's wife, Pru, and Idina's two granddaughters,
    Davina and Laura (author's photograph)
280 Idina's son Gerard Wallace, "Gee," at his wedding to
    Elizabeth Koch de Gooreynd (author's photograph)
288 Idina by one of her landscaped ponds in front of Clouds
    (courtesy of the 24th Earl of Erroll)
290 Portrait of Idina, 1922 (courtesy of the 24th Earl of Erroll)
293 Idina's brother, Buck (courtesy of the De La Warr Pavilion)
301 Idina Sackville (private collection)

THE BOLTER

Claridge's Hotel, Mayfair, 1934

DIARY OF DAVID WALLACE, AGED NINETEEN:

BALLIOL COLLEGE, OXFORD, FRIDAY 11 MAY 1934

Had letter from Sheila, saying had seen my mother, who wanted to meet me. All v. queer. . . . Not seen for 15 years. In some ways indifferent. Yet in others I long to see her. I certainly look forward to it immensely. I objectify it all, picture to myself. Young Oxford graduate, meeting mother after 15 years, moving scene, and not me.

BALLIOL COLLEGE, OXFORD, THURSDAY 17 MAY 1934

Letter from my mother; I knew it at once; suggesting meet Claridge's next week; had to write to Sheila to find out her name.[1]

On Friday, 25 May 1934, the forty-one-year-old Idina Sackville stepped into Claridge's Hotel in Mayfair shortly before a quarter to one. Her heels clipped across the hallway and she slipped into a chair in the central foyer. The tall, mirrored walls sent her back the reflection of a woman impeccably blond and dressed in the dernier cri from Paris, but alone. She turned to face the entrance and opened her cigarette case. In front of her, pairs of hats bobbed past with the hiss of a whisper—she remained, it was clear, instantly recognizable.

Idina tapped a cigarette on the nearest little table, slid it into her holder and looked straight ahead through the curling smoke. She was waiting for the red carnation that would tell her which man was her son.[2]

IT HAD BEEN TWO WEEKS since she had been told that David needed to see her, and a decade and a half since she had been banned from seeing him and Gee, his younger brother. All that time, she had stayed away. Had it been the right thing to do?

Would she do it the same way again?

That afternoon at Victoria Station when she had said good-bye to a husband she still loved was a lifetime behind her. And the reality of what that life might have been was minutes, maybe seconds, ahead. The cigarette finished, Idina lit another.

And then, as she leant forward, a disheveled young man came through the revolving doors. Six foot two, lean, she could see that he had her high cheekbones and unruly hair. His eyes, like Euan's, were a deep brown.

In his buttonhole was a red flower.

For a decade and a half Idina had been searching for something on the other side of the world. Perhaps, all along, here was where it had been.

BOOK ONE

EDWARDIAN LONDON

Chapter I

Thirty years after her death, Idina entered my life like a bolt of electricity. Spread across the top half of the front page of the *Review* section of the *Sunday Times* was a photograph of a woman standing encircled by a pair of elephant tusks, the tips almost touching above her head. She was wearing a drop-waisted silk dress, high-heeled shoes, and a felt hat with a large silk flower perching on its wide, undulating brim. Her head was almost imperceptibly tilted, chin forward, and although the top half of her face was shaded it felt as if she was looking straight at me. I wanted to join her on the hot, dry African dust, still stainingly rich red in this black-and-white photograph.

I was not alone. For she was, the newspaper told me, irresistible. Five foot three, slight, girlish, yet always dressed for the Faubourg Saint-Honoré, she dazzled men and women alike. Not conventionally beautiful, on account of a "shotaway chin," she could nonetheless "whistle a chap off a branch."[1] After sunset, she usually did.

The *Sunday Times* was running the serialization of a book, *White Mischief,* about the murder of a British aristocrat, the Earl of Erroll, in Kenya during the Second World War. He was only thirty-nine when he was killed. He had been only twenty-two, with seemingly his whole life ahead of him, when he met this woman. He was a golden boy, the heir to a historic earldom and one of Britain's most eligible bachelors. She was a twice-divorced thirty-year-old, who, when writing to his parents, called him "the child." One of them proposed in Venice. They married in 1924, after a two-week engagement.

Idina had then taken him to live in Kenya, where their lives dissolved into a round of house parties, drinking, and nocturnal wandering. She had welcomed her guests as she lay in a green onyx bath, then dressed in front of them. She made couples swap partners according to who blew a feather across a sheet at whom, and other games. At the end of the weekend she stood in front of the house to bid them farewell as they bundled into their cars. Clutching a dog and waving, she called out a husky, "Good-bye, my darlings, come again soon,"[2] as though they had been to no more than a children's tea party.

Idina's bed, however, was known as "the battleground." She was, said James Fox, the author of *White Mischief,* the "high priestess"[3] of the miscreant group of settlers infamously known as the Happy Valley crowd. And she married and divorced a total of five times.

IT WAS NOVEMBER 1982. I was thirteen years old and trans-fixed. Was this the secret to being irresistible to men, to behave as this woman did, while "walking barefoot at every available opportunity" as well as being "intelligent, well-read, enlivening company"?[4] My younger sister's infinitely curly hair brushed my ear. She wanted to read the article too. Prudishly, I resisted. Kate persisted, and within a minute we were at the dining room table, the offending article in Kate's hand. My father looked at my mother, a grin spreading across his face, a twinkle in his eye.

"You have to tell them," he said.

My mother flushed.

"You really do," he nudged her on.

Mum swallowed, and then spoke. As the words tumbled out of her mouth, the certainties of my childhood vanished into the adult world of family falsehoods and omissions. Five minutes earlier I had been reading a newspaper, awestruck at a stranger's exploits. Now I could already feel my great-grandmother's long, manicured fingernails resting on my forearm as I wondered which of her impulses might surface in me.

"Why did you keep her a secret?" I asked.

"Because"—my mother paused—"I didn't want you to think her a role model. Her life sounds glamorous but it was not. You can't just run off and . . ."

"And?"

"And, if she is still talked about, people will think you might. You don't want to be known as 'the Bolter's' granddaughter."

MY MOTHER WAS RIGHT to be cautious: Idina and her blackened reputation glistened before me. In an age of wicked women she had pushed the boundaries of behavior to extremes. Rather than simply mirror the exploits of her generation, Idina had magnified them. While her fellow Edwardian debutantes in their crisp white dresses merely contemplated daring acts, Idina went everywhere with a jet-black Pekinese called Satan. In that heady prewar era rebounding with dashing young millionaires—scions of industrial dynasties—Idina had married just about the

Idina as painted by Sir William Orpen in 1915

youngest, handsomest, richest one. "Brownie," she called him, calling herself "Little One" to him: "Little One extracted a large pearl ring—by everything as only she knows how," she wrote in his diary.[5]

When women were more sophisticated than we can even imagine now, she was, despite her small stature, famous for her seamless elegance. In the words of *The New York Times,* Idina was "well known in London Society, particularly for her ability to wear beautiful clothes."[6] It was as if looking that immaculate allowed her to behave as disreputably as she did. For, having reached the heights of wealth and glamour at an early age, Idina fell from grace. In the age of the flappers that followed the First World War, she danced, stayed out all night, and slept around more noticeably than her fellows. When the sexual scandals of Happy Valley gripped the world's press, Idina was at the heart of them. When women were making bids for independence and divorcing to marry again, Idina did so—not just once, but several times over. As one of her many in-laws told me, "It was an age of bolters, but Idina was by far the most celebrated."[7]

She "lit up a room when she entered it," wrote one admirer, "D.D.," in the *Times* after her death.[8] "She lived totally in the present," said a girlfriend in 2004, who asked, even after all these years, to remain anonymous, for "Idina was a darling, but she was naughty."[9] A portrait of Idina by William Orpen shows a pair of big blue eyes looking up excitedly, a flicker of a pink-red pouting lip stretching into a sideways grin. A tousle of tawny hair frames a face that, much to the irritation of her peers, she didn't give a damn whether she sunburnt or not.[10] "The fabulous Idina Sackville," wrote Idina's lifelong friend the travel writer Rosita Forbes, was "smooth, sunburned, golden—tireless and gay—she was the best travelling companion I have ever had . . ." and bounded with "all the Brassey vitality" of her mother's family.[11] Deep in the Congo with Rosita, Idina, "who always imposed civilization in the most contradictory of circumstances, produced ice out of a thermos bottle, so that we could have cold drinks with our lunch in the jungle."[12]

There was more to Idina, however, than being "good to look at

Nancy Mitford

and good company." She was a woman with a deep need to be loved and give love in return.[13] "Apart from the difficulty of keeping up with her husbands," continued Rosita, Idina "made a habit of marrying whenever she fell in love . . . She was a delight to her friends."[14]

Idina had a profound sense of friendship. Her female friendships lasted far longer than any of her marriages. She was not a husband stealer.[15] And above all, wrote Rosita, "she was preposterously—and secretly—kind."[16]

As my age and wisdom grew fractionally, my fascination with Idina blossomed exponentially. She had been a cousin of the writer Vita Sackville-West, but rather than write herself, Idina appears to have been written about. Her life was uncannily reflected in the writer Nancy Mitford's infamous character "the Bolter," the narrator's errant mother in *The Pursuit of Love, Love in a Cold Climate,* and *Don't Tell Alfred.* The similarities were strong enough to haunt my mother and her sister, two of Idina's grand-daughters. When they were seventeen and eighteen, fresh off the Welsh farm where they had been brought up, they were dispatched to London to be debutantes in a punishing round of dances, drinks parties, and designer dresses. As the two girls made their first tentative steps into each party, their waists pinched in Bellville Sassoon ball dresses, a whisper would start up and follow them around the room that they were "the Bolter's granddaughters," as though they, too, might suddenly remove their clothes.

In the novels, Nancy Mitford's much-married Bolter fled to Kenya, where she embroiled herself in "hot stuff . . . including horse-whipping and the aeroplane"[17] and a white hunter or two as a husband, although nobody is quite sure which ones she actually married. The fictional Bolter's daughter lives, as Idina's real daughter did, in England with her childless aunt, spending the holidays with an eccentric uncle and his children. When the Bolter eventually appears at her brother-in-law's house, she looks immaculate, despite having walked across half a continent. With her is her latest companion, the much younger, non-English-speaking Juan, whom she has picked up in Spain. The Bolter leaves Juan with her brother-in-law while she goes to stay at houses to which she cannot take him. "'If I were the Bolter,'" Mitford puts into the Bolter's brother-in-law's mouth, "'I would marry him.' 'Knowing the Bolter,' said Davey, 'she probably will.'"[18]

Like the Bolter, Idina famously dressed to perfection, whatever the circumstances. After several weeks of walking and climbing in the jungle with Rosita, she sat, cross-legged, looking "as if she had just come out of tissue paper."[19] And her scandals were manifold, including, perhaps unsurprisingly, a case of horsewhipping. She certainly married one pilot (husband number five) and almost married another.[20] There was a white-hunter husband who, somewhat inconveniently, tried to shoot anyone he thought might be her lover. And, at one stage, she found an Emmanuele in Portugal and drove him right across the Sahara and up to her house in Kenya. He stayed for several months, returning the same way to Europe and Idina's brother's house. Idina then set off on her tour of the few British houses in which she was still an acceptable guest, leaving the uninvited Emmanuele behind. This boyfriend, however, she did not marry.

Even before that, the writer Michael Arlen had changed her name from Idina Sackville to Iris Storm, who was the tragic heroine of his best-selling portrait of the 1920s, *The Green Hat,* played by Garbo in *A Woman of Affairs,* the silent movie version of the book.[21] Idina had been painted by Orpen and photographed by Beaton. Molyneux designed some of the first ever slinky, wraparound dresses for her, and her purchases in Paris were reported throughout the American press.[22] When Molyneux had financial difficulties, Idina helped bail him out. In return he would send her some of each season's collection, delicately ruffled silk dresses and shirts, in which she would lounge around the stone-and-timber shack of the Gilgil Club.

A FARM HALFWAY UP an African mountain is not the usual place to find such an apparently tireless pleasure-seeker as Idina. Clouds was by no means a shack: by African mountain standards it was a palace, made all the more striking by the creature comforts that Idina—who had designed and built the house—managed to procure several thousand feet above sea level. It was nonetheless a raw environment. Lethal leopard and lion, elephant and buffalo, roamed around the grounds of its working farm, where "Idina had built up one of the strongest dairy herds in Africa," according to a fellow farmer who used to buy stock from her.[23] Idina took farming immensely seriously, surprising the Kenyans who worked for her with her appetite for hard work. Like them, too, she camped out on safari for weeks on end. But then, as Rosita put it, Idina "was an extraordinary mixture of sybarite and pioneer."[24]

Up at Clouds, Idina filled her dining table with everyone visiting the house. She made no distinction between her friends and the people working for her, "including the chap who came to mend the gramophone etc."[25] The gin flowed. She was "always most hospitable . . . absolutely charming and put one completely at one's ease and I was bowled over by her," wrote an acquaintance.[26]

However, behind this hard work and high living lay a deep sadness.

When the poet Frédéric de Janzé described his friends (and enemies) in Kenya alphabetically, for Idina he wrote: "I is for Idina, fragile and frail." When Idina is described, sometimes critically, as living "totally in the present,"[27] it should be remembered that her past was not necessarily a happy place. Driving her wild life, and her second, third, fourth, and fifth marriages, was the ghost of a decision Idina made back in 1918, which had led to that fall from grace. On the day the First World War ended, she had written to her young, handsome, extremely rich first husband, Euan Wallace, and asked for a divorce. She then left him to go and live in Africa with a second husband, in comparison with Euan a penniless man. She went in search of something that she no longer had with Euan. And when, not long after, that second marriage collapsed, Idina was left to go on searching. In the words of Michael Arlen's Iris Storm, "There is one taste in us that is unsatisfied. I don't know what that taste is, but I know it is there. Life's best gift, hasn't someone said, is the ability to dream of a better life."[28]

Idina dreamt of that better life. Whenever she reinvented her life with a new husband, she believed that, this time round, she could make it happen. Yet that better life remained frustratingly just out of reach. Eventually she found the courage to stop and look back. But, by then, it was too late.

When she died, openly professing, "I should never have left Euan,"[29] she had a photograph of him beside her bed. Thirty years after that first divorce she had just asked that one of her grandsons—through another marriage—bear his name. Her daughter, the boy's mother, who had never met the ex-husband her mother was talking about, obliged.

At the end of her life, Idina had clearly continued to love Euan Wallace deeply. Yet she had left him. Why?

The question would not leave me.

MY MOTHER TOLD ME almost none of the above. In fact, she told me barely anything at all. She simply said that Idina's first marriage had been to her grandfather, Euan Wallace, and that Euan Wallace was, by all accounts, breathtakingly handsome, heartbreakingly kind, and as rich as Croesus. Their first child, David, had been my mother's father. A year later Euan and Idina had had another son, Gee. Idina had then gone to Africa, leaving the two boys. Euan married the famously beautiful eldest daughter of the architect Sir Edwin Lutyens and had three more sons. Later, within three years during the Second World War, Euan Wallace and four of his five sons, including my mother's father, had all died. My mother had been two years old, and had no memory of her father. None of the other sons had any children, including Billy, who was the only one to survive the war but died of cancer before the age of fifty. My mother had barely crossed paths with him, she said. The Wallace family had come to an abrupt end.

After this much, my mother raised a wall of noisy silence.

Idina was not, she said, a person to admire.

IN 1990, WHEN I WAS TWENTY-ONE, Billy Wallace's widow, Liz, died and we received a pile of photograph albums and some cardboard boxes. I sat on the floor of my parents' London sitting room and ferreted through them with my mother. The albums fell open to reveal endless pictures of Billy and his mother, Barbie, picnicking with the Royal Family; the princesses Elizabeth and Margaret as children outside Barbie's house; and a large black-and-white photograph of a young and beautiful Princess Margaret in the passenger seat of an open-topped car, Billy behind the wheel.

My eyes widened.

"Aah, is this why your paths didn't cross?"

My mother nodded. "Different lives," she added. "Now I need your help with this."

She lifted the lid off one of the cardboard boxes and scattered the contents on the floor. In front of me lay the photographs of five young Second World War officers. Their hair was slicked down under their caps, their skin unblemished, noses and cheekbones shining. The portraits were unnamed.

"There must," my mother continued, "be some way of working it out."

She could identify her father from the other photographs she had. She had also known Billy well enough to pick him out. The three who remained were all RAF pilots: bright-eyed, smiling pinup boys in their uniforms. They were my mother's uncles, Johnny, Peter, and Gee Wallace. Yet we didn't know who was who. Each one of them had died shortly afterward, and this was all of their brief lives that survived. Apart from my mother and her sister, who had been toddlers when they had died, the only relative left to ask was my mother's mother. And, even fifty years on, these deaths still upset her almost too deeply to raise the matter. After a couple of hours of puzzling, we slipped the pictures back into the mass grave of the box.

"I was only two when my father went," my mother murmured.

"Not went, died. Nobody left you. They all simply died, one by one."

There was a theory, my mother continued, that it was the pink house. Pink houses are unlucky. They moved into that pink house and then they all went.

I nodded. My mother was not having a logical moment. The best thing to do was to nod.

Then, softly, I broke in. "Idina didn't die then, though. Did you ever meet her, Mum?"

"No, I didn't."

"Why not?"

"Well, it would have been disloyal to Barbie, who brought up my father. In any case, Idina wasn't interested in my sister and me. She didn't care."

"Oh."

"She was not a nice woman."

"Why, Mum? You're not that old-fashioned. Just having a few lovers doesn't make you a bad person."

"Well, it's not exactly the best, or happiest, way to behave,

Idina and Euan's sons, Gerard ("Gee"), left, and David

but you're right, that didn't make her a bad person."

"Then what did?"

My mother turned and looked me straight in the eye. "My grandmother was a selfish woman, Frances. In 1918, when my father was four and his younger brother, Gerard, just three, she walked out on them and her devoted husband and disappeared to live in Kenya with someone else."

Then she went upstairs and came down again with another photograph. It was a black-and-white picture of two tiny boys in thick woolen and collared jerseys and knee-length shorts. Their hair has been tidied for the photograph but on each it is bounding back in its own direction. Instead of looking at the photographer, they are huddled next to each other, eyes wandering up and to the side.

It took me another decade and a half to realize the full horror of that photograph and what I had been told Idina had done. Another decade and a half of simmering fascination until, in the first years of this century, I had two small children of my own, of whom I possessed innumerable photographs standing side by side, at the same age that my grandfather and his brother had been when Idina had left. I thought of those little boys often at my own children's bedtime, which caused me to linger, casting excess kisses into my little ones' hair and giving in to their unending "Mummy, I need to tell you something. Just one last thing." Idina, the person whom I yearned most to meet in an afterlife, had, according to my mother, done something that now made me feel quite sick.

But Idina was beneath my skin.

Just as I was beginning to fear the wear and tear of time myself, stories came to me of Idina's ability to defy it. In her fifties, she showed not a trace of self-consciousness when removing her clothes; even after three children "she still had the full-breasted body of a thirty-five-year-old."[30] At parties, she would walk into a room, "fix her big blue eyes on the man she wanted and, over the course of the evening, pull him into her web."[31]

One evening, in the 1940s, Idina sauntered into the rustic bar in the Gilgil Club, where an officers' dance was in full swing. She slipped off her gold flip-flops and handed them to the barman, Abdul, asking him to "take these, and put them behind the bar," walked across the floor, showing off still-perfect size five feet, and folded herself on a pile of cushions next to the twenty-something girl who would later tell me this story. Idina raised her hand, always heavy with the bulbous pearl ring she wore, lit a cigarette, and, blowing immaculate smoke rings, informed the girl that "we share a boyfriend,"[32] making it clear that she held both a prior and a current claim that she did not intend to relinquish. The boyfriend in question was a twenty-four-year-old Army captain, thirty years younger than she was.

A great-grandmother sounds a long way away, but in Idina's case it was not. Most families grow into a family tree branching out in several directions. The family between Idina and me, however, had been pollarded until all that was left was my mother and her sister, and several ungainly stumps where living relations should have been. Far from driving me away from her, the horror of what Idina had done in leaving her children magnified my need to know why she had left a husband she loved, and what had happened to her afterward.

And, oddly, stories abounded of that kindness referred to by Rosita Forbes and also of a woman who exuded maternal affection, wearing a big heart on her sleeve. "While my parents were away," said one female friend, younger than Idina, "she looked after me so tenderly that I find it impossible to believe that she was anything but an adoring and excellent mother."[33] This same woman made Idina godmother to her eldest child. So what had made her bolt from a husband she loved? Was there a story behind it, or was it just some impulse, an impulse that one day might resurface in me?

EVENTUALLY MY MOTHER HANDED ME a large tin box containing Euan Wallace's diaries—a regimented set bound in blue and red—together with two worn briefcases overflowing with photographs and letters. Some were from Idina. She always wrote in pencil. She couldn't stand the mess of ink.

Her script was long and fluid, each letter the stroke of a violin bow, curling at the end. Her words, reaching across the page, thickened in my throat. "There is so little I can say for what are words when one has lost all one loves—thank God you have the children . . . How unutterably lonely you must be in your heart"—her words to her daughter-in-law trembled upon her son's death.[34] Even within the breezeless still of a shuttered dining room, I held her letters tight, folded them, put them back in a pile weighted down, lest they should flutter away.

And out of these, and the attics of several other people's houses and minds, tumbled the story of a golden marriage slowly torn apart during the First World War, and a divorce that reverberated throughout Idina's life and still does today.

Chapter 2

The first upheaval in Idina's life came early. She was four years old and her younger sister, Avice, called by all Avie at most, and Ave at worst, had just been born. Their mother, Muriel, exhausted from childbirth and her breasts overflowing with milk, was therefore not at her most sexually active. Idina's father chose that moment to leave her for a cancan dancer.

Gilbert Sackville, Idina's father and the eighth Earl De La Warr (pronounced Delaware) left the manor house in which he was living with his family in Bexhill-on-Sea. He moved a couple of streets away and into another property he owned. In this second house he installed the "actress" whom he had first espied through a haze of whisky and cigar fumes in the music hall on the seafront; a seafront which had been heavily subsidized with his wife's family's money. The year was 1897.

Idina's parents had married each other for entirely practical reasons. Idina's mother, Muriel Brassey, had wanted to become a countess. Gilbert, known as Naughty Gilbert to the generations that followed, had wanted Muriel's money.

In a society that valued the antiquity of families and their money, Gilbert's family was as old as a British family could be. Eight hundred years earlier they had followed William the Conqueror over from Normandy and been given enough land to live

*Idina's great-grandfather
Thomas Brassey*

off the rent without having to put their hands to earning another penny. This is what was expected and, with just a couple of exceptions, in the intervening centuries the family had done an immensely respectable little other than live off the fat income generated by its vast estates. The exceptions were two crucial flashes of glory in the now United States. One Lord De La Warr had rescued the starving Jamestown colonists in 1610, had been made governor of Virginia, and then had given his name to the state of Delaware. Another ancestor had been an early governor of New York, earning the earldom as a reward. But these men of action aside, Gilbert's family had been remarkably quiet and, after eight hundred years, the money was running out.

Muriel's family money had, in contrast, been made very recently and in the far less respectable middle-class activity of "Trade," as it was snootily referred to by the upper classes who did not have to earn a living. And Muriel's family's Trade was now, far from discreetly, crisscrossing Britain in brand-new thick black lines. Muriel's grandfather, Thomas Brassey, had employed eighty-five thousand men, more than the British Army, and had built one in every three miles of the railways laid in his lifetime. He had been an extraordinary man, for, despite the vast number of his employees, he had employed no secretary. Instead he had gone everywhere, even for a country walk, with a writing case, insisting that all correspondence be brought to him personally and immediately—even if he was standing in a field. He had opened each letter upon receipt and then sat down and composed an equally immediate reply. In the process he had made more

Idina's grandparents Annie and Tom Brassey Jr.

money than any other self-made Englishman in the nineteenth century. Upon his death, in 1870, his financial estate, excluding any of his properties, was 6.5 million pounds, "the largest amount for which probate has been granted under any one will," as Lord Derby wrote.[1]

Muriel's own parents, Thomas Junior and Annie, had also pushed the boundaries of the world in which they lived. Annie was plagued by chest infections throughout England's damp winters. Rather than spend the winter months lingering in a deck chair in a hotel in the South of France, she decided to turn this handicap to her advantage and travel more adventurously. By the time that Thomas Senior died and bequeathed Idina's grandparents a share of his substantial fortune, Annie had already traveled extensively in the Near East. She recorded her adventures with the recently invented photographic camera. Now in possession of near limitless funds, she commissioned the building of one of the world's largest private steam yachts, the *Sunbeam*. The specifications included a library of no less than four thousand books and a schoolroom. Breaking with Victorian traditions of keeping children out of sight, her four surviving children moved on board; the youngest was barely a year old. Annie had long suffered from debilitating seasickness, but she was determined to ignore it, and started on a voyage that would make her the first person to circumnavigate the globe by steam yacht. The *Sunbeam* was 157 feet in length and had both captain and commander, a resident doctor, and even an artist—as well as a crew of thirty-three. The journey that Idina's grandparents embarked upon took eleven months. The *Sunbeam* set sail from Southampton, England, on 1 July 1876 and traveled west across the Atlantic to Rio de Janeiro, which it reached by mid-August. Thomas Junior and his son, also Thomas, then returned to England. The son went back to school at Eton, the father went back to Parliament, to which Annie had dispatched him to promote the cause of female suffrage. Over the next nine months, Annie and her three daughters, Muriel, Mabelle, and Marie, visited, among other countries, Brazil and Chile. They rounded the Strait of Magellan at the tip of South America, spent Christmas and New Year's in Hawaii, a further month in Japan, weeks in China and Sri Lanka—all interspersed with months at sea—before slipping up the Suez Canal and through the Mediterranean and back to the British holiday resort of Hastings. The five-year-old Muriel and her siblings had thus spent formative days quite literally being washed overboard and rescued as they collected botanical specimens in the South Seas, and their evenings climbing volcanoes to feast with local chieftains and, in between, learning to scrub the decks. Annie kept a detailed diary of these adventures, which she published under the title *A Voyage in the "Sunbeam."* The book was a success—partly, perhaps, because the trip had not been without incident. The *Sunbeam* caught fire three times, including one long, terrifying blaze that lasted all night, recounted in detail by Annie. In the Magellan Strait, she and the girls had come across a cargo ship carrying coal that had started to burn. Almost as soon as the fifteen-man crew had been hauled up onto the *Sunbeam* their vessel burst into flames. *A Voyage in the "Sunbeam"* was also packed full of the domestic detail of traveling for so long with a young family on board. The book was reprinted and published in several editions in the United States and Canada and was translated into several languages.[2]

Idina's mother and aunts were catapulted into worldwide celebrity, accustoming them to living in the glare of publicity. In Muriel's case, this appeared to have a lasting effect. Seven years old when *A Voyage in the "Sunbeam"* was published, she was

Annie and children pulling specimens out of the South Seas

almost too young to remember any other way of living. When in adult life she was faced with decisions that most of her contemporaries would have shied away from for fear of drawing unwelcome attention from the newspapers, Muriel barely blinked and steamed ahead.

Annie went on to travel for a further decade. In 1887 she died of malaria, off the coast of Mauritius. However, even from beyond the grave, she appeared to live on. A quarter of a century after it was first published, *A Voyage in the "Sunbeam"* was used as a school textbook—and it is still in print today.[3] Annie's husband, Thomas, went on with the crusade she had set him: using his parliamentary position to argue for votes for women.

Thomas Brassey was a member of the British Liberal party, known as the Whigs, whose leader was the morally austere William Gladstone. Gladstone is regarded alongside Winston

Churchill as one of Britain's greatest prime ministers—an office that he held four times. However, he is also known for his curious private life, in which he practiced self-flagellation and invited prostitutes into his home, as he explained, to talk them out of their profession. Gladstone believed in the extension of suffrage, but only to a wider group of men, not to women. Thomas Brassey sought to persuade Gladstone otherwise.

To that purpose he entertained Gladstone and his entire Cabinet at Normanhurst Court, his sprawling mock-French château in Sussex, and at his double-width house in Park Lane. At the back of the latter he had put up a two-story Indian palace, known as the Durbar Hall, bought from a colonial exhibition in London. He used it to display the trophies Annie had collected from her travels and, after her death, proudly opened it to the public twice a week. And, by the time Muriel married Gilbert, her father, Thomas Brassey, son of a railway builder, Member of Parliament, had become Sir Thomas, then Lord Brassey, and was on his way to being an earl himself.

But he still wasn't grand enough for Gilbert's parents. Eight hundred years on, the Sackvilles remained ardent courtiers. Their darling son had, after all, been a childhood playmate of the next king but one[4] and should not be marrying into a nonaristocratic family who had been obliged to make their money in Trade. Even more upsetting for them was that this Trade and the newness of the Brassey money were so obviously displayed. For a start there was all the soot and dirt and steam of the railways. And then there was Normanhurst Court, with all its bright-red brick, ornate ironwork, gratuitous church spire, general Francophilia, and even its name, reeking of ill-judged effort. And it was right on the De La Warrs' doorstep in Sussex: the two families vied constantly over who should be Mayor of Bexhill. The old Earl and Countess De La Warr refused to attend their son's wedding.

Thus disapproved of, Idina's parents had careered through their marriage at speed. Idina arrived within a year. She was named after the wife of Muriel's brother, Tom, but was fashionably given a first name, Myra, by which she would never be

Idina's father, Gilbert Sackville, and her mother, Muriel (née Brassey)

called. By the time Idina was three, Muriel, like her own mother, was herself pushing the boundaries of traditional society by opening Britain's first mixed-sex sea-bathing area at Bexhill; hitherto men and women had been separated not just by balloonesque bathing dresses and machines, but beaches too. And, together with her husband, she had started racing the brand-new motorcars along the seafront. That same year, Gilbert's father, perhaps reeling from the shock of all these modern goings-on, died. Gilbert therefore inherited the title of Earl De La Warr and Muriel became a countess.

The following year, Muriel's second child, Avie, was born and her husband left. Three years after that, in 1900, Muriel surprisingly gave birth to her husband's son and heir, Herbrand, called Buck as a shortening of his earl-in-waiting title of Lord Buckhurst. She then, as if to prove her parents-in-law's prejudices right, launched what was seen as an attack upon the upper-class establishment by divorcing Gilbert.

For Muriel, divorce promised both practical and political progress. Practical because divorce would prevent Gilbert from spending any more of her money on other women. Political in that it would show that a woman need not be tied to an unsatisfactory husband.

For Idina, however, her parents' divorce would be less beneficial. It set the example that an unsatisfactory husband could be divorced and introduced her to the idea that husbands and parents can leave. Both patterns of behavior Idina herself would repeat, while reaching out for constant physical reassurance that she herself would not be left alone.

For a young child of divorced parents in Edwardian England, life was not easy. The divorce immediately set Idina and her siblings well apart from their peers, for it was, in 1901, extremely rare—even though, among a significant tranche of the Edwardian upper classes, adultery was rife. Along with hunting, shooting, fishing, and charitable works, adultery was one of the ways in which those who did not have to work for a living could fill their afternoons. The term "adultery" is chosen carefully, for it applies only to women who were married. And it was married, rather than unmarried, women who were likely to pass the couple of hours between five and seven (known as a *cinq à sept*) in the pattern set by Queen Victoria's pleasure-loving son, King Edward VII, and his coterie of friends. This group had been named the Marlborough House Set after the mansion Edward had entertained in as the Prince of Wales before becoming king.

The choice of this hour of the day was purely practical. It took some considerable time for a lady to unbutton and unlace her layers of corsets, chemises, and underskirts, let alone button and lace them up again. Lovers therefore visited just after tea, when ladies were undressing in order to exchange their afternoon clothes for their evening ones.

Where the King went, society tended to follow. If he took mistresses among his friends' wives, then so could and would those of his minions with both the time and the inclination (although many remained appalled by his behavior). Married women were safer. First, they were not going to trap a man into marriage. Second, if they became pregnant, the child could be incorporated within their existing family. For this reason a married woman was expected to wait until she had produced two sons for her husband ("an heir and a spare") before risking introducing somebody else's gene pool among those who might inherit his property—thus "adulterating" the bloodline.

As long as a high-society married woman followed these rules of property protection and kept absolute discretion, she could do what she liked. In the oft-cited words of the actress Mrs. Patrick Campbell, "it doesn't matter what you do in the bedroom as long as you don't do it in the street and frighten the horses." The boundary between respectability and shame was not how a woman behaved, but whether she was discovered. If she was, her husband could exercise his right to a divorce: for a man to divorce his wife, she had to be proved to have committed adultery.

A woman who wanted a divorce, however, not only had to be wealthy enough to support herself afterward but also needed to prove one of a handful of extreme grounds. A man's infidelity counted for nothing, since any illegitimate children he produced would stay outside both the marriage and inheritance rights. A woman who wanted to escape an unhappy marriage had therefore to choose between two equally difficult options. The first was to prove not only that her husband had committed adultery but that the adultery was incestuous or that he had committed bigamy, rape, sodomy, bestiality, or cruelty, or had deserted her for two years or more. Or she had to be branded an adulteress herself.

Even if she was the innocent party, a woman who obtained a divorce faced exclusion from the somewhat hypocritically bedhopping high society. She was seen as spoiling everyone else's entitlement to fun, because once affairs had the potential to lead to divorce, the stakes of illicit sex were dangerously upped. And, by taking a case through the divorce courts, she opened her bedroom door to the eyes of anybody who could read a newspaper. The reaction of Queen Victoria to her son's being called as a witness in a divorce case summed up the upper classes' fear of divorce: his "intimate acquaintance with a young married woman being publicly proclaimed will show an amount of imprudence which cannot but damage him in the eyes of the middle and lower classes."[5]

Countless scandals bubbled just below the public's line of vision, and that is where, on the whole, they were kept. Unhappy couples were expected to put up with it, quietly arranging their lives to live apart if necessary. Before the First World War, only in the very worst, unavoidably public cases did couples part, in the process miring both themselves and their children in scandal.

Idina's parents did.

Muriel cited adultery and abandonment. Gilbert and his can-can dancer were spending her money like water. In order to prove her case she had to write to her husband begging him for the restoration of "all my rights as a wife" and offering to live with him. After "careful consideration," Gilbert replied immediately, by return of post, that he would not.[6] When the case was heard, the newspapers printed both letters in full. For a countess with one of England's oldest titles to divorce her earl was scandal enough to shake the foundations of British society, and Idina found that, even though her mother was legally the wronged party, her childhood friends were no longer allowed to come and play with her. Now nine, Idina was old enough both to miss her friends and to realize that it was some change in her family life that had taken them from her. At least she had her cousins to keep her company. In this she was lucky. Muriel's two sisters, Mabelle and Marie, had both had sons, Jack and Gerard, within a few months of Idina's birth. And, after Annie's death, Thomas Brassey, Jr., had married again, producing a daughter, Helen, just six months older than Idina. This small group might have been enough for a childhood. However, if she wanted to find a husband, when she reached eighteen Idina would have to make her way into the society of the outside world. And then, unlike her peers from conventional families, she would have to battle for acceptance in order to succeed.

AFTER THE DIVORCE, Muriel moved her children out of the small manor house she had occasionally shared with Gilbert and into the countryside nearby. Five miles down the road from the medieval De La Warr stately home, which Gilbert had been forced to rent to a family of newly rich bankers, she bought a nearly identical house and called it Old Lodge. She surrounded Old Lodge with a picturesque farm and became a champion breeder of diminutive black-hided Kerry cattle. While Gilbert married twice more, Muriel never married again. She had enough money of her own not to need the burden of a husband. She did, however, devote the rest of her life to another man: the future leader of the Labour Party, George Lansbury.

Lansbury's father had been one of Muriel's grandfather's huge workforce. Muriel and Lansbury shared a fervent belief in female suffrage and Muriel rapidly added trade-union rights to her quiver of causes. She opened Old Lodge to Lansbury and his other campaigning friends, such as Beatrice and Sidney Webb. Hitherto it had been widely argued that people were poor because they were morally inadequate. Now the Webbs were proposing the near-revolutionary thesis that people were poor as a result of how the economy was organized. In due course the Trades Union Congress decided to field its own parliamentary candidates for election, creating the Labour Party, and in 1910 George Lansbury was elected Labour Member of Parliament for Bow and Bromley.

Muriel worked hard. Pound by pound she siphoned money out of her own pockets and those of her friends, including the American railroad families the Osborns and the Dodges, to whom the Brasseys had become very close. This was used to pay for strikers' and suffragettes' food, bail, and printing costs and, when necessary, to keep the trade unions' mouthpiece, the *Daily Herald* (now the *Sun*), afloat—at one stage funding an outright buyout for Lansbury. She also hosted key meetings between Lansbury and the leading militant suffragettes, the women of the Pankhurst family. In his autobiography, Lansbury wrote:

Of all the women, outside those belonging to my family and the working classes, whom I have known and worked with, none stands higher in my memory and esteem than

Muriel, Countess De La Warr. I never heard her make a speech, though she must have attended hundreds of public meetings and many private gatherings of committees.

Over and over again her friends saved the Daily Herald from death in the old days when it was independent, and often it was her example and her work which helped women suffragists to hold on in the darkest days of defeat.

Her love for human rights and duties kept her very largely out of society. She spent her days almost secretly doing good. Many, many people like myself owe her a big debt of gratitude for the continuous help she gave to causes in which we worked.[7]

Lansbury was a married man. Muriel is said to have had an affair with him. This may have been the only explanation society could find for her politics, but Muriel and Lansbury certainly spent several decades in a close working partnership. And, during this time, Muriel's former sister-in-law and Idina's aunt, Margaret Sackville, was having an affair with the future socialist prime minister Ramsay MacDonald. It was all very cozy. In 1923, MacDonald would put Idina's younger brother, Buck, into his first government.

But the coziness may have started even earlier. For it was and still is a suspicion among some of the family that Buck, conceived remarkably close to Gilbert's departure for South Africa in 1899 and some two years after he had taken up with the first of his cancan dancers, may have been Lansbury's, or even some other man's, son. And upon his return to England after Buck's birth, Gilbert did not move back home.

Muriel then took to a new religion. Her mother had brought her up to pursue two things: the vote for women and scientific knowledge. Muriel now made her own mark by breaking away from the latter dramatically. She took up with an Irishwoman called Annie Besant, who was in the process of attempting to overturn almost every convention she encountered. Besant, who had long been separated from her own husband, had been an advocate of Marxism, then social democracy. She had organized a groundbreaking strike by the young women working for the match manufacturer Bryant and May, in which she succeeded in helping them improve their pay and conditions. She had then been put on trial for publishing a book advocating birth control. She was freed on appeal, but the court case had lost her her own children; full custody of them was given to her estranged husband. She then published a book, *The Law of Population*.[8] This also argued for birth control, and declared that abundant recreational sex within a marriage was healthy for women.

In the late 1870s, when *The Law of Population* was published, it ran in direct contradiction to the belief of the Victorian establishment that women did not and should not enjoy sex, which was considered an unavoidable moment of regrettable bestiality unfortunately necessary to produce children. The work was condemned in the *Times* as "an indecent, lewd, filthy, bawdy and obscene book." Besant, who rapidly became one of Muriel's closest friends, continued to preach her views; her audience included the adolescent Idina. Despite the scandals, Besant was nonetheless elected to the London School Board in 1889. In the same year, she converted to the cult of Theosophy. Theosophy had been brought to Europe in the late nineteenth century by a Ukrainian mystic, Madame Blavatsky. The underlying principle of Theosophy, a combination of Hinduism and Buddhism, was that the dogmas of revealed religion had corrupted pure communication with God. Within a very few years, Besant was president of the British Theosophical Society, and Muriel followed her into the cult.

Theosophy was widely recognized but was veiled in scandal on several counts. One was its association with Besant. Another was its link to Besant's former publishing partner Charles Leadbeater, who had also become a Theosophist. Besant and Leadbeater declared themselves clairvoyant, and said that they were searching for the New Messiah, who would be a young boy whom their clairvoyancy would enable them to identify. Shortly afterward, Leadbeater was accused of interfering with the sons of Theosophists and had to flee to India to escape arrest. Besant remained in Britain and, perhaps spotting the depth of Muriel's

*Idina, her sister, and her brother in their pony cart, drawn by miniature
Shetland ponies bred by their mother*

open purse, suggested that Idina's brother, Buck, might be the
New Messiah. Muriel was attracted to the reforming zeal of the
Theosophists, and their acceptance of her despite her divorce.
She went along with the plans for Buck to be anointed, and
funded whatever was required.

Muriel was not alone in her conversion to Theosophy. Lady
Emily Lutyens, daughter of the Earl of Lytton and wife of the
leading British architect, Sir Edwin Lutyens, was also a keen
Theosophist. The late nineteenth century had seen a vogue for
spiritualism, with fashionable parties procuring a mystic for
postprandial entertainment, which often included table-turning.
Theosophy caught this wave of fashion.

By 1911 Besant's society had sixteen thousand members.
Besant and Leadbeater had changed their minds about the New
Messiah. In a move that managed not to offend Muriel or any
of the society's other keen donors who had sons in the running
for the title, they chose an eleven-year-old Brahmin boy from

India, called Krishna-murti. Muriel, her own son rejected, nonetheless deepened her bonds with Theosophy. She offered Krishnamurti a home at Old Lodge with her children—all of whom, including Idina, were still living there.

All these political, social, sexual, and religious theories had inevitably played a huge part in Idina's childhood. While Muriel ricocheted between London and Sussex, preoccupied with politics and religion, the

From left to right: Idina; her sister, Avie; and their brother, Buck

formal part of the children's education had been looked after in the upstairs schoolroom by a golden-hearted governess, Miss Rowden, whom Idina, Avice, and Buck called Rowie or Row and visited until the day she died.[9] After the morning's lessons were over, the afternoons had been spent on rumbustious ponies, careering through picturesque fields and either over or through their bottle-green hedges. Then, from teatime on, after most other Edwardian children had been banished back to the upper reaches of their homes, Idina and, as soon as they were old enough, her siblings, had remained in the drawing room, where they were plunged into the cut and thrust of the politics of the day. All grew up able to maintain a conversation with anyone, about anything.

Despite the social fallout from the divorce, it had been a childhood that Idina clearly enjoyed. And, later, the moment she had an opportunity to build a house for her own family, she built one that bore more than a passing resemblance to Old Lodge. But then, having spent her adolescence debating workers' and women's rights with the politicians of the day, in her mid-teens Idina had been sent to board at a "finishing school"—an institution where girls with ink-stained fingers were transformed into future society hostesses.

School was not an enjoyable place for Idina. After the discussions she had become used to at home, she had found her fellow pupils intellectually disappointing and quickly earned a reputation for being "already precociously educated and easily bored."[10] But these girls and their lifestyle and traditions were part of the environment in which Idina would make her way when she left school and joined the adult world, which she did just after Krishnamurti arrived at Old Lodge.

The "way" for both Idina and her colleagues was to make themselves as attractive as possible and to marry well. These, after all, were the only means by which they would be able to determine the lives ahead of them. Idina had to have been very aware of the shadow cast over her by her parents' divorce, but she clearly decided that she wanted to close the gap between herself and her contemporaries and she made the most of what she had in the marriage market that awaited her. She may not have been a natural beauty—that shotaway chin haunted her—but she had high cheekbones and, above them, a pair of wide, blue, bedroom eyes. Knowing that if she wanted to succeed in making men fall in love with her she needed to make the most of her appearance by dressing beautifully, she used the funds at her disposal to do so. She enjoyed the process, teaching herself how to walk and stand so that the folds of material hung just so, making her clothes, as they should, appear a second skin. And, thus dressed, Idina shone among her peers. She had "a much-envied gift for wearing clothes attractively," as the *Daily Express* would later write. "It has been remarked of her that the simplest gown becomes distinguished when she puts it on."[11] Yet all that precocious education and easy boredom rapidly led to a potentially sharp tongue. Idina soon learnt that she could make other girls "terrified" of her.[12] And years later, when a former classmate and new arrival in Kenya approached her with a "Do you remember me, we were at school together?," the sharpness would still be there. Idina turned to her, half smiled, and replied, "Oh, yes, you never powdered."[13]

Idina, it was clear, was never going to meld with the other girls around her. However, she was now armed with a fast wit and the ability to turn every head in the room. If she could not join them, she would beat them: she would take the few advantages nature had given her and make herself the most attractive young woman in town.

The wave of change of the Edwardian age had begun, along with its political causes, a fashion for female independence. The age of chaperones had more or less vanished. Young women whose fathers could afford to keep them in style stayed single. They traveled the world, attended lectures and political meetings, bought motorcars, hung around in groups, smoked, and stayed out late at friends' houses, listening to the gramophone. And they had boyfriends, known as dancing partners. Unmarried, they didn't dare go all the way, for fear of becoming pregnant. But that still left open a wide field of sexual behavior—usually limited to the back of motor taxis since they still lived with their parents in their families' London town houses. But for the "Saturday-to-Monday," as Edwardian weekend house parties were known, the young could rely on the older generation's exodus to the countryside.

Nonetheless, real freedom came only with marriage. In families where there were any boys to leave money to, most of it went to them. When girls were left money, they were not usually allowed access to the capital until they married. A young woman who wanted to buy or rent her own house therefore needed a husband either so that she could access her own money or so that he could pay for it.

In Idina's case, joining the marriage market was far from straightforward. The slurry of scandals in which her parents wallowed threatened to muddy the white of her dress. Socialism, suffrage, and divorce had combined to earn Muriel a reputation as a "class traitor."[14]

The first hurdle for Idina was practical. Muriel had been presented at Court herself but, as a divorcée, was now excluded.

In February 1911, Muriel therefore took Idina to London to stay with her sister Mabelle, now the Hon. Mrs. Egerton, in her house in the highly fashionable St. James's Place, on the very edge of Green Park.

Muriel adhered to what traditions she could. Mabelle presented Idina at Court and then cohosted with Muriel "a small dance"[15] for her at the Ritz. Mother and daughter returned to London again for the start of the Season at the beginning of May. Muriel put an announcement in the *Times:* "Muriel, Countess De La Warr and Lady Idina Sackville have arrived at 11, St. James's Place,"[16] indicating where invitations could be sent. Idina was "out."

And Britain was fractured with strikes. The gap between rich and poor was acute. While the wealthy and idle partied, workingmen struggled to feed their families on their weekly wages. In the East End of London, whose slums teemed with just short of a million inhabitants, more than three hundred thousand people lived in what was acknowledged to be extreme poverty. Here there was a single, and inevitably unpleasant, lavatory for every twenty-five households, along with one trickling standpipe, its meager flow of water slowed yet further by the drought settling in to rainless Britain. As the heat in the shade rose to more than 100 degrees Fahrenheit and temperatures in the sun were melting lead at 130 degrees, the stench in these slums rose, fostering unrest. In the summer of 1911, this disquiet over the irregularity of employment (and the fact that the jobs that were available were low-paid, with nothing extra for overtime) found a voice in a man called Ben Tillett. Tillett had been born the son of an alcoholic cart polisher but had succeeded in educating himself in the evenings after work not only to read and write but to do so in ancient Greek and Latin as well. He was now the leader of the union of dockworkers, the men who unloaded Britain's numerous ships and kept the harbors they berthed in open. Shipping provided island Britain with crucial contact with the outside world. The threat of a dockworkers' strike was a threat of ceasing all international trade and halting much-needed food supplies to Britain. In addition to this the British government was acutely aware that Tillett could call on the support of the railway union. A rail strike would hit Britain hard, interrupting the transportation of goods and, more important, food, around the country.

Eventually, in the middle of the Royal Ascot racing week, the high point of the British upper classes' social season, Tillett called a strike, dramatically preventing a vast new transatlantic liner, the *Olympic*, from sailing. By the end of the week dockworkers all over the country were on strike. The bustling, noisy harbors of Britain were ominously silent. Even the wharfside cranes on the River Thames, whose long bridges usually rose and fell throughout the day, were still. Instead the dockworkers took to the streets; the wide merchant avenues of Britain's port cities filled with the million laborers who had created their wealth. In London, the strikers marched on Trafalgar Square—as the gunmakers of St. James's Street and Pall Mall sold out in forty-eight hours. In early August, the railway workers went on strike. Riots began to break out among demonstrators, followed by widespread looting, leading some to fear that Britain was on the verge of revolution. A 2,300-man warship was sent to moor just outside the Liverpool docks, and in London, detachments of troops camped in Hyde Park, ready for action. Finally, the prime minister, Lloyd George, asked the dockworkers to reopen the ports, calling on their patriotism in the face of Germany's recent territorial move of sending a warship to the strategically positioned country of Morocco. As British society trembled, Idina's mother and George Lansbury very publicly acted—for the strikers.

By mid-August it was over. Wages were raised, and the dock owners gave guarantees of regular employment. Britain slowly jolted back to normal.

Meanwhile, Idina and her fellow debutantes were fully absorbed by the trial of staying cool in rib-crushing and stifling corsets as they attended the round of dances varying from Idina's small do to the Duke and Duchess of Devonshire's ball for several hundred.

Idina, however, breezed through both the heat and the dictates of fashion. She quickly worked out what suited her and how to wear it. When it came to the dances, having grown up with her male cousins as almost her only friends at home, she was very much at ease with the opposite sex. And sex, or rather sex appeal, was what Idina, both confident yet longing to be reassured and thus willing to go a little further toward extremes than anyone else, promised from every pore.

Where convention demanded cool reserve, Idina threw herself into the rounds of debutantes' *bals blancs* with abandon. Nobody forgot a dance with her—her partners were still recounting those moments to her children thirty years later.[17] Idina was followed by the newspapers even in the United States, being pictured alongside extraordinary combinations of Prime Minister Asquith's daughter and the leading actresses and showgirls of the day[18] and being written up by papers as far away as the *Oakland Tribune* as "very accomplished" and "a great favorite of Society."[19]

But Idina perhaps pushed boundaries a little too far. The constant company of Satan, the black Pekinese tucked under her arm, may have been too much for many. And, dazzling as she was, Idina was nonetheless not entirely proper. Whereas British society has always adored the eccentrics whose differences celebrate the values they cherish, it has been less keen on those who might upset the extremely comfortable order of things. Idina was of the latter set. For as Idina danced, her mother's support for both the Socialist George Lansbury and the strikes crippling Britain immersed Idina in further scandal.

Even during her first Season in London, this showed through. The desire for political change had been very firmly ingrained in Idina's upbringing. Between debutante dances she returned to Old Lodge and its maelstrom of ideas and, in July 1911, she cofounded the East Grinstead Women's Suffrage Society. And, by the end of the Season, although she had been a "success" as a debutante, she was not yet engaged to be married.

Rather than let her daughter appear secondhand by doing the same social round again the following year, Muriel packed Idina off to the United States. On 30 August 1911, Idina sailed to New York on the *Olympic,* released by the strikers.

It was a glittering voyage. Every cabin was full[20] and the passengers' fortunes were as vast as the new ship aboard which they were sliding across the Atlantic. Among them was a Miss Emilie Grigsby, who declared eight hundred thousand dollars' worth of extravagantly set diamonds, rubies, and pearls to the U.S. customs officials. Amid the storm of publicity that Miss Grigsby's arrival in New York caused, one of the other passengers, Mr. Carlisle, the chairman of Harland & Wolff, the shipbuilders who had constructed the *Olympic,* saw fit to boast that "the *Titanic,* a sister of the *Olympic,* would be ready next March to enter the Atlantic trade."[21]

Idina was accompanying a middle-aged couple, both of whom were scions of American industrial dynasties. William Church Osborn, who was heavily involved in New York politics, was the son of railroad entrepreneur William Henry Osborn, and both the grandson of another railman, Jonathan Sturges, and the nephew of the banker J. P. Morgan. Osborn's wife had been born Alice Dodge and her grandfather had been founder of the Phelps Dodge mining fortune. This had made enough money for one of the partners' widows to leave the impressive sum of more than thirty-six million dollars in her will.[22] Alice's sister, Mary, who never married, was one of Muriel's closest friends and the greatest donor to all her causes.

The Osborns were traveling with three of their four children: their two younger sons, Earl and William, and their daughter, Aileen, who was a few months older than Idina. When Idina arrived in New York she went to stay with Aileen's twenty-year-old cousin, Josephine Osborn.

Josephine had even more glamorous family connections than her cousin Aileen. Her father, Henry Fairfield Osborn, was William's brother but, rather than devote himself to politics, he had become a paleoanthropologist and was now president of the American Museum of Natural History. While Josephine's father absorbed himself in the past, her mother, Lucretia, who was the sister-in-law of another of J. P. Morgan's nephews, used her "spacious"[23] house on Madison Avenue to host a series of balls for family members.[24]

Josephine's own coming-out dance had been held at home two days before Christmas in 1908. Mother and daughter, in pink

Idina the debutante, as depicted in the newspapers, February 1913

chiffon and white satin, "received their guests in the ballroom entrance" at 11 p.m. The orchestra had been large enough to play "throughout the affair," the "dining and other rooms" took thirty tables at which each one of the three hundred guests had been seated for a 2 a.m. supper. Then the dancing resumed. The guests included Kermit and Ethel Roosevelt, children of the former president.[25]

Lucretia Osborn's coming-out dance for her niece Aileen, just a few months before Idina arrived, had been more modest. It was "small and informal," and the guests, who had "included a number of young married people and many of the debutantes," had been few enough to be fed in just three large dinner parties before arriving to dance at 10:30.[26] However, at the end of the autumn in which Idina arrived, her hostess threw a debutantes' dance for another niece, Josephine's cousin Sarah Spencer Morgan, the granddaughter of J. P. Morgan's sister, after whom she was named.

This dance, like Josephine's, was held just before Christmas, and the house was an explosion of seasonal decoration, "the staircase being festooned with greens and holly. The library and dining-hall . . . were decorated with cut flowers in vases, including hyacinths, carnations, lilies of the valley and American Beauty roses. The ceilings were hung with evergreen, broken by poinsettias."[27] The mass of red and green and polished wood and books, along with the sense of impending occasion and limitless wealth, must have given the house almost as charmed a period atmosphere as possible. Still, this, for the Fairfield Osborns, was a small dance, for the beautifully decorated library and dining hall were where the dancing was. The ballroom wasn't even needed.

Nonetheless, it was certainly an exciting evening for Idina. By now she had been in the city for almost four months, becoming "not unknown as a visitor in New York," as the *Washington Post* would later write.[28] It was long enough to collect a chain of admirers, and this dance, at the house in which she was resident, was one to which she could ensure every single one was invited.

While Idina remained in the United States she careered up and down the East Coast, turning heads and adding Newport and the Berkshires[29] to the list of places in which she was "not unknown." Twelve months later she came back to England, and as the spring of 1913 rolled in, she returned to London. But just as the round of parties started, almost as if they no longer presented a challenge, Idina turned back to one of her other interests: the campaign for Votes for Women.

The previous eighteen months of campaigning had seen a wave of violence by militant "suffragettes" who were committed to realizing female suffrage by any means. They had smashed windows, burnt pillar boxes, and chained themselves to prominent statues with such frequency that the protests started to disrupt everyday life in the capital. In February 1913 they had even firebombed the house of David Lloyd George, the chancellor of the exchequer.

In trying to control the protests, the government had been facing the additional problem that many of the suffragettes, once imprisoned, were hunger-striking. Once a prisoner neared death she had to be released. In the spring of 1913 the government passed a bill colloquially and pejoratively known as the Cat and Mouse Act. This allowed it to release prisoners about to die and to reincarcerate them once they had recovered. The suffragettes' protests increased in fury at this until, on 4 June 1913, Emily Wilding Davison dashed out in front of King George V's horse in the Derby. She was crushed, and three days later died.

Idina was not a militant suffragette. Instead, her East Grinstead organization was a branch of the NUWSS (National Union of Women's Suffrage Societies), which believed that women's suffrage should be achieved by peaceful means. NUWSS members called themselves "constitutionalists" or "suffragists." Davison's death shook them into making a mark for peaceful persuasion. They instigated a six-week campaign of local rallies around the countryside which would culminate in a mass demonstration in Hyde Park at the end of July.

The East Grinstead Women's Suffrage Society organized its own local rally, set for 23 July, just three days before the final rally of the evening, ten protesters marched off, a silk banner billowing overhead. But when they turned into East Grinstead's High Street they met a mob of fifteen hundred antisuffragists marching against them, hurling "pieces of turf, a few ripe tomatoes and highly-seasoned eggs," as the *East Grinstead Observer* reported.[30]

The suffragists took shelter in a house, but it was charged by the mob and its front door slowly and steadily bent until it cracked. The police dragged the women out the back to the branch's headquarters at the top of the Dorset Arms pub, where they were trapped for several hours, listening to the crowd outside continuing to bay for their blood.

It was the only violent outburst in the entire six-week campaign, but Idina and her mother's involvement in the group was enough to confirm society's unfavorable opinion of Idina.

Ironically, all this outward rebellion meant that Idina was conforming to her mother's version of normality. Deep down, something in Idina kicked against this. In her mother's less than full emotional life, the only male figure, George Lansbury, belonged not only to a wife, but also to the electorate and his causes. Idina, having grown up with an absent father and a preoccupied mother, yearned for someone to shower her alone with attention. Three months after the riot in East Grinstead, Idina embraced society's conventions instead of her mother's and decided to live a more normal life than she had been brought up with. Now aged twenty, she became engaged to a twenty-one-year-old Cavalry officer who was one of the most eligible bachelors in Britain. He was a man with whom she would fall deeply in love and who, she believed, would belong to her.

Chapter 3

Idina's fiancé was called David Euan Wallace and known, like Idina, by his second name. Euan, it is still repeated today, some ninety years later, was an exceptionally good-looking man. In the portrait photograph I have of him, taken at the time, he poses sitting in his then modern khaki Cavalry officer's uniform, buttons shining, polished leather straps crossing his chest. His nose, cheeks, mouth are all neat, perfectly formed in a young face that looks designed for first love. And, it is also still said, he was kind, charming, and funny.

Euan was a social animal. He liked to go out and about incessantly to gathering after gathering, noting with whom he had lunched, tea-ed, and dined.[1] In 1910, at eighteen, he had gone to the Royal Military College at Sandhurst. The best part of a year later he joined the 2nd Life Guards. The 1st and 2nd Life Guards, together with the Royal Horse Guards, known as the Blues, formed the King's Household Cavalry. As wars were few and far between, the Household Cavalry were expected to spend most of their career guarding the King's Household, which involved appearing at London's society balls and dancing with both debutantes and their disaffected mothers. This is how Euan spent his evenings. The daytimes were busy with parades and polo. Traditionally the officers in these regiments were supposed to be aristocrats and therefore, in theory, gentlemen. Euan Wallace was not, however, in any way aristocratic: he was simply rich.

Euan's great-great-grandfather, a Lanarkshire Scot called Alexander Baird, had founded one of the fastest-grown industrial fortunes in the world. In 1816, finding his income as a tenant farmer too meager to support his wife, eight sons, and two daughters, Baird had taken a lease on a coalfield and given it to his twenty-year-old eldest son, William, to run. By the time his sons died in the 1860s, William Baird & Co. was running Gartsherrie, the largest ironworks in the world, producing three hundred thousand tons of iron a year. Murray's *Handbook* for Scotland describes Gartsherrie as "a group of blazing Iron Furnaces . . . [in] a desolate, black district—of smoke, coal, ashes—treeless, sunless."[2] Between thirty and forty thousand people depended upon the Bairds, who built them houses, schools, and churches, donating over half a million pounds to the Church of Scotland directly. But they could afford to: Gartsherrie made them a million pounds' profit each year. They had become the richest family in Scotland and, at one time, it was said, the richest in Britain. The family spent its money carefully—in land. The brothers Baird bought up hundreds of thousands of acres of country estates and houses across Scotland, so establishing themselves as the new landed gentry.

Far from spreading the fortune between innumerable descendants, the Baird dynasty then shrank. The seven of the eight Baird sons who went into the family business spent their lives working too hard ever to find wives. Instead it was their elder sister Janet who produced two sons and a son-in-law to take over the firm and its profits. The son-in-law was Euan's grandfather David Wallace. However, at the age of just fifty-four, David Wallace died, leaving Euan's father, John, known as Jack, with the best part of a million pounds at the tender age of fifteen.

Jack therefore saw no need to follow his father into the family firm. Instead, to the disapproval of his Glasgow peers,[3] when he reached twenty-one and received the money, he started to divide his time between the estate of Old Glassingall (it inspired the setting for Robert Louis Stevenson's *Kidnapped*), which his father

Euan Wallace

had bought, and a house he bought himself in Mayfair, London. Armed with a fortune and a great deal of time, Jack Wallace began to turn himself from newly rich Scot to high-living English gentleman. He married, had a single son, Euan (whom he sent to the English boarding school Harrow), and lived well. But, by the age of forty-six, Jack Wallace, too, was dead. Euan was, just as Jack had been when his father died, only fifteen. The million pounds had shrunk to a mere 250,000 (worth 25 million today). It was a fraction of the sum Jack had inherited. But 250,000 pounds was enough to make Euan a rich young man—certainly rich enough for the Cavalry.

Being a Cavalry officer was an expensive occupation. Applicants needed no less than two thousand pounds a year in private, unearned income. An officer needed a manservant to maintain his uniforms, both khaki by day and glittering red and gold by night. He needed at least one groom to look after his string of a minimum of four horses: two chargers, on which he would occasionally parade, and polo ponies. He also needed to be able to afford to behave like a gentleman and pick up the bill whenever one appeared.

And thus Euan had behaved until September 1913, when as a twenty-one-year-old lieutenant slipping across London's ballroom floors in a flash of burnished leather, polished brass, and crimson, his fortunes had taken a dramatic turn. His great-uncle William Weir, then still a senior partner of William Baird & Co., had turned up at his beloved mistress's a little early one afternoon to find her in the arms of one of her fellow actors. Uncle Willie had turned on his heels. On 15 September 1913 he had drawn up a new will. Eight days later he had died from a fatal combination of heart-break and shock. Child-less, he had left almost a hundred thousand acres of Scottish estates and two million pounds to be divided equally between Euan and one other nephew. Overnight, in an age overflowing with mil-lionaires, Euan became one of the richest young men in Britain. He was rich enough for his social ambi-

Idina's engagement photo

tions to withstand marrying a girl from a scandalous family. Within a fortnight he had proposed to Idina.

Putting the scandals to one side, Euan and Idina appeared a perfect couple. They were both glamorous and seemingly dedi-cated to a nonstop social life. They were enough in love to call each other pet names.[4] Moreover, the vastness of Euan's fortune was seen as a match for the antiquity of Idina's family name.

But, in the rush and blush of sexual excitement and first love, they overlooked a fundamental difference in their approach to life. They may both have been startlingly energetic, and the life and soul of any party, but for Euan this social life was the be-all and end-all. For Idina, whose eyes had been opened a little wider in her youth by a mother who lived "very largely out of Society,"[5] it was no more than passing entertainment. Instead, like her grandmother, Annie Brassey, what Idina wanted from life was adventure. Yet all couples have their differences and, for as long as things are going well, these are, for the most part, trifling.

And, at the beginning, things went very well. Indeed, in the world that Idina and Euan inhabited, their life could hardly have been better. Their engagement was announced in the *Times* on 13 October 1913 and their families' solicitors immediately set about drawing up a marriage contract. This set up a Marriage Trust into which Euan put the then impressive sum of one hundred thousand pounds for Idina. Among other conditions, the contract stipulated that if Idina left the marriage she would forfeit the lot.

The customary six weeks later, Idina and Euan married "very quietly"[6] in Christ Church in Down Street, in London's wealthiest residential area, Mayfair. This is a curious church that remains invisible until you are upon one of its two side doors, through which you angle your way to the altar (there is no straight route to God even for the wealthy). Idina, wearing a traditional bridal blue serge traveling dress, was given away by her grandfather, by now Earl Brassey.[7]

The best man was one of Euan's Cavalry colleagues, a fellow Scot in the 2nd Life Guards called Stewart Menzies. Stewart was two years older than Euan and his closest friend. He was not only best man at the wedding, he was also the trustee of the Marriage Trust.

Menzies was someone who could slide through any social situation. He was well connected—his mother was lady-in-waiting to Queen Mary—and he basked in the notoriety of the (now discredited) rumor that he was the illegitimate son of King Edward VII. He was also a person who knew how to spot an opportunity and turn it to his advantage. Within a few years he would become a legendary chief of British Intelligence. The head of the British Secret Service is called Control, or C for short. For thirteen years it was Stewart Menzies. Ian Fleming, creator of James Bond, called his hero's wise, tolerant boss M instead of C, after Menzies. John le Carré based George Smiley's faithless wife, Lady Anne, on Menzies's own first wife.

In 1913 Stewart Menzies was already one of the most influential officers in the 2nd Life Guards, as he had been appointed to adjutant, the right-hand man of Colonel Ferguson, who commanded the regiment. As adjutant he was responsible for the day-to-day organization of the troopers and officers, disciplinary affairs, and matters relating to the general well-being of the regiment—whom the officers married being one of these. An officer, for example, could on no account marry a divorcée. Idina, as the daughter of parents who had not just divorced but who continued to make headlines for their less than conventional behavior, was a borderline case. Nor was it usual for young junior officers, as Euan was, to marry at all. But Stewart was ferociously fond of Euan. And there is one law for the rich, and another for the phenomenally rich. Euan was now one of the latter.

After the ceremony the guests—the women's buttoned-up ankles flashing under their hobble skirts—tripped along Curzon Street to the Brasseys' house at 24 Park Lane. They wafted up the curving staircase and through the drawing rooms to the Durbar Hall. There Idina's wedding presents, an array of diamonds and star sapphires twisted into tiaras, bandeaux, watches, and rings,[8] had been spread out among her grandmother's spears and botanical specimens from the South Seas.

That afternoon Idina and Euan left for Egypt. Honeymoons usually lasted a month or more. It was long enough to ride around the Pyramids and float down the Nile to the temple of Karnak. It was long enough, too, to go deep into the Sahara, followed like pharaohs by a caravan of cooks, tent-riggers, and armed guards. At night they could lie out under the stars and bathe in the emptiness of the desert, the only sound the distant clatter of pans and the Bedouin hum. Newly wed, and the fear of pregnancy diminished, Idina completed her introduction to sex: an activity not only for which she discovered she had a talent, but which she clearly found so intensely enjoyable that it rapidly became impossible for her to resist any opportunity for it. And, in an untypically British way, she had grown up listening to her mother's great friend, the Theosophist Annie Besant, pronouncing that abundant sexual activity within marriage was good for a woman's health.

She was pregnant within the first month.

This, however, was still an age in which the less said about a woman's waistline, or lack of it, the better. A lady simply uttered a small prayer of thanks for the just-invented brassiere[9]—which was considerably less uncomfortable than a corset—altered the style of her clothing, and continued with life until she became too undisguisably large to be seen in public. In any case, when she returned from Egypt, Idina was busy. She had two homes to create.

The first of these was in London, where she and Euan would spend most of the year. From here he would motor back and forth to the Life Guards' barracks in Windsor. In 1914 it was still the age of the motoring enthusiast and, rather than seeing the journey as a chore, both Idina and Euan regarded motoring as an intense pleasure. Euan's diaries are littered with references to how well a particular car or motorcycle performed when he took it out, and Idina was the daughter of two motor racers. While her parents had still been together, they had instigated motorcar races along the mixed-sex seafront at Bexhill. Once they were apart, Gilbert went on to be chairman of Dunlop Tyres. Muriel became an active member of the committee of the Ladies' Automobile Club. This was a controversial position. As late as 1908 the *Times* felt obliged to mention that "doubts have been felt—no opinion is expressed here—on the question whether feminine nerves are as a rule, so well qualified to stand the strain of driving as those of men. . . . Of course they can learn at least as much as men can, and the more they learn the better."[10] Idina inherited a disdain for such prejudice and the enthusiasm of both her parents, gaining a reputation for driving flat out in fast cars.[11]

In choosing their London home, Idina and Euan clearly felt they had to live up to their fortune. None of the houses on Park Lane was for sale, so instead they slipped just around the corner of Marble Arch, still more or less at the top of Park Lane, and still overlooking Hyde Park. Their new home was in a terrace of just under a dozen houses in Connaught Place. The houses in this street were wide, deep, and tall. Stretching over seven floors, they provided several thousand square feet of high-ceilinged living space, with the floors joined by a wide stone staircase. The entrances were in the quiet, Connaught Place side, but the main rooms were on the other, facing Marble Arch and Hyde Park. It was a cavernous space for such a young couple, even if a family was already on the way.

Compared with Idina and Euan's other home, however, Connaught Place was a pied-à-terre. William Weir had left Euan three adjoining estates in Scotland: Kildonan, Arnsheen, and Glenduisk. Weir had made his home at Kildonan, which surrounded the south Ayrshire village of Barrhill.

Spy *cartoon of Idina's father, Earl De La Warr, the motoring enthusiast*

A couple of hours' drive south of Glasgow, Barrhill was an old staging post, where travelers and coaches had changed horses, on the single road cutting through the center of the region from coast to coast. The village itself was a handful of houses astride the River Duisk, which ran along the bottom of the valley. Surrounded by purple-tinged moorland, it was a world away from London. And there, a few feet above the Duisk, amid a riot of elephantine rhododendron and manicured lawns, spread Kildonan House. The west-facing front consisted of a small two-story eighteenth-century manor house: just three windows across on the first floor and one on either side of a pillared and porticoed front door. To the rear of this neat, pretty house spread a monstrosity of an L-shaped Victorian extension, all Gothic stone and ivy on the outside, and on the inside a jigsaw of windows, brick, tile, and half-timber. A way in which to rid themselves of some of the weight of their fortune presented itself to Idina and Euan.

Twenty miles away on the coast, a Glaswegian architect called James Miller had built a vast new golfing and seaside hotel in the village of Turnberry. The hotel had been commissioned by the Glasgow and South Western Railway, which had extended its line along the coast for the purpose. Miller specialized in designing large public buildings such as town halls, hospitals, and railway stations. Idina and Euan commissioned him to build them a new house at Kildonan.

Old Kildonan was to be razed to the ground and the new house erected on the same site. As this was a leveled-off area on the hillside where the valley bottomed out, bounded by the river on one side and a ferocious burn and a brook on the others, it did not allow Miller a great deal of room to maneuver—especially when it came to Idina and Euan's plans for the house.

Ayrshire was a long way for their friends from London to travel. It required an overnight sleeper to Glasgow and then a couple of hours' drive into the wilderness. It was too far for a Saturday-to-Monday visit and possibly too far for any stay of less than a week—for the entirety of which they would need to keep their friends entertained. The estate burgeoned with sporting opportunities: pheasant and foxes in the winter, grouse on the moors, and salmon and trout in the Duisk in the summer. When these failed, there were also the beaches and golf course at Turnberry. The one element, however, to which Idina and Euan and their guests would be hostage was the weather.

When the sun shone, there seemed no brighter place in the country. When it chose not to, the skies clouded and rain fell thick and vertical in prison bars, keeping them indoors. They would need space in which to spend days at a stretch, amusements to fill the hours, and dozens of bedrooms in which to house the crowds of friends whom they, aged twenty and twenty-one, clearly could not imagine spending any time without.

By the time Miller had finished he had drawn up plans for a house with five wings and with sixty-five rooms on the ground and first floors alone. These included dozens of larders and kitchens, servants' bedrooms and laundry rooms, butlers' rooms, a plate room (a walk-in safe for silver), drying rooms, linen rooms, even a flower room—all required to keep the house and its sporting activities running. On the ground floor there was an oversized squash court, a dining room, a drawing room, a billiard room, a smoking room, and a sixty-foot-long, double-height baronial hall with a minstrels' gallery peeping over from the top of the main staircase next door.

On the first floor, in an L along the two principal wings, and linked by no fewer than five staircases to the ground, ran two 120-foot-long passageways. Off these were eight main guest bedrooms on the outward-looking, lawn side of the house, half with dressing rooms attached in which a husband could sleep, allowing couples used to different partners to separate for the night, and serviced by a row of bathrooms on the courtyard side of the house—which in themselves provided a reason for guests to be wandering the passageways after lights-out. At the far end, separated from the rest of the house by the upper half of the great hall, were Euan and Idina's rooms.

Ignoring the custom for separate rooms in one's own house, they had just one bedroom leading to a large bathroom. On the far side of this, with an entrance between three vast walk-in cupboards in the passageway, was a large dressing room for Euan. Next door to this, just outside the entrance to the apartment from the first floor, was Idina's maid's bedroom, within, as was customary, calling distance during the night.

There was one more floor above this. Here another pair of 120-foot passageways linked a long Elizabethan gallery and a rabbit warren of dozens of nursery bedrooms and servants' rooms to house not just Idina and Euan's own staff but the ladies' maids, gentlemen's valets, drivers, and loaders for the pairs of Purdey shotguns that their guests would bring with them. In all, Idina and Euan's plans for their new house contained over a hundred rooms. In the age of the great Edwardian house party, it was designed to cater to every creature comfort their guests might require—in an understated way. The exterior, instead of display-

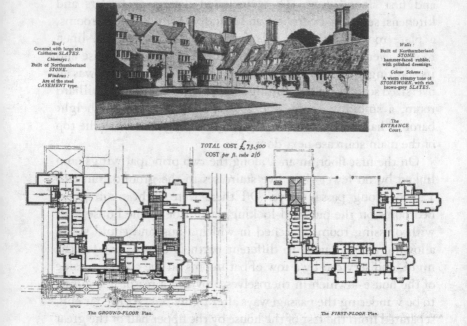

Roof:
Covered with large size
Caithness SLATES.
Chimneys:
Built of Northumberland
STONE.
Windows:
Are of the steel
CASEMENT type.

Walls:
Built of Northumberland
STONE
hammer-faced rubble,
with polished dressings.
Colour Scheme:
A warm creamy tone of
STONEWORK, with rich
brown-grey SLATES.

The
ENTRANCE
Court.

TOTAL COST £73,500
COST per ft. cube 2/6

The GROUND-FLOOR Plan.

The FIRST-FLOOR Plan.

Kildonan House, Ayrshire: the home that Idina designed for her life with Euan and their children. She worked on the plans but never saw the house completed.

ing the vastness of the house inside, did everything it could to conceal it.

For a start, each floor was markedly, almost overly, low-ceilinged, keeping down the overall height of the building. In addition to this feature of the design, most of the second floor of the house and some of the first were to be hidden within sloping roofs dotted with dormer windows. These roofs were to be covered with soft brown slates from Caithness in the north of Scotland. The walls themselves were to be constructed from creamy yellow Northumbrian stone, each irregularly sized brick carefully chosen. Each façade was to be broken up by an equally carefully planned irregularity of porches, loggias, gables, protruding extensions, bay windows, and the vast double-height window of the great hall. It would look not unlike a larger, newer version of Idina's childhood home, Old Lodge. The overall effect from the rolling lawns outside was one of a romantic, rambling late-medieval manor house. Yet it was totally modern. Each stone brick was hammered flat, its edges polished. The stone-mullioned windows contained steel casements. Inside, the numerous bathrooms were equipped with the latest plumbing. And the decoration was near-monastic—white plasterwork and exposed brick surrounded pale, unpolished, gray oak paneling. It would cost more than seventy thousand pounds, an astounding expenditure at that time.

The first task in this great project was, as these plans were being drawn up, discussed, and redrawn, to take down the old house. In the spring of 1914, as the thick layer of winter snow cleared, the tiles were pulled off the roof of Old Kildonan.

IDINA NOW HAD EVERYTHING in place for a magnificent life. She, Little One, had the Brownie she loved, and soon they would have a child. Euan had embedded himself at the heart of Idina's family. He popped in and out of their houses alone, and had become an elder brother to the fatherless Avie[12] and Buck. The Sackvilles and Brasseys in turn spun in and out of Connaught Place.

Meanwhile, together, Euan and Idina were one of the most sought-after couples in town. He was rich and handsome, she was glamorous and daring. They were invited out in several directions each night. They were building a vast home that epitomized the Edwardian country-house dream. The only financial worry they might ever have would be that they had too much money rather than too little. And once they had had a couple of children they would be able to spend that money traveling the world in limitless adventures. For a girl who had been shunned by society as a child, it was almost too good to be true.

Until the new house was built, Idina and Euan entertained their friends in London. When Euan returned from watching saddles being soaped, stirrups polished, and swords sharpened at Windsor, Idina welcomed him to a drawing room overflowing with young people. Their unmarried friends still lived with their parents. Idina and Euan's house, however, was gloriously free of any parents at all. It was spacious, rule-free, and had endless supplies of food and drink being produced by innumerable staff, together with the very latest gramophone records. Night after night Idina and Euan dined in a great gang at the Ritz, the Carlton, or Claridge's, went to the latest show, and then returned to Connaught Place. There their friends and Idina's younger sister, Avie—just seventeen and so almost "out" in society—sang and listened to ragtime and blues until the early hours, perfecting their steps in the shockingly intimate tango or the latest "animal" dance from the United States, inevitably popularized by being denounced by the Vatican. They ground their bodies against one another in the Bunny Hug; hopped and scissor-stepped in the Turkey Trot; yelled, "It's a bear!" as they swayed to the Grizzly. And, as spring turned into summer, the new Fox-trot arrived from across the Atlantic.

But, on 28 June, the heir to the Austro-Hungarian throne was assassinated in the Serbian city of Sarajevo. Within a few weeks the world was at war.

For a young Cavalry officer, it promised to be a glorious chance of an adrenaline-fueled charge for King and Country, followed by a glorious return to the stately life Euan and Idina were constructing. As war was declared, a line of twenty horse-drawn carts laden with stone were on their way from the station at Barrhill to the Kildonan building site.[13] But, by the time the war had ended, and the house had been built, both the world they were building it for—and Idina and Euan themselves—would have changed irrevocably.

Chapter 4

On 14 August 1914 Idina watched a single squadron of the 2nd Life Guards line up two abreast along an avenue running north-south just inside the eastern edge of Hyde Park. They wore their modern Cavalry uniform of khaki, only distinguished from foot soldiers by the leather of the cross belts that lay diagonally over their chests, broadening their shoulders.

As the band struck up and Euan and his fellow officers moved off, rows of women lining the route in white dresses raised their arms and voices in euphoric excitement. Those chaps on horses, it was being whispered, were the lucky ones, the ones chosen to go to France. They had a chance of seeing the first action since the Boer War, which they had followed as short-trousered schoolboys. This was a token land force going over. Britain's great strength, where surely it would flex its muscles in the fight to come, was at sea. In any case, it wouldn't go on for long. The last war on the European mainland had been between France and Prussia more than four decades ago. It had lasted a year. The word on the street was that this one would be "over by Christmas."

The word being muttered along the corridors of power, however, was a little different. There the extravagantly moustached Lord Kitchener, victorious veteran of the fight against the Boers and Field Marshal of the British forces worldwide, thought it might last a little longer. He took as his example not the Franco-Prussian War of 1870–71, which he had joined as a field ambulance volunteer, but the slightly earlier American Civil War. That had lasted four years and taken the lives of more than six hundred thousand men. In August 1914 Kitchener was already forecasting that this new European war would last three.

Euan left with the single "composite" Household Cavalry regiment—made up of a squadron of each of the two Life Guards regiments and one from the Blues—as railway stations throughout Britain filled with man-boys slouching on kit bags, knocking their heels against the canvas as they smoked and nodded, wondering whether they, in the glorious adventure that awaited them, would prove themselves to be men.

And the men and women they left behind in England went to war on the Home Front. On 8 August the Defence of the Realm Act had come into force, giving the government powers to commandeer economic resources, imprison without trial, and exercise widespread censorship. The streets of London were flooded with families of Belgian refugees: young children and their gray-clad parents, their heads low, dragging suitcases behind them. Lord Kitchener's famous finger-pointing poster "Your Country Needs You" appeared up and down the country, drumming up vast numbers of volunteers, who were being marched to and fro through London's parks until enough uniforms and rifles could be found for them. A handful of duchesses and countesses were setting up their own Red Cross hospitals to take to the Front. Nursing was the grandest way for a lady to help the war effort. But the young Lady Diana Manners, the famously beautiful and daring daughter of the Duke of Rutland, and a contemporary of Idina's, found herself forbidden to race across the Channel too, lest "wounded soldiers, so long starved of women, inflamed with wine and battle, ravish and leave half-dead the young nurses who only wish to tend them."[1] Idina, eight months pregnant, could do none of these things. Instead she moved back into her grandfather's house in Park Lane, where the extended family had gathered both themselves and what food supplies they could, to await the birth of her child.

For the next few weeks news of skirmishes, parries, and victories seeped back to London: first in the news posters plastered around the city and soon afterward through the details written up in the newspapers. Although the British Cavalry had discarded the old-fashioned armor and costumes still worn by their French and German counterparts, they were nonetheless mounting charges, one Cavalry officer writing that even his "old cutting sword . . . well sharpened . . . went in and out of the German like a pat of butter."[2] In the first week of September the Allies counterattacked at the River Marne and stopped the German advance, but the British Expeditionary Force, a tiny army compared with the million Frenchmen and million and a half Germans, was severely weakened. The BEF was left holding a thin line, unsupported from behind and desperately awaiting reinforcements before the Wagnerian wrath of "the Hun" reached them. Just as the news came back that the Cavalry had dismounted and were fighting alongside the infantry in the trenches, the dreaded telegram boy rang the bell at 24 Park Lane.

Idina's cousin Gerard had been killed. He had been fighting in a battle at the River Aisne in northern France. Like Euan a lieutenant, he had been in the 1st Battalion of the Coldstream Guards. This infantry unit had been engaged in heavy fighting both in the trenches and on open ground—with fatal results.

For Idina this was deeply upsetting news and almost certainly the first big shock of the war. She was resolved that if she had the opportunity she would name a child after him.

Just a fortnight later, on 3 October, Idina's baby was born at 24 Park Lane. It was a boy. However, when, a few days afterward, she received the inevitable elated letter from her husband, the news cannot have been entirely encouraging. Euan had been putting his own life at risk so often that his commanding officer had told him that he was being "Mentioned in Dispatches"— mentioned by name in one of the Commander in Chief's reports back to Kitchener, the recently appointed secretary of state for war. It was the lowest military recognition for bravery but it was still a tempting first step toward a medal for some daring act.

Euan also wanted his new son, as the eldest Wallace male in

his generation, to have a Wallace name. He wanted to name him, as he himself had been named, after his father and grandfather, and father and grandfather before that. Euan's first name was David, and Euan was a Scots variant of his father's name, John. And now that the Wallaces had—sporting seasons aside—come south, John it would be. David John. Nor would they have any of that now passé fin-de-siècle fashion for children being called by their second name. Finally, in order to firmly entrench his son in the bosom of English society, his name should be put down for Eton, where Idina's brother, Buck, had just started school. It would take Idina another son to have the name she wanted.

A little over a week after this, it was Idina's turn to receive a telegram.

Euan had been manning one of the outposts at Warneton in Belgium, ahead of the main line. Sheltered as the spot was within the undulations of the cloud-hung Flemish hills, the morning of 20 October began quietly, promising another hour-counting game of sitting, watching, waiting. When Euan levered himself out of his bunk, he had a chance to feel the length to which his stubble had grown, and settle down to breakfast.

At 0800 hours the silence exploded—and a piece of shrapnel embedded itself in Euan's leg. Behind the shells twenty-four thousand German riflemen and four motorized Jäger divisions were advancing toward him. Within seconds Euan was soaked in his own blood. He had a pearly-white bleeder's skin; knock it and a great bruise would spread.[3] But, at least at this moment of his not very long life, he was lucky. The stretcher-bearers strapped him into one of their stained, sagging canvases and started to bump him back, slipping and skidding again and again in the knee-deep mud. From time to time, between the stinking dark-gray clouds of smoke and flesh and the wobbling sky above, the clenched jaw of one of the bearers would swing into view, a vial of morphine hanging from his shoulder. If Euan had been in too many pieces to cobble back together in a stretcher, the bearers would have simply given him as much of it as they could spare.

The stretcher-bearers took him to the Regimental Aid Post, a muddy, bloody, rainy sprawl of bodies around a single tent, a good number of them in no state to go any further: some calling for their mothers; others begging "for the love of God" to be shot. The Post had been packing up, or trying to pack up, and move back toward Ypres in a general retreat, but men were still being tipped out onto the ground around it left, right, and center.

"What's his trouble?" was the medics' question.

"Leg, shrapnel," came the reply.

And then they had lifted him out onto a ground sheet and, within a couple of seconds, had turned and gone back for another.

Before the Germans reached the Aid Post, Euan had been moved back, via the Advanced Dressing Station, to the Casualty Clearing Station. There his wound was judged severe enough for him to be sent back to England. Three days after he had first been wounded, Euan reached England on a hospital ship and was transferred to the barracks hospital at Windsor.[4] Although in what must have been severe pain, he was nonetheless fortunate. He had been hit in the initial few days of the long First Battle of Ypres, before all those posts and stations and tents had become clogged with the tens of thousands of mutilated bodies that followed him. And he had escaped the trenches. Not all the lieutenants in the 2nd Life Guards had.

By mid-November five of the regiment's officers had been killed. Seven, including Euan, had been wounded. Eight were missing, of whom only one would turn out to be alive, and two had been sent home sick from France. Only six out of the total of twenty-eight 2nd Life Guards officers who had been sent to the Front remained there. More broadly, the British Army, which had set off to certain, glorious victory, had been all but destroyed. A month later Euan, still convalescing but looking fit enough to return to France soon, was promoted to captain to fill a gap.

By Christmas he was well enough to be sent to live at home. Two months after the birth of her son, Idina would have been more than ready to resume a sexual life. It was also clear that she would have Euan in her bed only until he was fit enough to go

back to the Front. As he was making just the occasional trip to
the barracks at Windsor, she made the most of having him
around. And within the first few weeks of their reunion, barely
three months after giving birth for the first time, she was pregnant again.

During the day Idina trotted and Euan hauled himself up the
long stone stairs of Connaught Place, plotting and planning Kildonan, the home they would have when this was all over. By
night, they stepped out into the dark London streets. The few
lights still in use had been covered over, leaving only a dim glow.

They scampered to that night's dance—inevitably busy, full,
frantic. The excitement of war was already dissolving into des-
peration to seize any remaining moments. A great many of Idina
and Euan's friends had been professional soldiers. By now over
half of these had been killed or crippled. The colleagues they had
left behind could make no sense of the fact that they, so far, had
been spared. Those soldiers, on returning to England and passing
through town, needed to be entertained, danced with at every
opportunity. The new captain Euan Wallace, proud bearer of not
just dashing good looks and an immense fortune but also a war
wound and a Mention in Dispatches, inevitably found himself
surrounded by a flock of femininity longing for a dance, at the
very least.

Euan, a lifelong admirer of attractive women, was not a man
to resist working his leg back into shape by taking to the dance
floor with each and every one. And, in a succession of other
women's arms, he showed Idina the direction in which her marriage would eventually shift when her husband, following the
established pattern, took lovers among her friends.

Her own childhood having been shaped by her father's departure, Idina clearly settled upon a strategy to keep her marriage
together. This was not to hide the extent to which she, too, was
in demand. At the beginning of March 1915, as Euan rejoined
his regiment in France, she accepted an invitation to sit for the
society painter William Orpen. The portrait had been commissioned by an admirer of hers: the multimillionaire industrialist

Sir James Dunn, a collector of many things, including vivacious women.

Dunn paid an unheard-of 750 pounds for the portrait. Idina wore a black velvet evening dress that had a plunging neckline and fell in folds to the floor. Orpen sat her up on a raised throne of a chair, the thick black material of her dress sweeping the black-and-white tiles of his studio floor, and her Pekinese, Satan, peeping out from underneath.

Orpen was a flirt, and more. Idina looked across at him, chin upward, defiant. When Euan had left Idina the previous August, she had been eight months pregnant and not in a position either to want or find a lover. This time her pregnancy was, as yet, barely visible and she had suddenly gone from having frequent and satisfying sex to an empty marital bed. Ninety years on, electricity still fizzes from the portrait.

And when she next met with James Miller to work on the plans for Kildonan, Euan's dancing with every girl in town before returning to France was obviously fresh on Idina's mind. As the rooms had been arranged, their bedroom apartments in the new house would allow Euan to retreat to his dressing room and then slip off down the passageways without passing her door.

In those first plans, the line of the outside wall in Idina's bedroom allowed for a deep cupboard, repeated in the smoking room below. Now, however, a staircase was sketched into this space instead. It would allow a friend to detach himself from the rest of the house party with the excuse of heading off for a final cigarette, and then slip straight upstairs to her.

Unlike her mother, Idina was not going to allow herself to be left while her husband was out having fun elsewhere. If Euan wasn't going to be there, Idina needed somebody else to be.

Chapter 5

The first diary is smaller than my outstretched hand. It is
bound in smooth-grained leather, navy blue and worn away
on each corner. It is a traveling diary, with a flap that comes over
the open edge and a broken strap that once held it down. Inside
it is pristine, with a rigid wormhole of a holder for one of those
impossibly thin diary pencils. The endpapers are stiff and mar-
bled in rich swirls of blue and gold. The pages within are pale
blue, featherweight, but tightly woven. Frank Smythson's, I
read, "PREMIER" DIARY. 1917. Nineteen seventeen was a terrible
year in British history. Not a year to be a soldier.

Euan's name comes first, inked with neat flamboyance. Then
come seventeen printed pages of useful information: the calen-
dars, the important information that gentlemen, or ladies, in
possession of a private income and struggling to fill their waking
hours, had needed to know before the war: lists of the royal children's names and birthdays (seven forenames for the Prince of
Wales, shrinking to a mere three for his youngest brother);
Empire Day, Queen Mary's Birthday, the King's Birthday, and
the Prince of Wales's Birthday. When the Royal Academy closed
for the summer. When grouse, partridge, and pheasant shooting,
and foxhunting, began. When the dividends on the government
stocks they lived off would be paid; that black-bordered mourn-

ing envelopes could not be insured; that their male servants needed a fifteen-shilling license; and a comprehensive table of servants' annual salaries (between a pound and one hundred pounds), showing what had to be paid them each day, week, and month.

But by the time Euan started to write, many of the hunters and shooters such diaries were produced for were themselves riddled with bullets and shrapnel. For over a year the two sides, each stuck in its own stinking, mud-filled trenches, had faced each other across an Armageddonesque wasteland, with soldiers occasionally venturing out to be mown down by machine guns within seconds. Kitchener's entire volunteer army had crossed to France and been slaughtered in the Somme. Asquith had given way to a new prime minister, the sprightly David Lloyd George. Controversially, unhappily, and reluctantly, the government had issued an order for compulsory conscription. Not even the horses were spared. Any four-legged equine that could pull a cart was shipped over to the battlefields. Gun carts and mess trucks were given the first available horses. Euan's gleaming Cavalry received the last. It was shrinking to a regiment that marched on two legs like the rest: the new mechanized tanks crawled steadily past them on the shell-pitted tracks that led men to the front line and brought only memories of them back.

AT THE BEGINNING OF 1917 Euan was stationed on the coast of northern France, spending day after day exercising horses on the sands, inspecting troops, and waiting, just waiting, for the next attempt to leap the trenches and barbed wire a week's march east—and the inevitable short, sharp exchange of a few hundred yards of territory for tens of thousands of lives.

1917. MONDAY, 1 JANUARY.

Idina's name was on the first page of Euan's diary: "DOG TAX DUE." Then a thicket of ink: "Rode around by Cregny & C. Vieille in the morning. Had large post. At lunchtime . . ."[1] At lunchtime she appeared. Not in person in the wet-dog smell of damp khaki wool in Euan's makeshift, windswept, here-today-gone-tomorrow Army camp, but back in London, in the choking pea-souper fog belched out by the coal smoke of hundreds of thousands of worn brick chimneys. Idina was wandering up and down the wide stone staircase of Connaught Place with their now two tiny sons and aching for Euan. "At lunchtime got Dina's wire saying she had 'every reason to hope' I would be home in the middle of Jan. So I suppose the CO has really arranged for me to change places with him."

In this war without end, leave was all Euan had to look forward to. It took just a day to return to England and be able to pull the blankets up over himself and Idina and pretend that the war was nothing but a freezing, muddy dream. Each day trains rattled along the veins of the French railway system to Calais, where the Leave Boat, a wide, tarpaulin-topped ferry, its nooks and crannies hiding illicit games of Crown and Anchor, rocked its way to Folkestone over the heads of the U-boats. There Euan sent a wire to Idina, asking her to meet the Victoria train he was about to leap on.

But now, here in January 1917, that last leave, last touch of each other's skin, clearly seemed a long way away. Euan was trying to get home. "Tuesday, January 2, CO is going to send me back for 10 days to Windsor!!" But four days later: "Saturday 6 January, Mark rather threw cold water on my chances of going home: but I am still hopeful." And for the next fortnight Euan's and Idina's hopes and fears flew across the Channel. Every spare minute that Euan had he spent scribbling to Idina: "wrote to Dina until lunch . . . wrote to Dina until dinner . . . wrote to Dina for a couple of hours and then bed." Idina's letters had come flying back, and each day that the post failed to arrive was marked glumly on Euan's pages, followed by elation when, at last, they arrived: "good mail, got 3 letters from Dina!!"

At the beginning of 1917 Euan and Idina were dangerously in love. Dangerously because at any moment Euan might ride into a hail of bullets and never return: enough to make a man, or his woman, a little reckless, inclined to take a step too far toward anything that might dispel this thought. Dangerously because their marriage, a tender, three-year-old shoot of a marriage between two people still in their early twenties, was precariously top-heavy with grandeur—that mansion in London, the estates in Scotland—and time apart.

"1917. Saturday 20 January, General Portal rang up at 9 pm and told me that W had decided I could not go home 'on duty' as all CO's had been recalled. Hell!"

Hell. A year earlier Euan had been promoted again. Stewart Menzies and his infinite capabilities for knowledge, finding it out, harboring it, and knowing just when to pass it on, had been requisitioned by Intelligence. Euan had been promoted to adjutant in his place. He was now the right-hand man of Lieutenant Colonel Algernon Ferguson, the commanding officer. Ferguson was a cousin by marriage to Menzies and an officer of the old school who, in the face of tanks and machine-gun fire, still clung to the belief that no modern method of warfare was a match for a Cavalry charge. So far he had been wounded seriously enough twice to be sent back to England. Both times he had bounded back to duty.

Under his charge, Euan was responsible for all regimental administration, discipline, and requests for leave from HQ. And now that Ferguson had gone back to Windsor, Euan was the one officer who couldn't go too.

Another month passed. February arrived and the weather turned cold. Back in Connaught Place, deep fires were lit. Euan and Idina's sons, David and Gerard, two and a half years and eighteen months old, scampered down the stairs, over the road to the park, and back with their cavalcade of starched-hatted nan-

Idina and Euan's sons, David and Gerard ("Gee") Wallace

nies, nurses, and nursery maids. A few familiar faces came to the house, the piano keyboard was bared, bottles were cracked open. And then Idina and her friends went out: there were shows to see, those dinners out in great gangs, as they had had before the war, and dancing back at home.

But Euan wasn't there.

He was still in France, with the snow and the threat of a more permanent whiteout falling thick around him.

"The General and I motored to Royon, where we picked up his golf clubs and Ricardo and then on to Torcy. We found too much snow to play." So he had tried something else. "Nib Pill Miles Dragon Alec Marc and self went tobogganing on a hill NW of the town in the afternoon. We have now 2 toboggans and very good sport was obtained."

And then, on 20 February, Euan bumped into Idina's uncle, Tom Brassey, at the Divisional School, where they were both attending a lecture. Tom told Euan that Muriel was coming over to meet him in Paris the following Monday, six days away.

Euan leapt at the idea. "I decided to try and get Dina too." Paris leave, it appeared, was easier for Euan to come by. He would be only a few hours away from the regiment, not potentially stuck on the other side of the Channel while the U-boats wreaked havoc. "Squared the leave with Bill on the spot." That afternoon he wrote out a wire to Idina and "took it into Berck on the bike."

Would she come over, could she come over? A night of hoping was followed by a morning of panic. All it took was a passing comment in the officers' mess: was he luring his wife to a watery grave? Germany had declared unrestricted submarine warfare at the start of the month. Not even civilian ships would be spared. Not that they had been, in any case. The moment the early-afternoon drill was over, the brigadier gone, Euan was up and off. Full tilt on the bike. The wind bit into his cheeks and chin, the goggles pressed into his face. "Sent another wire to Dina from Berck warning her not to attempt to come out if it was considered unsafe."

1917. TUESDAY, 27 FEBRUARY. "Left Rang du Fliers by 3 pm train for Paris. Slow journey but punctual. Train not very crowded. Arrived 11 pm and got a share of a taxi to the Ritz where I found Dina wide awake."

Idina had been waiting for her husband for a day. A day and a half if she counted back to the time on Monday morning that her mother strode out of 24 Park Lane and swung herself against the thick upholstered back of the car beside her.

By the time the two women reached Victoria Station they had joined the war. Idina and Muriel picked their way across a concourse swarming with brushed khaki and polished leather. Above them high glass arches reverberated with a low-pitched murmur.

They flitted like shadows into a first-class carriage. It was three hours to Folkestone: stopping and starting and chuffing and grinding, their heads knocking into the high, padded seat backs. Three hours of repeatedly tugging and releasing the leather window strap to see where they had reached, what was happening outside; then yanking the window up again as soot and steam curled back along the train.

The boats were running. The women followed their leather suitcases and hatboxes up the gangplank. The crossing took ninety stomach-turning minutes of the hull rocking up to one side, pausing, and falling back again with the swell as the boat steamed slowly over the black water. At Calais they were swept with the soldiers off the Leave Boat and onto the Army trains heading east to Flanders. They peeled themselves away to the Paris train, escorted by a handful of officers, the red tabs on their uniforms revealing their smug administrative and noncombat staff postings in Parisian HQs.

Paris was a city of façades: brushed pavements, manicured parklets, rows of little shop fronts and grand colonnades. Its web of cobbled alleyways, passages, and tiny streets led from the damp, sweet air of bakeries to the rich aromas of cafés before tumbling out into long, wide boulevards. Here proud, pale-stone buildings descended in classical lines to the ground, where suddenly the archways and wrought-iron gates broke into curls and twisted vines—pure, shivering, Parisian elegance.

Before the war, before her marriage, Idina had been to Paris with her mother half a dozen, maybe a dozen times. They had gone for exhibitions, concerts, balls, and to order their clothes.

Before the war, every good idea had been had in Paris. Marcel Proust had pushed the literature to extremes; André Gide had taunted the establishment; Debussy had ignored every operatic tradition; Picasso had started to paint in the straight lines of Cubism; and Paul Poiret had started to design his new, corset-free dresses. The Café de Flore and the Deux Magots on the Boulevard Saint-Germain bubbled with smoke and ideas. On the pavements outside, women had stepped past, every detail of their costume at the perfect angle. Paris had been at the cutting edge of all that was new. "*Ici même les automobiles,*" wrote the poet Apollinaire, "*ont l'air d'être anciennes.*"[2] But, on the afternoon of Monday, 26 February 1917, Idina stepped out of the railway terminus of Saint-Lazare into a strange city.

Shell craters dotted the avenues, the perfect terraces now broken by buildings turned to rubble. Shop after shop was shuttered, messages that the proprietor had gone to war chalked on the doors. Here and there flashed traces of military uniforms. Empty sleeves pinned to their chests, crutches and canes at the ready, the war-wounded advanced slowly along the streets. Around them the women walked slowly, too, their pace weighed down as if by the heavy black of their mourning clothes.

The first few streets of grand apartment blocks beyond the station were still, their owners cowering in their country houses. In the early days of the war, as the German Army had bombed the city, the wealthy had fled. Even now, the guns were not much further away. Close enough, on a fine day, for the sound of the thudding of shells to drift across the rooftops. Nonetheless, over the previous twelve months, as the war had grown into a way of life, Paris had started to fill again. The theaters and music halls, the cinemas and galleries, had begun to reopen. The cafés were once more overflowing onto the streets, every table crammed with glasses and coffee cups, croissant-covered plates, a boulevard beach of military caps in every shade from pale blue to black nodding above them.

Half a day's journey from the Front, close enough to make something of forty-eight hours' leave, Paris had become a soldiers' city. Even the long hallway of the Ritz was crammed. Men in khaki uniforms perched on red velvet benches and sofas, mirroring the marble statues of classical heroes in the patio garden that ran alongside. Water cascaded through stone lions' mouths in the garden, while alcohol, which had been banned, arced out of the silver spouts of teapots indoors.

Above the rows of desks and doormen, a wide staircase curled steeply up to vast, silk-wallpapered rooms. Most heavenly of all, however, were the bathrooms. The Ritz had been the first hotel in the world to attach one to every room. No maids and steaming buckets carried up six flights of stairs, but swimming pools of enamel tubs with swan's-head taps producing endless hot water en suite.

When Idina arrived, she was caked in soot, steam, and saltwater, and must have been longing to slip into a hot bath. There she could just reach out for the tap and spend hours submerged until the tips of her fingers had blanched and shriveled. The only trick to master was keeping her cigarette dry on its way to the holder and the ash out of the water.

All that was missing was Euan.

In the year since Gerard had been born, Euan had found it hard to come home. The long months in between had been lonely for Idina. Euan's diaries show that she and Euan were still very much in love.[3] Nonetheless, she had taken other lovers. Friends home on leave. Friends who hadn't gone over the Channel at all. All had, as was quite proper in the circumstances, been transient and passed unnoticed.

Now, however, she was waiting for the man she loved.

He hadn't come on Monday. Idina and Muriel had dined downstairs in the hotel and found there a couple of familiar faces with whom to celebrate Idina's twenty-fourth birthday, fingers crossed that Euan might turn up ahead of a wire—a birthday surprise.

The next day she had waited. She couldn't stray too far from the Ritz—just in case. An afternoon, or even an hour or two, was too precious to waste. At least it gave her time to prepare the room and ask the hotel to push together the twin powder-and-gilt beds, making them up into a vast bouncing double. He could appear at any moment, her Brownie,[4] the husband she'd come to save from the trials of taking his turn with the dancing partners at the charming Madame de la Barondière's, or traipsing all the way to Passy to visit the exotic-sounding woman he would refer to in his diary simply as "Solange!!"

Then, on Tuesday night, just as Idina was not quite asleep, Euan had slipped through the door.

And when, the next morning, Euan started spending some of their precious moments bent over a small volume on his knees, scratching away, Idina slid her fingers over the book he was writing in and pulled it from him.[5] When she flicked through the pages she could see the days rolling by under her eyes, packed with polo matches, toboggan runs, exercising the horses on the sands, lunches in Le Touquet, and long dinners in the officers' mess. And she suggested that, while they were together, she would write the diary for him.[6]

Breakfast arrived. A feast of coffee, croissants, eggs if available spread out over a thick, white, starched tablecloth that hung to the floor. Then she dressed for a city whose wartime fashion, like London's, preached the art of the subdued: a tunic coat, a single row of buttons running down over her left breast to just below her knee, a small hat—for a small woman. Little One, she called herself in a penciled French script that curled between the lines on Euan's pale-blue diary page.

They set off apace. Paris was made for walking. And they "walked miles," arm in arm in the freezing cold, heels ringing on the pavements, the echo bounding up the shuttered buildings on either side. They searched for open shops, peering into each one, looking for something, anything, to buy together. Searching in vain. The city of glittering treasures was tarnished, as dull as the sky that hung above them. Even the boulangeries were empty—

The salon d'essayage *at Lanvin in Paris*

the making of pâtisserie, those featherweight, sugar-topped cakes, was now against the law.

"Desultory shopping," wrote Euan.

They went back to Callot Soeurs, an Aladdin's Cave of stores.

The Callot sisters were famous for twisted lace around the edges of blouses, camisoles, and cami-knickers, gowns cut out of swaths of gold and silver lamé. The store was known to glisten. There had to be something in there.

But the shelves were bare. Here and there the odd pile of dark fabric, mourning cloth, beckoned like a sad song. It was, wrote Euan, a "bloody dreadful sight."

They lunched at the Ritz and after lunch, wrote Idina, "Antoinette picked us up and we went to Lanvin" in the rue du

Faubourg Saint-Honoré, five minutes' walk around the corner from the Ritz. Lanvin, unlike Callot's, was overflowing with samples of silks, muslins, and beading in the latest designs, its eighty seamstresses' fingers still flying in its workrooms. With fighting spirit, Jeanne Lanvin, the top French couturier, had even designed a nurse's uniform, with its Red Cross armband, for the best-dressed Parisiennes doing their bit. The skirt this year, Madame, ran the vendeuse's patter, will be a little straighter, to meet with the new fabric restrictions, *très simple, très chic*. Paris, "Antoinette" had revealed to them, still had its treasures. At least for those who knew where to find them—and had the money to buy.

The *salon d'essayage* was the size of a small drawing room, paneled to waist height and scattered with prints of drawings and designs from this season and last. Euan and Antoinette sank back into the wood and velvet armchairs and the heady scent of polish and rose oil, as the tassels on the lamp shades swung with the to and fro of women clutching fabrics, feathers, and measuring tapes. Yes, Madame, the sales assistant continued, in a week your order will be cut, stitched, embroidered, fitted, and finished. And "a small one," wrote Idina in their hotel room later, "ordered 2 dresses and a hat! Came back for tea."

That night they dined at the Café de Paris, with its huge gilt mirrors and low, tasseled lights on each table, theirs covered with plates of escargots and mousses that slithered down their throats, the band blasting in the corner. "Little One," wrote Idina, "realised she liked Champagne. After a large dinner, among all the other cocottes, we came home to bed."

"Cocotte," a neat pun, was French for both "pet" and "tart." In Euan's company, Idina styled herself the latter, and a "little one" at that. In the Café de Paris, however, they were surrounded by professionals. Some company for the evening, others just for the hour. Underneath its veil of restraint, Paris, like any soldiers' city, was a town where sex was in demand and for sale. Sometimes in private, where widows and hardened veterans of skirmishes between the sheets priced themselves for an overheated market at an astronomical eight pounds an interview. Elsewhere, on the stage, in a variety of cabarets deemed "unsuitable for ladies" by the travel guides of the time.[7] The thigh-flashing cabaret at the Folies Bergère was too crowded to find a seat. At the Mayol, the women on stage did not bother to wear any clothes at all. That night, when the restaurant closed for its nine-thirty curfew, Idina, her husband's *cocotte,* took him straight back to bed.

And so it went on. Idina, self-styled cocotte by night, rose each day and, she wrote, "walked miles in the morning." Then they went to a lunch party and, giggling, off to the cinema or "Grand Guignol in the afternoon." "The Big Puppet Show," as its name translated, had become a theater of horror, the success of each short piece measured by the number of people who fainted. From a box fenced in by a jail-like iron grille, Idina and Euan watched children being murdered by their nannies and heroines scalped, disemboweled, and guillotined—the convulsions on the decapitated faces played out in full. "2 very bloodcurdling pieces," wrote Euan, who turned to find "Muriel and Tom . . . in the next box."

Afterward, wrote Idina, "all had tea at the Mirabeau" and then the Café de Paris again, followed by the real theater, where they "went to see Guitry's play Jean La Fontaine—very good." They feasted at Ralph Lambton's, at Madame Ste. Allegonde's and with "Sturges" who, the next day, after their Sunday outing to the British Embassy Church, brought his lion cub to lunch with them at the Ritz.

That night, Sunday, it was just the two of them again, once more at the Café de Paris. Idina had wrapped him back around her little finger—"very amusing," wrote Euan. But, when she awoke the next morning to discover that a cold had wriggled its way through layers of linen and blanket, he was up, off, and out without her. His last precious days of leave were not, after all, a time to stay in and nurse a sick wife: a man needed to enjoy himself before heading back to war. And he rushed off to find a telephone to call Stewart, his best man and closest friend.

He told Idina that he'd be back at twelve-thirty. Wallace Cuninghame was coming over then, to go to lunch at Madame Barrachin's.

And he was gone.

Two days later, on Wednesday, the two of them went first to the permit office, then to the prefecture "to get her Passports done," wrote Euan. Not that Idina could travel yet. The U-boats were hitting their targets and the boats to England had been stopped. "Harben promised to let her know when they would start." They lunched "upstairs at 12." For forty minutes they chattered about everything except the war and when, or if, they might see each other again. And at twenty to one precisely Idina grazed her lips on Euan's moustache, closed the door behind him, and listened to the sound of his motor taxi rattling across the cobbles of Place Vendôme and away.

But it was not the war that would take him from her.

Chapter 6

The next time Idina saw Euan was in London, on 1 June 1917. He arrived more or less straight from a week in the trenches which, this time, hadn't been as bad: "Nice little dugout: no rats."[1] And he was only a day late coming home. The relief hadn't arrived until a quarter to three the morning before, and by the time he had reached HQ there were no cars left to take him to the station that day. So he had come on Friday, in the General's car and via GHQ. He caught the 7 p.m. boat from Boulogne and reached Victoria at 11 p.m. "Dina had got my wire from Folkestone and was there to meet me."

London at night was quiet. The streets were dark, windows blacked out and lamps extinguished or covered in dark-blue paint. The traffic, which had thinned by day, was, by the evening, barely evident. A week earlier the first bomb-bearing airplanes had reached the Kent coast and opened their carriages, killing just short of one hundred. London—today, tomorrow, in a week or two's time—would be next.

The few who ventured out in the blackness scuttled between darkened doors. Barely a household remained untouched; many held an empty bed or chair of somebody who was no longer there. Those who were at home, khaki cuffs scratching their wrists, white knuckles clenching rolled-up cigarettes, felt their names churning in the great lottery of death across the Channel. Which would it be: slowly, "from wounds," in a French field hospital; mustard gas—the worst, especially if it didn't take a man at once; or the swift, merciful obliteration of a direct shell that would leave not a shred of skin at all?

Yet life went on. One hundred feet underground, Tube trains rumbled through the city's veins. Behind the scarred front doors and blinds, lights flashed on and off, babies were born, old folk died, and young couples married, quickly, desperately, before they said good-bye. Restaurants, limited to two courses at lunch, three at dinner, and no meat on Tuesdays, were still open until their 10 p.m. curfew. And they were full.

Any man home on leave deserved to enjoy himself. Great groups of friends gathered in the best place they could afford. The women fluttered around, at lunch, at tea, then dressed for the evening, in elegant, subdued hues and long, dark lines that dropped from below their busts to a few inches above the floor. They ate early and went to one of the dozens of lighthearted musicals in town: *Bing Boys, Bing Girls, Bubbly, Topsy Turvy, The Maid of the Mountains,* or *A Daughter of the Gods.* But even these were curfewed, and at half past ten they were out on the streets again, hunting for the hidden entrance to one of Soho's hundred-odd illegal nightclubs where they could sip whisky from coffee cups until dawn.

The young drank anything, and anywhere they could. When the government imposed curfews on the serving of alcohol, and the nightclubs had opened, patrols were sent around the streets to stop drunken behavior and heavy petting in public. Where they could, friends piled into houses for "bottle parties,"[2] even to inject morphine together—and to spend the night. Fearful of not seeing each other again, some couples seized what might be their only chance to share a bed. The new duty to show a man who was about to die a good time began to override the old mores of virginity until marriage. Especially as marriage itself became an ever-retreating possibility. There were fewer and fewer men left to marry. Girls began to call themselves by boys' names as nicknames: Euan's diary reverberates with Jonathan and Charles in quotation marks. Any man who came back from France in more or less one piece found himself surrounded by a gaggle of girls. Even the married women became more predatory in a near-frantic need to prove themselves still able to attract a new man, should their own not return. Any man, single or married, was fair game.

Some nights there were dances in private houses. One of the great hosts of the day, the writer George Moore, strewed white lilies over dozens of tables, hired two bands, and kept his guests dancing until dawn. He opened his doors almost as often as it was still decent. Each time, some guests would go back to France and never return. The evenings became known as the Dances of Death.

Idina, glowing, at the front of the crowd on the station platform, watched Euan walk toward her. His cap was straight, shoulders still square, feet stepping briskly forward. Idina had a glorious twelve days with her Brownie[3] ahead of her: almost two whole weeks of strange wartime married life, in which Euan's duty was to have as good a time as he could and Idina's was to keep him entertained with a frenzy of social and sexual activity.

They rattled back through the empty streets to Connaught Place and ran upstairs.

Euan's diary records how the next day the social activity began: on Saturday it was just a lunch party, an afternoon walk in the park with friends, dinner at the Carlton, and the hit show of the year, *The Maid of the Mountains*, "where we occupied the enormous stage box!" On Sunday they set out "in the Rolls," picked up two friends, and drove west out of London and into a barely recognizable countryside. Every inch of rolling green field and sloping lawn had been plowed brown and planted with corn now turning gold. Baggy-trousered Land Army girls wearing knotted headscarves and with rolled-up sleeves were bent double at work.

Outside Slough they burst a tire and "had some trouble putting on the new wheel!" Half an hour later they reached Maidenhead Boat Club for lunch, where they then went on "the river in an electric launch until 7 pm. Took tea with us."

For a wartime afternoon, it was idyllic. Idina had succeeded in her task of entertaining Euan: "Dined at the Club (Lags joined us for dinner) and had a ripping run back after: car going beautifully." It must have appeared the perfect start to a perfect fortnight.

But, on Monday morning, after barely more than a scrabbled-together twelve months of married life in the same country, the trouble began.

It began with Idina's sister, Avie. Avie came to lunch at Connaught Place. Now nineteen, she was tiny like Idina but heavier-boned. Her shoulders were square, her cheekbones, nose, and jaw heavier. She was not, as the press rather unkindly pointed out, as attractive as her elder sister. However, the friend she brought with her was beautiful: given her ambition and the extent to which Euan enjoyed her company, disturbingly so.

Barbie Lutyens was eighteen years old and the eldest child of the most renowned architect in Britain, Edwin Lutyens. Lutyens had designed dozens of "modern" country houses in Britain and public buildings all over the British Empire. He was now working on the new Viceroy's Palace in Delhi, a monumental building with several miles of passageways. Like Idina and Avie's mother, Muriel, Barbie's mother, Emily Lutyens, was an ardent Theosophist. When Krishnamurti had come to England in 1911 he had left Idina and Avie's house to spend his summer holiday with Barbie's family. There was also another connection between the two families.

Emily Lutyens had formally broken off sexual relations with her husband. And over the past year Edwin Lutyens had become close friends with one of Idina and Avie's Sackville cousins: Victoria, Lady Sackville. Unlike the Sackvilles, however, the Lutyens family was, comparatively, frustratingly poor, and Barbie's family and her parents' relationship were constantly beset by money worries.

Barbie was tall and slender with endless legs, ice-blue eyes, and dark hair. Her skin was porcelain, her jaw sculpted. Her mouth was wide, childlike, giving her the air of a doe in some woodland glade. But this aura of treat-me-like-a-Ming-vase concealed a determination of steel. Barbie was embarrassed by her mother's Theosophy and social reticence and by her father's endless jokes.

She was irritated at the way in which the family lurched from financial crisis to crisis, moving into ever-smaller homes. She wanted a rich husband and a glamorous social life. As her sister, Mary, wrote in her biography of their father, Barbie "was determined to get out of her milieu" and had an "ambition of being accepted in smart society."[4]

After leaving the coeducational King Alfred School in Hampstead the year before, Barbie had gone to Miss Wolff's, a smart finishing school in South Audley Street, Mayfair. Upon leaving she had joined the middle- and upper-class nursing service of the Voluntary Aid Detachment and trained at a hospital near Aldershot. The moment her training was complete she had moved to Mayfair, where her aunt, the Countess of Lytton, had started a nursing home for officers in Dartmouth House, a mansion in Charles Street. Barbie had found Avie working there. The two of them had become firm, inseparable friends: Avie bitterly aware of being less attractive than her sister, and Barbie bitterly aware of being less wealthy than her friends. For Idina, this was to prove a fateful combination.

Two tennis-packed days later, Barbie reappeared. She accompanied Avie to tea at Connaught Place. Tea—the great British at-home social moment of the day—continued unabated, almost as an act of wartime defiance. Flour was gray, butter, sugar, and eggs scarce. Nonetheless, ashen sandwiches, scones, and transparent jam were arranged around the gently diminishing stacks of an empty cake platter, carried in by uniformed servants also bearing engraved trays laden with silver teapots and delicate porcelain cups and saucers.

Barbie, with her swan neck and big eyes, folded herself into a chair for an hour or so. It was not a long visit, but it was long enough: Euan was clearly hooked.

He had to spend the next day, Thursday, at his barracks in Windsor, and Idina went with him to keep him company. But back in London on Friday morning, Euan dashed out by himself first thing. He took Idina's small Singer car and "visited Avie and Barbie at their hospital."

Slowly, a gap seemed to open up between Idina and her Brownie.

In Paris they had been living together in a hotel room, with nobody but each other to talk to, every moment of their day in tandem. In London, however, they were in a house spread over seven floors and twenty rooms, with children to see—although in his diary Euan mentions only David and only once—and a stream of servants and daily business. This time he didn't give Idina his diary to write in. He had reason not to: Barbie appears on every single page for the rest of his leave.

That Friday evening Euan and Idina had fourteen for dinner and fifty to dance. "A great success," wrote the ever socially aware Euan, "cutting out three other dances which were taking place the same night." Barbie took herself home at dawn but, the following afternoon, when he and Idina drove down to Wimbledon to play tennis they "found Avie and Barbie there."

And so it went on. On Sunday Barbie arrived shortly after breakfast for a lift to the Maidenhead Boat Club, where she slipped herself into Euan and Idina's punt. When the boats stopped for tea, Idina succeeded in swapping Barbie for one of her own girlfriends. But the next day, Euan's last in London, Barbie came back to tea at Connaught Place with Avie, and Euan asked both girls to say good-bye to him over lunch the next day. They came. By the time they went back to their nursing home, Idina had less than an hour with him left.

But Idina had not yet lost Euan. When he returned to France he continued to write at length, if marginally less frequently than before. And, ten weeks and several dozen scribbled letters later, he was given some Paris leave. On Friday, 24 August, Idina crossed the Channel to meet him. After the near-constant presence of her younger sister's eager single female friends in London, Paris offered Idina a chance to spend some time alone with her husband.

However, when Idina reached the Ritz she discovered that she and Euan would not be alone after all. Instead of a flock of single girls, wings flapping, beaks at the ready, she found Stewart Menzies—Euan's almost ever-present and too adoring friend. Stewart and Euan were bonded by the Life Guards and their Scots blood. Away from each other for too long, one would twitch, make his way to the nearest telephone, and track the other down. Stewart could be found through GHQ. And GHQ could always find Euan for Stewart. If Euan needed a hard-to-find car ride, a pass, a

Stewart Menzies, future spy chief and the best man at Idina and Euan's wedding

place for the night, he called Stewart. And Stewart provided. Now, having not seen Euan for several weeks, Stewart had come to Paris to meet him.

Idina dined with Stewart in the hotel while waiting for Euan to arrive.

The following morning Idina managed to take her husband out alone and they were back as they had been six months earlier, only this time baking, not freezing, as they trotted around the streets, the wide brim of Idina's sun hat waving as they strutted along. They lunched at the Ritz, spent the afternoon walking again, in the Bois de Boulogne. That night they went back to the Café de Paris. Stewart, however, came too. The three of them went on to a show and back to the hotel. Idina and Euan went up to their room. Stewart followed them. And, frustratingly for Idina, he stayed—for hours. He "talked until about 1 am!" wrote Euan, as if his friend's prolonged company was almost too much even for him.

Eventually Stewart left. But that night Euan fell sick. The following morning he was still unwell. "Felt very ill," he wrote the next day; "have got poisoned by something." He spent the morning in bed but a lunch party—irresistible to Euan—beckoned. Shortly after noon he and Idina were heading south to Versailles for lunch and on to the tennis club at St. Cloud. Euan's illness receded: "We had some excellent tennis." They came back for dinner in the hotel, for which Stewart joined them. This time, at least, he did not follow them upstairs, but by the time Idina and Euan reached their room Euan was again as white as a sheet: "another bad night," he wrote.

Idina was struggling to find time alone with her husband. But the next day, at last, Stewart left and they went out shopping. They wandered off to Callot's, whose shelves had barely improved, and then to a jeweler's. Idina led Euan in. She gazed, asked, tried, admired—and they left. They dined à deux at Larue, went on to the nude show at the Mayol, and went straight back to the hotel.

When Euan sat up to write his diary the next morning, Idina again tugged it from him. Here in Paris she was going to make the most of the proximity of living together in just one room. And here, as she wrote, Idina "extracted a large pearl ring—by everything as only she knows how!"

A large pearl ring. One of the things a woman does when she wants to know how much a man loves her is see how large a piece of jewelry she can persuade him to buy. One of the things a man does when he feels guilty is to buy it. The next morning Idina led Euan back to the jeweler's, where she had seen a vast pearl ring. She left the store with it on her finger.

Idina wore that pearl ring through thick and thin. After four more husbands, the ring Euan had given her was still on her hand.

The morning after Euan bought Idina the ring, she wrote in his diary again, filling the bottom of the page. It wasn't the done thing for a woman to worry about fidelity in an upper-class marriage. Their money and property were bound for life. But Idina, as much as she enjoyed her sexual freedom, had had a father who had simply left.

She wrote, "Little One the only woman, wicked little creature," reminding him that no glacial beauty could offer what she did in bed.

They had three days left in Paris: more shopping, more lunching, more tennis. They visited Sturges and his pet, now more lion than cub. They dined in a group and found a gramophone to dance to. Little One and Brownie dined alone together at the lowbrow streetside café-concert of Les Ambassadeurs on the Champs-Elysées, just around the corner from the Ritz. They watched the vaudeville, listened to an operetta, and slid on to a show called *Hello Boys*. But Idina clearly still felt insecure. She tried to see just how much money she could persuade Euan to spend on her on an evening out—and then made a point about it. "Little One very sweet," she scrawled in his diary, pretending to be Euan, "but I was certainly taken for my high class keep."

But, as entertaining as Idina made herself, Euan was still drifting from her. This time he resented having to escort her around the permit office, the prefecture, and the railway station for all the pieces of paper she needed to travel back to England: "took all morning," he wrote. And at breakfast time the next day he packed her onto the London train.

WITHIN THREE WEEKS Euan was back in London. On 25 September he reached Victoria at six for another fortnight's home leave. Idina's first move was to order herself a new car to be brought around for a test drive. It was a Calcott and the latest wartime fashion accessory: a small car, half the size of the Rolls, it was powered by a four-foot-high rectangular gas bag perched above the roof. The Calcott arrived at Connaught Place at lunchtime. As soon as they had finished eating they leapt into it, "tried it for half an hour," wrote Euan, and then drove off in it to play a couple of sets of tennis. At teatime they returned home, where "the man from Cambridge" who had brought it down was

Idina's gas-bag-powered Calcott car: all the rage in fuel-conscious wartime London

still waiting. They persuaded him to exchange the Calcott for their old Singer.

At first the arrival of a fun new car seemed to have done the trick. For the next few days, as Euan wrote in his diary, he and Idina were barely out of it. They went shopping "in the Calcott," they drove out to lunch, to tea, to dinner, "in the Calcott." They went off to play tennis at Queen's Club, at the Ranelagh, at Prince's, "in a covered court, in the Calcott." They "went out again" and drove around for the hell of it "until tea, in the Calcott." On Sunday the two of them took off together in it "down the Guildford Road." They ended in Ockham, found somewhere to eat and "went for a walk in the woods after." And their gas-powered Calcott was such an intensely fashionable car that it was photographed for the *Illustrated London News.*[5]

Even back in London, with her husband in reach of all those young girls, Idina appears to have been enjoying a new honeymoon with Euan, and the shadows that had crowded in on their marriage three months earlier seemed to have faded away.

But halfway through Euan's leave Barbie reappeared.

She was brought to tea by Avie. Euan immediately set up the gramophone and they all "danced till nearly 7." The next eve-

ning, when a crowd of friends gathered at Connaught Place to go
to a party at the Tagg's Island Hotel, in the middle of the
Thames at Molesey, Euan handed over the keys to his Rolls and
he and Idina climbed into the cozy Calcott. Barbie climbed in
with them.

And Barbie vanished again. For the next four days, his last
in London, Euan didn't mention Barbie. He and Idina threw
another dance for fifty, "kept up till nearly 4," and went out in
small groups, great groups, and by themselves. They decided to
move the boys out of London away from the air raids and rent a
house for them, their nanny, and nursery maids, an hour and a
half west of London in the tiny Buckinghamshire village of
Sandhill.

As Euan left for France, Idina asked her sister to move in properly, treat the place as her own, ask her friends round. Whether
she extended the invitation out of loneliness now that the children had gone or in a miscalculated attempt to keep her potential enemies in sight, it would turn out to be an unwise move.

IT WAS JANUARY 1918 before Idina had a chance to see Euan
again. For him the three months in between had been long, cold,
and miserable, punctuated by an influenza that had been making
its way around the army. Throughout October and November
his regiment was moved, on horseback and in buses, in and out
of the trenches. By the time they were relieved from the trenches
in mid-December, the lorries were not able to drive the troops
home: "the snow in places up to our waists and mules' bellies,"
he wrote. And they had had to walk. Eventually back at base, he
had "sat up till 10.45, talking about the war, and cursing the
people in high places."

A couple of days before Christmas 1917, Euan received a wire
promoting him to the post of Brigade Staff Captain. This was a
post for which he had been lobbying for some time, since as a
member of the General Staff he would stay away from the front
line. It was not, however, the glorious job he had been hoping for. He joined the General Staff on Christmas Eve and the
next afternoon found himself alone and lonely in the Orderly

Room, "going through old files and taking over." He had an early dinner, wrote a letter, and went to bed at 10:30 p.m.: "It snowed again in the afternoon and was a very cold night." It was also Christmas Day, but Euan doesn't mention it. As New Year approached, the snow deepened and the temperature dropped still further. Euan's new workload—much of it either financial or the unhappy task of summarizing prosecution evidence for courts-martial—"three 1st LG are being tried for sleeping on sentry"—now stretched into the evenings. He had little time for long mess dinners and, in any case, none of his old colleagues with whom to make them jolly. When, in the third week of January, Idina cabled him suggesting that they meet in Paris in ten days' time, he applied for leave on the spot.

Two days before Euan was due to set off for the Ritz to meet her, Idina cabled him again to say that she was too ill to travel. It was not like Idina to be ill. She may have been small in stature but she was physically tough. Euan waited three long weeks but, to his surprise, Idina didn't make a quick recovery. She had had a cough that had turned to bronchitis and now stubbornly sat on her chest. Instead of going to Paris, she had to go to Brighton to gasp the sea air and have her chest pummeled for an hour a day to prevent it turning fatally pneumonic.

In mid-February Euan gave up waiting for his wife to recover and decided to go to Paris with one of his unmarried fellow officers. The two of them took rooms at the Ritz, breakfasted in bed, had their hair washed and nails done by M. Combes, did a bit of shopping, popped into a lunch party or two, and by midafternoon were at the first of their day's shows of scantily clad dancing girls. At the Folies Bergère "there was such a crowd we couldn't get a seat." On the second night the two of them ended up with the dancing partners at Madame de la Barondière's. By teatime on day three Euan had whisked his young friend "off to Passy & introduced him to Solange!!"

Euan returned from the whirl of Paris to Brigade HQ to find some astounding news waiting for him. He was, at last, being posted back to England. He would be there for almost four months.

Chapter 7

Short of the whole beastly war coming to an end, the prospect of four months with Euan was about as good news as Idina could hope to receive. He was being sent back to England to attend a training course for Staff Officers. The course was a twelve-week affair that would mean living as a student at a Cambridge University college, dining in the college hall, attending lectures, and writing essays. In a rapid-fire exchange of letters and wires, Idina, although not yet fully well again, planned to join him. It was a taste of the university life that neither of them had experienced. Idina would take a house or some rooms in a hotel, and they would spend as much time as they could together. And, on either side of the course, Euan would have a whole fortnight's home leave. In theory it should have given the two of them much-needed time together to strengthen their relationship. But Euan's return would not save their marriage, but destroy it.

On 21 March 1918 Idina took a late-lunchtime train from Brighton to London. She reached Victoria just after three, hailed a taxi, and arrived at Connaught Place half an hour later to discover that Euan had wired from Folkestone at one. One of their household servants, driving the Calcott, had already left to pick him up from Victoria, giving Idina just a few minutes to do her face and conceal how ill she was still feeling. On her dressing table was spread an array of silver-topped glass jars and pots, an armory of brushes, pencils, and powder puffs between them.[1]

Whatever she did, it was not enough. When, twenty minutes later, Euan came in he was dismayed: "Found Dina had just got up from Brighton and is still not looking at all fit,"[2] he wrote that evening.

It was not a thunderbolt of a reunion. Euan was disappointed that Idina was not yet well. In a sense it had been her wartime duty to recover for her husband's return. She appeared to have neglected it. Brighton, where she had supposedly been recuperating, was full of fresh sea air, but it was also full of bright young things on jaunts out of London. Once they realized what precious little entertainment the town held for them, these jaunts would end in drunken and often morphine-fueled bottle parties in hotel rooms. Idina had been there, a beacon to their friends, waiting to be visited, cheered up, and entertained.

Euan insisted they dine "quietly upstairs" at a small table at the end of the drawing room, and when the evening paper arrived he seized it. Idina watched him pore over its pages. The long-expected great German offensive had begun. He had made it back to England just, and only just, in time. Here in London all he had to fight for—apart from avoiding the bombs—was palatable food. Not only bread, but now meat, butter, and sugar were tightly rationed and, first thing the next morning, before Idina had had time to dress, Euan was off to hunt down his ration tickets. Then, he told her, he would visit his mother.[3] Idina stayed in bed.

Euan's mother, Minnie Wallace, was a disapproving, dour, and tightfisted woman, ironically so, given that she lived at 9 Grosvenor Street, an elegant town house barely twenty yards from the extravagances of the Bond Street shops. Since the death of her husband, Jack, Minnie had depended on her son for money. She had been widowed ten years earlier at the age of forty after a twenty-year marriage that had produced a single son: her darling Euan. She spent her days exercising her terrifying memory in the playing of bridge and labeling every item in her possession with her name and address. On one occasion a small black umbrella was returned to her after she uncharacteristically left it on one of her many economical journeys on London's buses.

She could not have been more different from her daughter-in-law, Idina, and her eccentric family. Socialism and suffragettes, cults and cancan dancers, not to mention divorce, all sent shivers down Minnie Wallace's spine.[4] If Euan had not been twenty-one and therefore of age when he married Idina, Minnie's consent might well have been withheld.

Euan came home for lunch. Idina, still obviously in need of rest but equally obviously determined to show her husband she was well enough to keep him company, was up and dressed.[5] After lunch Euan drove her out in search of milk. The supply of fresh milk had come to a standstill, so there was no need to ration it. It simply wasn't there. Instead the two of them drove to the Nestlé shop. Powdered milk it was, or no milk at all. Idina went in alone and bought as many tins of milk as they would allow her. It would be mixed with water for breakfast in London and for the children, who were still down in the country. Then, as if to prove that she was not as ill as she looked, Idina set off with Euan and "walked to various shops." They had friends to tea and went out on the town with others, dining at Claridge's with a couple of women, one taking the name of Charles to even the numbers, before going on to the theater.

However, even this first day of keeping Euan entertained had proved too much, too soon, for the still-unwell Idina. When they awoke on Saturday morning she looked terrible and could barely move. Euan insisted that she see a doctor. Doctors, however, were thin on the ground. Anyone young enough to be sent to the Front had been. One of the household knew of a doctor just around the corner in Connaught Square. Euan sent for him.

Dr. William Beecham came that morning. A man in his sixties, he was neither a general practitioner nor a society doctor. Instead he specialized in skin diseases and gynecology.

Nonetheless, he examined Idina's chest and, as surgeons often do, diagnosed her as in need of bed rest and, Euan recorded, "a small operation next week." Beecham also announced that Idina was so unwell that she "could not possibly come to Cambridge."

This was devastating news for Euan and Idina. Their plans for a riotous four months together were dissolving before their eyes. If this doctor was right, Idina would be stuck in bed and Euan would be alone in Cambridge. Clearly desperate to rescue the situation, Idina refused to accept his recommendation. And when he left, she got out of bed.

That evening Idina went out with Euan. They dined at the Berkeley Hotel and went to a show called *Nothing but the Truth,* which Euan thought "most amusing." For three more days, darting here, dining there, she kept up the pace. On Sunday morning they went to church at the chic Chapel Royal at the Savoy, and then took three friends to lunch at the Ritz. That night they dined at Claridge's again and, the theaters being closed for Sunday, had "a small party" afterward at Connaught Place, "some people playing Poker and some singing." And on Idina went.

Two days later Idina and Euan "motored down to Sandhill to see the children." They left at ten-thirty and "got there before one."

Almost as soon as the car stopped the boys came bounding up, "both looking very well and in good form." The straight-haired David, at three and a half no longer a baby at all but very much a boy, was growing lean and stretched, old enough to chatter nineteen to the dozen. A year younger, Gerard, his head a mass of fair curls, still had legs fat enough to make him lollop from one side to another as he ran. Idina and Euan stayed for two hours: time for nursery lunch and a romp around the lawns. At three-fifteen they left in order to reach London for the evening, as a couple of friends were coming to dine.

After five hours of windswept motoring along country lanes at full tilt, Idina lasted through dinner and then, already dressed to go out, hair up, gown to the floor, white arms bare, she sank. Euan stood clutching four tickets for the theater that night. "Dina," he wrote, "felt too tired to go, so I picked up Barbie and she filled the vacant seat."

Idina stayed in bed on Wednesday morning. Euan, ebullient after his evening with Barbie—"awfully good play"—went out to a lunch party at Dorchester House in Park Lane, the home of Stewart's stepfather, the multimillionaire Sir George Holford.

Euan lunched and went up to St. John's Wood to play tennis with Barbie. The rest of the day in his diary is blank.

On Thursday Idina hauled herself out of bed again. She went with Euan to dinner at a friend's house and then on to *Carmen* at the Royal Opera House in Covent Garden. In the second interval, her legs buckled. Euan, missing the climactic last act, "brought her away."

The following day was Good Friday, a bank holiday. Idina was still unable to get up after the night before. Avie entertained Euan and that night the two of them dined quietly together at a supper table set up at one end of the drawing room "as Dina went to bed, feeling rotten again."

By Saturday Idina had agreed to Dr. Beecham's "small" operation. It was booked for Monday morning, requiring Idina to go into the nursing home the night before, Easter Sunday. Once this had been fixed she hauled herself out of bed and spent the morning out shopping with Euan in the Calcott. They went back home to have lunch with a couple of friends and then afterward, as Idina lay down to rest, Euan climbed back into "the little car" and headed out of London. He and Idina had been invited to a weekend Easter house party. Even if Idina could not go, he did not want to spend the holiday weekend kicking around an empty London with a sick wife. He drove off.

The operation was postponed. Idina, sitting alone in Connaught Place, called Euan's house party just before dinner, and at noon the next day he scooped her up from Connaught Place and took her to a family lunch at 24 Park Lane. Avie was already there. She needed, she said, a fourth man for tennis that afternoon. Euan volunteered. After lunch he and Avie dropped Idina back home and headed up to St. John's Wood. Barbie was waiting there.

Euan didn't see Idina again until Friday. He went from the tennis courts to the Ritz to the sleeper for Glasgow without going back to see his wife.[6] When he returned on Thursday evening it was straight out to the Ritz, with another man, Avie, and, of course, Barbie. The four of them went on to a show, *The Boy*, "which was excellent again." Euan then came back to Connaught Place. But he didn't go up to Idina. Instead he dashed up to the first floor, picked up the gramophone, carried it back out to the car, and drove to Barbie's new house in Montagu Street, just the other side of Marble Arch.

Barbie still lived with her parents. The Lutyens family had, until a week or two previously, been living in a vast house in Bloomsbury's Bedford Square. However, financial pressures had forced them to sell and move on—in this case to a smaller house but far closer to Park Lane and Mayfair and the fast set to which Barbie yearned to belong.

Barbie had the house in Montagu Street more or less to herself. Her mother had taken the younger children to Shropshire to escape the bombs. Her father meanwhile was spending most of his time during the week in London with Idina's cousin, Lady Sackville,[7] and every weekend at her Sackville ancestral home of Knole—a palace of seven courtyards, fifty-two staircases, and 365 rooms. This left Montagu Street empty and a perfect venue for an impromptu party.

Euan set up the gramophone and the four of them "danced till 12:30 am."

The following day, Friday, was Euan's last before going up to Cambridge, and one of Idina's greatest girlfriends came to tea. Eva Belper was godmother to Idina's elder son, David. She was just a few months older than Idina, and the two women had been "out" as debutantes at the same time. They were both from industrial dynasties (Eva's family had discovered vast coalfields under their Glamorganshire estates) who had become Liberal politicians and then peers of the realm in the new industrial aristocracy. However, within a couple of months of Idina's launch into society, Eva had married. Her husband was Algernon Strutt, the eldest son of the second Lord Belper and another scion of a Liberal political dynasty that had risen from an industrial fortune. Shortly before the war Algernon's father had died and

Algernon had succeeded him as the third Lord Belper. Algernon and Eva's marriage was not, however, running smoothly. The two of them were heading, slowly and steadily, toward divorce.

Through all this Idina and Eva had remained close and, after Idina had wandered back upstairs, Eva stayed and "talked" to Euan "for half an hour." That night Euan went out again with Avie, Barbie, and another man and ended up at Barbie's house, where, with the slight thrill of being servant-free, "we made some supper & danced & played the gramophone." The gramophone was Euan and Idina's, which he had installed in Barbie's home. "Stayed till nearly 2 am," he wrote.

Sometimes it is not what is recorded in a person's diary that counts, but what is not. Idina's operation was on 8 April, two days after Euan left for Cambridge. The operation went well and Euan scribbled at the end of the page in his diary: "Heard Dina alright after op." But Idina did not make a rapid recovery. She remained bedridden and needing daily "treatment" by a physiotherapist called Mrs. Rigden to try to dislodge the infection from her lungs. And as she lay in that again near-empty cavern of Connaught Place, she slowly slipped out of her husband's consciousness.

Euan came back to London from Cambridge every weekend. On a Saturday night he had an early dinner in his college, Caius, and then caught the 9:10 p.m. train to Liverpool Street, arriving just after eleven-thirty. The first Saturday, Avie met him at the station and whisked him straight to Barbie's house, "where an informal party lasted till pretty late." Euan eventually reached Connaught Place in the early hours, long after Idina had fallen asleep, and he crept into his dressing room to sleep. He then appeared in Idina's room for breakfast the next morning, "at 8:45." But she was still indisputably an invalid.

After an hour Euan left. It was inconceivable that Idina might ask him to stay longer with her when he had so little time to enjoy himself. Stuck in bed, Idina was powerless to do anything but watch her husband dash out of the house to keep up with his new crowd of lively young girls.

Euan went to visit a Cavalry colleague of his, Viscount Ednam, the eldest son of the Earl of Dudley, who had been invalided home and was coming out of hospital that morning. He and Avie drove around to Eric Ednam's family's town house to join the party to welcome him back and listen to his "thrilling account of the Brigade in recent fighting." Eric had an audience of half a dozen: Euan; Avie; Barbie; Cimmie Curzon, the younger, beautiful sister of Irene, both celebrity debutantes and daughters of the former viceroy of India, Lord Curzon; and Eric's sister, Morvyth Ward, who called herself Dickie. Dickie was a statuesque English beauty with well-defined features and a well-defined sense of have-a-go fun. That night Euan rounded up a couple of other officers on leave and took all the girls out to dinner at Claridge's before catching the train back to Cambridge.

The next Saturday was Euan's birthday. After "a bottle of champagne for dinner to celebrate" at Caius, he again caught the evening train to London, "came by tube from Liverpool Street to Marble Arch" and, instead of walking fifty yards west to Idina in Connaught Place, turned north to Barbie's house, "where Avie and Barbie had a small party lasting fairly late, which was great fun."

He had breakfast in Idina's room the next morning, the news of what he had been up to inevitably revealing how much he was enjoying being caught up in his new gang of her younger sister's friends. But this Sunday, at least, it was "raining like the devil," wrote Euan. For once he stayed in. Idina started to spend a precious morning with him. But it was a short morning. By lunchtime Barbie had dropped in.

Euan then vanished. He went out to lunch with another crowd and Barbie came back at teatime with Avie, Dickie, and three or four others: "they played piano and danced and sang till after 6!" Idina meanwhile was upstairs, again being pummeled by the brutal arms of Mrs. Rigden.[8]

The following weekend Euan again went "to Barbie's" for what had become "the usual Saturday evening party." The next morning, Sunday, he awoke at ten, immediately "did some telephoning," and was at Barbie's house at eleven. That night, when he left the gang's Sunday-night dinner at Claridge's halfway through to catch the train back to Cambridge, "Barbie came to see me off."

This weekend there was no mention of Idina.

BARBIE WAS BEAUTIFUL, interested, yet tantalizingly unavailable. She wanted a rich husband, not a rich lover. Fooling around in bed with a man would not guarantee her position in society. Misbehaving in that way was for the girls who did not have to make a journey up the social ladder as she did. And while Idina lay in bed and Barbie kept herself just out of reach, Euan began an "Edwardian friendship" with somebody else. According to the mores with which both Idina and Euan had been brought up, having a passing affair with a married friend was accepted behavior. However, the new wartime morality had stretched this to "friendships" with single girls. While a single girl might not risk pregnancy by having full intercourse, that still left open a wide field of sexual behavior.

Ten days later, in the second week of May, Euan received a letter from Dickie Ward inviting him to Dunkeld, her family's sporting estate in Scotland, for the coming long bank-holiday weekend. Dickie was not as beautiful as Barbie but she was both attractive and lively and, unlike Barbie, was socially and financially secure. Her father was an earl and her family was in possession of not only, like Euan, a vast industrial fortune, but also of a country home regarded as one of the very finest houses in Europe. Witley Court in Worcestershire was a palace. Dickie's grandfather had reputedly spent more money on the house than had been spent on any other home in Britain or even in Europe. It had endless bedrooms and rows of columns, sweeping staircases, and balustrades linking them. Its gardens were laid out in great vistas of fountains and marble statues. An invitation to Dunkeld was not an invitation to Witley. But it was a first step along the way.

Euan rang Avie that morning to ask if she would, in effect, chaperone him. She "said she would decide by tea-time." When she agreed Euan proceeded to telephone Idina. This was his first mention of her in his diary for three weeks and it would be the

Euan (right) and friends (at Dunkeld)   *Avie, Dickie, and Barbie (at Dunkeld)*

Off for a ride over the Scottish hills

The Black Gang

Off for a walk

Picnic time

*Dickie, Barbie,
and Avie letting
their hair down*

last for another three. He told her that he would not be coming home for his leave after all.

It was not Idina's style to protest. She was clearly still proud and it was not the done thing to play the possessive wife—indeed, it would have been humiliating to do so.

On Friday, 17 May, Euan and Avie boarded the early-evening sleeper to Scotland. They reached Dunkeld at seven-fifteen the next morning and were met at the station by Dickie and Barbie in the car. On reaching the house they changed and walked over to the stables. By mid-morning the four of them, and another man, Ralph Burton, who was also staying, were riding out with a picnic lunch. For three days they lived the old, prewar life. They went for "glorious rides over the hills," fished and swam in the River Tay, played furious tennis on grass and hard courts, booby-trapped one another's bedrooms, and took the gramophone outside after dinner, danced until the early hours, and bonded themselves in a group that Euan tells us they named the Black Gang. On Euan's last day, Monday, the Black Gang spent several hours lounging in the shade as they posed for photos to commemorate the weekend. "The best 3 days I have had for many months," he wrote.

There were more "best days" to come. One week later, back in Cambridge, Euan "got a long wire from Dunkeld, suggesting Maidenhead on Sunday." He immediately wired Dickie to accept.

Chapter 8

Idina and Avie were both asleep upstairs at Connaught Place when, on Saturday, 1 June, Euan arrived shortly after eleven at night. One of the servants let him in but, before his footsteps had passed the first floor, the doorbell rang again. It was the Black Gang: Dickie and Barbie, together with two more of its members, Dickie's brother Eric Ednam and a friend of theirs called Lionel Gibbs. The four of them swarmed up to the drawing room, chuckling and whooping, and lifted the lid of the piano. Euan dashed upstairs. It was six weeks since he had last seen Idina but he came back down with Avie, leaving his wife undisturbed. This Saturday night the "usual party"[1] was at his house. But, aware that Idina was trying to sleep upstairs, he pushed them out after half an hour.

The next morning Euan picked up Dickie at ten-thirty and drove her to Paddington. By eleven, Euan, Dickie, Avie, and an admirer of Avie's called Mike were on the Maidenhead train. Shortly after noon, having signed in at the Boat Club and selected a punt, Euan was punting them upriver: "We lay under the trees and ate strawberries for a bit."

This time Idina followed her husband and her sister's friends. In the six weeks since she had last seen Euan she had recovered considerably and was now clearly determined to join in his social life. She dressed and picked up the telephone. Shortly afterward, she piled into a car with Barbie, Dickie's brother Eric, and a couple of others and arrived at Maidenhead Boat Club in time for lunch. Euan's punt came back to meet them. They ate in the packed dining room. "Saw lots of people at the Club," wrote Euan, "quite like old days."

After lunch they all went out in a flotilla of punts. They drifted in and out of the shade, closed their eyes, dangled their hands in the cool water, and listened to the quacks and whistles of the birds floating by. Then they bumped into another gang, "the Grenfell party," and the calm was shattered. The men pushed the punts to the banks, the two sexes disappeared behind their own bushes and emerged, the women in bloomers and camisoles, the men in underpants if anything at all, and "had a good bathe." Idina, having been regularly tossed into the English Channel from her mother's mixed-sex bathing beach in Bexhill since the age of three, and keen to prove that she was on her way to being as fit and well as any of the other girls, plunged in.

The Black Gang decided to stay and dine at the club, leaving Euan to go back to London ahead of them in order to reach Cambridge that night. He had agreed to travel there with Idina's brother, Buck. It was Buck's eighteenth birthday. Buck had, in anticipation of the date, long planned to remove himself from Eton that morning and, as a conscientious objector, head immediately to Great Yarmouth to enlist as an able seaman on a minesweeper.

"Dina and I went back by the 5:22 train," wrote Euan. The following week Idina was taking the children to the seaside for a month and this train journey was her opportunity to try to persuade him to join them. They were going to Frinton in Essex. Several other people she knew were taking houses there with their children. It was not far from either Cambridge or London. The boys would love to see him. So would she.

Idina was not a woman who either pleaded or threatened. She just made things sound as enticing as she could. But at this point her life and Euan's were running in barely parallel grooves. First Euan's absence had left Idina to build a life for herself and her children on her own. It was a life that Euan had played no part in, and the names of her own new friends held little attraction for him.[2] And when she had been ill, he had built his own life—and had done so with such success that he now appeared to forget that he had a wife and children.

The next weekend Euan went not to Frinton but to London to see the Black Gang. He arrived by teatime on Saturday and went to Dorchester House. He "dined with Eric E at Claridges—party 12. Ave, Dicks, Barbie etc etc," went to a show, and then, with Idina away in Frinton, held "the usual Saturday night party" at Connaught Place: "danced to the gramophone for 2 hours."

Euan didn't go back to Cambridge until Monday morning. On Sunday the dozen of the night before headed off for Maidenhead again. There, after a long lunch, and much to the consternation of the more traditional members of the Boat Club, they hired a motor launch and towed several punts up the river behind it. At the end of the day they squashed six into each car and motored back to London, ending up again at Connaught Place: "good dance to gramophone until 1:30." At 1:30 a.m. Euan left his own party and took a taxi to the hotel at Liverpool Street Station. He went to bed at five past two and was woken less than three hours later to catch the 5:53 train to Cambridge. It slunk him into the station at eight-fifteen, so he had time enough to rush back to his room and emerge again as though he had been there the night before. However, despite his efforts at discretion, Euan's weekend exploits had not gone unnoticed by his senior officers. Sunday's japes at Maidenhead had alerted a wide audience to the activities of the Black Gang.

On Tuesday evening around seven o'clock, just as he was changing for dinner, Euan heard a knock at the door of his room. He opened it to find his commanding officer, Gore Brown, standing there. He wanted "a word." Euan invited him in. Gore Brown asked Euan how he was, how things were generally, how were his wife and children? And then he started talking to Euan about the Black Gang. Gore Brown had heard that Euan was moving in a very fast set.

Now, a chap was entitled to enjoy himself on leave, but the

episode with the motor launch and punts on Sunday had upset quite a few people at the Boat Club. Not to mention all that bathing together the week before. He gathered that the antics didn't stop at that. It wasn't quite the done thing for a married officer to be careering around town and country with a group of young single girls. It was time, said Gore Brown, to start thinking about "breaking up the Black Gang."

Euan had little choice but to agree. In any case, there was only a week or so left of the course in Cambridge. He would stay up the next weekend and keep away from London. Then he had only a couple of weeks before he went back to France. And he followed Gore Brown in to dinner.

Nine days later, on Thursday, 20 June, "after a most excellent lecture on the Strategical Situation by the Duke of Northumberland" and "lots of drinking and bearfighting," followed by an impromptu "concert in Broadwood's room until 12:15 am," Euan packed up his things, said his good-byes, and caught the train to London. He arrived in time for a "dinner party of 12 at the Savoy ('Black Gang' & 6 others)."

Dickie, however, was not there. She was down at Witley, preparing the way for the Gang's arrival on Saturday for a week's haymaking on the farm. After this Euan would return to London for the Buckingham Palace investiture of the Military Cross he had just been awarded and leave for France the next day.

But on Friday afternoon Euan came back to Connaught Place after tea with his mother to find "a wire from Dickie altering all our plans for Witley. Frantic telephoning till dinner." Faced with an empty Saturday-to-Monday alone in London, Euan decided that he might as well visit Idina and the boys at Frinton.

Chapter 9

Caught 10am train from Liverpool Street to Frinton, arriving 12:33. Had to travel most of the way in the guards' van. Dina met me and we walked to St. Patricks.[1]

Idina was standing on the platform when the steaming seaside train, overflowing with children, hats, and brown-paper packages, pulled into Frinton. Engine and passengers screeched to a halt, doors were yanked open, string-tied suitcases and toddlers were passed through windows. For a minute or two the platform was swarming with life. And then the passengers cleared in search of lunch. Euan, her Brownie, was standing at the far end. He'd stepped out of the guard's van. Even there, as he later wrote, it had been standing room only.

Idina was now glowingly fit. She had walked to the station, as if to make the point to Euan. This weekend was her chance to prove how well she was and what a good time he could have with her.

It was good walking weather, good walking air, clearer than Cambridge, down in the Fens. They were lunching at the golf club, St. Patrick's. They walked there and as they strode, side by side, Idina was able to fill Euan in on who was around, what she'd been up to, what the children had been up to, and their plans for the weekend.

Waiting at the club were a man called Ian Maxwell and a girl-friend of Idina's, Dorry Kennard. Euan had heard of them but didn't know them. "Lady Kennard" was how he referred to Dorry in his diary, surprisingly formally, as she was barely a year older than he was. The year before, Dorry had published a book about her travels alone in Romania. She had completed her march toward independence by, just six weeks earlier, in early May, divorcing her husband. Sir Coleridge Kennard had been a former secretary at the British Legation in Stockholm. He and Dorry had met and married in Tehran in early 1911. When Dorry had given birth to their second son, in April 1915, Sir Coleridge was on "a motor-car tour" with an actress whom he had moved into the same block in which he kept a flat for "private literary work."[2] Dorry's petition for divorce "on the ground of her husband's desertion and adultery"[3] had therefore been easy to prove.

As the weekend passed, the gap between Idina's and Euan's lives widened. The talk at lunch was of travel: of the travels that Dorry had done, and of the travels that both she and Idina longed to do. When the war was over, if the war was ever over, they both wanted to go a long, long way away, as far from war-torn Europe as they could.

Idina and Dorry had other like-minded friends to talk of, too, such as Rosita Forbes: "Mrs. Forbes," Euan called her. Rosita had also divorced her husband and wanted to travel, traverse deserts and continents and write about it afterward. The prewar era had been the age of the "gentleman explorer." This new vogue for travel among Idina's girlfriends was the female response. For Idina, the company of these women pursuing lives beyond their families and social circles was one in which she could feel totally at home. The paths that both her mother and her grandmother had taken, providing them with fulfilling and meaningful lives, had shown Idina that motherhood did not have to be a woman's ultimate aim. The heritage of these two women reverberated through Idina's life. She had spent most of it surrounded by the political echoes of her mother's drawing room, and many hours wandering through the Durbar Hall museum at the back of the house on Park Lane, examining the costumes, weapons, and geological samples that Annie had brought back from her travels. It had left Idina with a longing for her own adventures.

When lunch had come to an end, and the conversation to a pause, the four of them played a round of golf. And on the day went, Idina making sure the hours were busy enough and social enough for Euan not to be bored. After golf there was a tea party back at Idina's house, and "good tennis after." Then they went out to dinner. Euan found a four for bridge. Idina played poker. "Home about 12." Now that she wasn't coughing so much, they could share a room again: a knot of Little One and Brownie in bed.

On Sunday morning Idina watched Euan play "with David in the garden." Playing "Bears" was their favorite game. Up and down the paths, round and round the bushes, on all fours, growling. It was raucous, squealing, three-year-old fun.

Idina took Euan down to the sands before lunch. She ran into the water, its ice-cold waves stinging her legs. Then she was bobbing several yards out, blinking salt out of her eyes, the wind whipping low across her cheeks. Dorry was beside her, both of them waving at Euan, laughing, calling him to come in.

"After some hesitation, bathed with Dina and Lady Kennard," he wrote later.

The whole glorious afternoon they played tennis, before and after tea. Idina and Euan were back in their old pair, playing their old game. They knew each other's serves and shots, which part of the court to cover, when to rush over, when to leave it to the other. Euan was having a good time. "Dina and I played Blake and Lady Kennard—3 of the best 'mixed' sets I have ever had."

Dinner was like it used to be. Their hostess, Mrs. Loeffler, knew how to lay on a spread: tender meat; vegetables from soil that hadn't yet been bled to a vacuum from overplanting; pastry that crumbled, that actually tasted of something. "Absolute prewar dinner!" wrote Euan. Then he and Idina "danced to the gramophone," its needle scratching away in the corner.

"Home 12:30." They were alone together again. And the next day was Midsummer's Day.

Euan wasn't going to spend it with her.

He was leaving, Idina learnt, the next morning on the 7:32. That way he could go to the War Office to arrange the investiture of his Military Cross, then have lunch with Avie, and the two of them would get down to Witley by the end of the afternoon. But he'd be back in London in a week. For the investiture and the whole charade. She needed to come with him to Buckingham Palace. Why didn't he meet her back there then?

Idina was now well, and fully able to keep her soldier husband entertained.

He, it appeared, felt his life was elsewhere.

Chapter 10

Euan and Avie reached Witley station at 5:30 to find Barbie and Dickie waiting for them. They drove to the house. When they arrived it was half shut up, half in use as a Land Army base. Here and there sheets hung out of the windows. Across former lawns and flower beds ran the corduroy lines of freshly turned earth. Nonetheless, in the afternoon light the house and its colonnades glowed.

The tennis court was still in use. They squeezed a good couple of hours in before "high tea" with the Land Girls. After eating, the four of them, Euan, Avie, Barbie, and Dickie,[1] went out again and walked around the park until sunset. Euan hooked a shotgun over his arm and the girls took it in turns to take pot-shots at rabbits. Back at the house they held their own Midsummer's party, singing and dancing until midnight when the girls, all three of them, announced they were going not up to bed but out to bed. They dragged mattresses out onto the vast, porticoed veranda, and slept there.

As at Dunkeld, it was just like the old times, a sweeter, simpler old times checkered with wartime novelties. With all the grooms off at the war, they caught their own ponies before breakfast: "some job!" wrote Euan afterward. They exercised them all morning and mucked them out themselves. After lunch they went haymaking on the farm—"real hard work"—until the heavens opened at teatime. There was more rabbiting after tea, followed by dinner, then a couple more hours out on the horses, cantering at hedges in the fading light. They came back to dance to the gramophone and for "a little piano." Then they fell into a deep sleep before midnight.

On Tuesday the enigmatic Barbie said she had to leave, and went. Euan walked to the village to find a telephone and make a call—not to Idina, but to Stewart. The rest of the week rolled by in a rural idyll. They went haymaking again. They helped out at a fête: Euan and Dickie staggered around together with a large picture, whooping with laughter and selling raffle tickets. Dickie and Avie "fixed up a 'ghost'" in Euan's room "with a string & reel of cotton." Various other friends came and went. And then, on Monday, Euan, Avie, and Dickie took the train back to London, lunched at Claridge's, spent the afternoon shopping together, and all went back to Connaught Place.

Idina was waiting for Euan when he tumbled into the house for tea with Avie and Dickie. He was leaving for France on Thursday—in three days' time. Idina gave it one last try. Tea duly arrived in the drawing room and in between the chatter Idina told Euan she had four tickets for *Fair and Warmer* that night and that she had asked a friend of his who had popped round, a chap called Whinney. Avie was staying at Connaught Place. They couldn't go out without her. Dickie withdrew. Idina won.

The show was good, very good. "Most amusing," wrote Euan. But when they returned to Connaught Place he didn't follow Idina upstairs. Instead, he stayed in the drawing room with Avie, going over their week at Witley and "talking till 12:45 am." And the following morning he went out shopping with Avie and Dickie.

On Wednesday, 3 July, Idina went to Buckingham Palace with Euan and his mother. For two hours Euan sat beside her tapping his heels and shuffling his cuffs to glimpse his watch. "Long slow business," he wrote. On the walls around her, over-sized portraits of rulers stared down on all sides, the decorated columns that separated each panel rising like imprisoning bars. She was sitting next to her husband, her first true love, whom she'd written to almost every day of the years they had been apart and who had now not only lost interest in her but was quite publicly pursuing her younger sister's unmarried friends.

Before the war an unfaithful husband showed his love for his wife by putting her first in public and only making love to married women who would return him to her. Extramarital affairs had been accepted because they were usually just passing things and would not break a marriage. That was the system. But that was not what was happening here. The situation had changed. People were starting to divorce and men were starting to become involved with not-yet-married women, making the relationships potentially more permanent and marriage-breaking. Over the next few years this would lead to a shift in morality that would make these new high-risk affairs no longer acceptable. But now, during the war, extramarital affairs were still acceptable and newly risky at the same time.

That evening was Euan's last night in England. He dined with Idina "quietly at home at 8," their conversation leaping the chasm between their lives. Then they went to "Ally's dance at the Beauforts' house." The dance floor was packed with giants in uniform and silk: "all the best and beautifullest there," Euan wrote. He disappeared into the throng, his big, brown eyes locking on to a succession of girls in Avie's crowd.

Given her own childhood, Idina clearly decided that, if her marriage was going to fall apart, it would at least be she who did the leaving rather than being the one left behind. And when Euan returned to France the next morning she left it to Barbie and her friend Cimmie Curzon to see him off.[2]

BACK AT THE WAR, Euan no longer bothered to write to Idina. When he picked up his pen in free time snatched between inspections and conferences and piles of paper, it was to Dickie that he wrote. Dickie, in whose Scottish and Worcestershire homes Euan had spent his most idyllic times since the war had begun. Dickie, besotted and hoping for some sign of a future together,[3] wrote back "a long letter." Euan, perhaps now remembering that he was married and officially taken, struggled to put together a reply and "spent half the morning answering" her. Dickie kept on writing.

Three weeks after Euan had returned to France, he received a letter from Idina: "An important letter," he wrote. But, however poor the state of his marriage, just three weeks after the best part of four months back in England, there was little that Euan could do about it now.

Even for those who hadn't been home, leave was thin on the ground. For the next three months everyone was kept busy with orders for "desperate schemes" and "death-rides" being proposed and most of them, "Thank God, cancelled." But not all. Stuck on the pit-scarred Somme battlefield, the ways ahead and behind jam-packed with troops and unable to move off the narrow tracks that divided the shell holes and trenches, the Life Guards found themselves sitting targets for the enemy: "heavily shelled for 35 mins. 2 OR hit: horses stampeded and several killed." They had lost several officers and men the day before when the Brigade HQ had been shelled. Now half of Euan's horses were gone and he didn't even have a saddle left. But at last the Allies were on the offensive.

Early on the morning of 11 November, the 6th Cavalry Brigade left its billets in the Belgian border village of Ramecroix, assembled in Barry, just a mile along the road, and set off east. At ten o'clock, just as Euan was entering the next town, Leuze, the "Cavalry Corps Car arrived with news that HOSTILITIES CEASE 11 AM!"

The streets filled. Every door opened and women stepped, children ran, infants toddled, old men hobbled down onto the cobblestones in a chattering, bubbling, screaming mass. "Great demonstration," Euan wrote, "in LEUZE square." The Cavalry left them to it. They moved east of the town "to clear road" and waited. At a quarter to one an "aeroplane message was dropped ordering us back to last night's areas." Euan returned to Ramecroix, "where we now have a lovely chateau and celebrated with a big hot bath and gala dinner; finished all the champagne."

Five days later, on Saturday 16 November, he "got two letters which decided me to go home as soon as possible." The first was from Stewart, asking Euan to be best man at his wedding to Avie in ten days' time.

The other was from Idina.

Eve.... later, on Saturday, November ... put two letters
which decided me to go home as soon as possible. The first was
from Sir Lan... King I am to be her maid at his wedding in five
or ... days time.
The other was from Dodge.

Chapter 11

Idina had taken a lover. His name was Charles Gordon and she had met him at the flat of a woman called Olga Lynn. Olga Lynn was a professional singer and singing teacher, and Lynn was not her real name. She had changed her surname from Löwenthal on moving to London from Germany.[1] Keen to be invited to the parties at which she was hired to provide the after-dinner entertainment, socially she was a busy bee of a woman, given to emotional outpourings and intense friendships, and was widely "suspected of being a Sapphist."[2] She lived in a large house in Catherine Street, a Georgian terrace in the shadow of Parliament. She filled it with guests, for drinks, for dinner, for the night. It was a crossroads where art collectors mixed with actors, dancers, and the pleasure-seeking end of high society. There was always some sort of party going on in the evening at Oggie's, as her friends called her.

When Euan went back to France, Idina found herself going round to Oggie's. Whenever Idina turned up, the tiny Oggie threw her arms open and let out a whoop of joy. And there, in a haze of cigarette smoke and champagne, Idina met Charles.

Like Euan, Charles Gordon was a Scot who had been sent south to Harrow School. He was four years older than Euan, and their time there had overlapped—Charles was in his last year when Euan was in his first—but the age gap had been too great for them to have been friends. Also like Euan, Charles was pale-skinned, dark-haired, good-looking. However, for Idina his attraction was very different from Euan's. Whereas Euan could hardly let a minute slip by without filling it with some social activity, Charles took a distinctly—perhaps overly—relaxed view of life.[3]

He and his slightly older brother, Jack, had been orphaned by the time Charles was eight. The rest of their childhood had been spent being shuffled between boarding schools in term time and maiden aunts in the holidays. At the age of twenty-one Charles and Jack had each inherited from their father a share of a house in Aberdeenshire and the money required to keep the house and land going. Unfamiliar with the property, the two young men had felt no attachment whatsoever to it. They therefore started to celebrate their newfound freedom from dormitories and spinsters by spending the money on a life free from labor and care.

Dormitories and spinsters had, however, ill equipped Charles and Jack for the pitted maze of London life. The money ran through their fingers as fast as they extracted it from the bank. Jack, who was the more insular of the two and tended to avoid romantic entanglements, found a steadying hand among the incense and reverberating chants of the Catholic Church. He decided that, if his pot ran out, he would take holy orders and retire to a monastery rather than dampen his brow in the world of wage-bearing work.[4] As a consequence, he battened down the hatches of expenditure and stopped passing over a single penny more than was strictly necessary.

Charles, by contrast, as his daughter later said, found a life of such fiscal and other abstinence less than appealing. His eye automatically followed an attractive woman as she crossed the room.

And, more often than not, the attractive woman, once she had noticed Charles, his dark hair, his height, his strong cheekbones and jaw framing a pair of twinkling, inviting eyes, recrossed the room toward him. With his air of falling back into a comfortable chair, Charles invited approach. He had broad shoulders, a long attention span, and an endless supply of handkerchiefs. If help was needed, he took enormous pleasure in providing it.[5]

Idina fell into Charles's comfortable chair. Here was a man interested in only her. He offered Idina the affection she craved but was no longer receiving from her husband. Instead of glancing over her shoulder for the next invitation he showed no ambition for anything except an easy, pleasant life. Charles showered her with attention and sympathy. With the prospect of her husband returning to her appearing unlikely, Idina slept with Charles not just once or twice but again and again and again. At first it was covert adultery: endlessly changing rooms and flats. But crossing town at unearthly hours was a tiresome business. They began to go out together, ceasing to care if anyone saw them, or what anyone said. They went down to Brighton, where Idina had spent so many weeks the year before, and moved into the Metropole Hotel. There the two of them could lie side by side and whisper of the life they might have had if Idina were free, if she had met Charles first, if there wasn't a war on. Charles told her about East Africa—which he had visited—and its gardens of Eden clinging to the slopes of its mountains, limitless fresh, sweet food that came in harvests not once but two, three, four times a year, and wide-open plains where animals ran free, uncaged.

Within a few weeks Charles had filled the space that Euan had left open.

IN OCTOBER IT BECAME CLEAR that there was not much of the war left. Euan would soon be home. Idina had to consider the prospect of trying to rebuild a life with a man whom she loved but who might any day leave. During her years apart from Euan they had developed lives so separate that it was hard to imagine pulling them back together again. Like Euan, Idina could have simply drifted from lover to lover. But she feared the future, and what old age might bring.[6] Her paramours would cease to visit.

Euan, if he hadn't already left her for another wife, would be out at the latest social occasion or in some mistress's arms, and with all that money, however advanced his years, he would never be short of either mistresses or would-be wives.

Idina had been scarred by Euan's semi-disappearance. She felt that there was something very wrong about her husband being targeted by women who wanted not just to be close to him (which she could put up with), but to take him away from her altogether and marry him. However many lovers she would have in the years that followed, it was said of her that "she never stole other women's husbands, but might pick them up if they were left lying around."[7] To Idina "left lying around" would show itself to mean either sanctioned by their wives to sleep with whomever they chose, or abandoned by wives adventur-

ing abroad. It would not mean husbands who were at a loose end while their wives were sick.

In the autumn of 1918 Idina was twenty-five. Her life had hardly begun, yet the life she had been planning with her husband appeared over. Twenty-five, however, was young enough to start again and, in the aftermath of a war that had broken both a continent and a generation, everyone who could was starting over, including several of Idina's closest friends, among them Dorry Kennard and Rosita Forbes. These women were not

Idina's friend the travel writer Rosita Forbes

retracing their steps to a time before the war in order to relive the same marital disharmony: they were setting off on great adventures and new lives.

Marriage to a handsome, rich Cavalry officer had been Idina's attempt to conform to the social norm of the day. It had also been a rebellion against her unconventional upbringing. Now, both convention and rebellion had failed her. After a fatherless childhood, she had been looking for a man who belonged to her. Euan clearly no longer did. And Idina's instincts turned her toward the examples of her upbringing. Like her mother, she was not going to take second place in an unhappy marriage. And the blood of her globe-circling grandmother, Annie Brassey, ran deep in her veins. Right now, the lives led by Idina's girlfriend explorers were more familiar territory to her than a loveless life with Euan. Somewhere there had to be a better life than this one, painfully married to a man she still loved but who no longer seemed to love her, in a country heavy with grief.

Idina's confidence, however, had been rocked by the failure of her marriage. She was not going to go abroad alone. She needed someone who loved her to come with her. There was Charles. And East Africa was now offering all former soldiers the chance to buy farms there. A farm would, again, offer Idina a life like the one she had grown up with.

Idina suggested to Charles that they go to Africa.[8] She had ten thousand pounds (the equivalent of a million today), which her mother had given her in her own name on her marriage to Euan. It was enough to buy a farm and live off of it until, on three harvests a year, they could make it pay. And there they could live the English idyll that this terrible war had fought so hard to destroy. They could spend their early mornings riding and the rest of the day on the farm in brilliant sunshine. It would be a life in paradise where what money they had would go a long way.

On 11 November, the day the Armistice was signed, as the nation celebrated and her sister, Avie, was planning her marriage to Stewart, Idina wrote to Euan asking for a divorce.

On Wednesday, 20 November, Euan reached Charing Cross Station at ten to three in the afternoon, surprised to find nobody there to meet him. "Got a taxi home: Dina had never got my wire,"[9] he wrote, as if unable to understand what asking for a divorce meant.

Idina was waiting for Euan at home. She hadn't seen him for almost half a year. Yet his face was still the same one that she had spent years wanting to reach out and touch.

Before either of them had a chance to talk, tea arrived. Rapidly burdened with a saucer and a cup full to the brim with scalding liquid in one hand, and a sandwich plate in the other, neither was able to say anything of any meaning whatsoever until after it had all been cleared away.

Then they sat by the window overlooking Hyde Park and its expanse of dulling green autumn grass pockmarked by brown mulch pools of leaves, bare-armed trees reaching above. The light was almost gone. They spoke about their marriage. "Important discussion with D after tea," Euan wrote. It would be five years the following week: five years, two children, a not yet half-built house several hundred miles away. Not quite a year and a half of that time had been spent on the same side of the Channel, during a war that they thought had been the beginning of the end of the world.

Idina did not want to remain married to a man who had so openly forgotten he had a wife. She didn't mind what anyone thought, but she wanted a divorce and a chance to start again. Euan would easily find witnesses to win him a divorce from her, if that was how he wished to do it.

The light outside had gone, but when Idina looked up she would have seen that this discussion had come as a relief to Euan: "explains much, thank goodness," he wrote later of their afternoon's conversation. His reaction was not surprising, considering that, if Idina had tried to divorce him by claiming desertion, he would have been thrown out of the Life Guards.

EUAN RETURNED FROM HIS BEST MAN'S dinner with Stewart, Avie, and Muriel just after eleven. Idina, too, had returned from dinner, dressed to the nines. She'd had time to have a drink or two. Euan had too.

He tried to persuade her to stay: "Long talk to Dina . . ."

Euan had some strong points to make. For one, Idina would lose any right to the money in the Marriage Trust. Her mother was still emptying her own bank account into the Socialists' and Theosophists' pockets. Charles Gordon couldn't have much left to rub together. That meant no Lanvin, no Claridge's, no Ritz. If Idina insisted upon going, she would be giving up a fortune.

But Idina clearly didn't give a damn about money. She wouldn't have been leaving Euan if she had. In any case, she had a little money in her own right. It wasn't a fortune, but if she went abroad it would be enough to live on.

The children were more difficult. Euan was, after all, the one with the money to support them and give them the best lives they could have. Besides, no gentleman wanted his children living in another man's house. Even if he had seen them just twice in the past twelve months, he certainly was not going to allow Idina to take them to Africa. What they needed was an English education. In any case, before they could blink the boys would be seven and off to boarding school. What would either see of them then?

For the past four years and a bit, the major part of their short pre–boarding school life at home, Idina had been the one making sure the children were well, taking them to the doctor, taking them to the seaside, finding somewhere for them to live when fevers struck and bombs fell, hiring and firing nannies, nursery maids, and cooks. She had done all that she was expected to do as an Edwardian mother. Yet, if she refused to leave them with Euan, he could refuse the divorce. And, as he had not in fact deserted her, Idina would have been extremely unlikely to win a divorce from him. An unhappy mother was not a good mother. Idina herself had grown up with only one preoccupied parent and Rowie, her divinity of a governess. It had seemed, happily, to be quite enough. Her mother was still at Old Lodge, as was Rowie, to keep an eye on things. And, now that the war was over, they would have Euan. When he was there he was very good with them. Africa, on the other hand, was not a place for children. As painful as it might be, giving her boys to Euan clearly seemed the best thing for them.

But Euan didn't just want the children to stay with him. He didn't want any coming and going. What they needed was stability. If Idina insisted upon leaving with Gordon, she would have to go and never return. She couldn't hop in and out of their lives on a whim.

The alternative to all this was to find a way to make their marriage work again.

Emotions deepen late at night. And it was "far into the night" by now.

Idina softened into indecision.

Their conversation was not over. Idina had been certain but now, seeing Euan again, she was not so sure. She had fallen in love with Charles and therefore believed she ought to marry him. But she still loved Euan too.[10]

The sky outside was late-autumn pitch.

It was not an hour to make promises that might be hard to keep.

IDINA SPENT THE NEXT DAY with her friend Eva. The moment Euan had left to grip his mother's shoulders while she wrung her hands with all the agony of a soothsayer ignored at the prospect of her adored son being tarnished with a divorce, Idina had called Eva, who had come round. The two women had talked all morning. Then, when Euan returned, they went out to lunch—Euan gave them a lift—and talked some more.

That night, when Euan returned from another pre-wedding dinner followed by a show with Avie, Idina was waiting for him again. "Another talk to Dina lasting two and a half hours."

Even though Idina had conducted her affair with Charles so publicly, as good as living with the man, Euan was prepared to have her back on a sole condition—that she never saw Gordon again. If she did, he would divorce her and she would never see the children.

It was a big promise to ask Idina to make. Euan gave her two weeks to decide.

The next morning Euan went to his lawyers, Williams and James, "eliciting a great deal of information about the general position." He could start divorce proceedings against Idina in Scotland, as far as possible from the Fleet Street press. A single hearing, a couple of witnesses, was enough.

He then went shopping, eventually returning to Connaught Place to talk to Idina for half an hour before a lunch party at Dorchester House. Behaving as though he thought his threats might work and Idina would be coming back to him, he returned "home at three and picked up Dina and drove her to Victoria in the little car," her own car, gas bag still teetering on top. He pulled up outside and called a porter for her bags.

They stood facing each other, the train whistles filling the space between them. The station was heaving, every step across the concourse blocked by muted tweed, worn leather and khaki still bobbing around. The air stank. Coal, grease, shoe polish, unfinished sandwiches, half-digested meat pies, and human sweat were being steamed up to the top of the high glass arches, where they condensed against the freezing air outside and fell back in erratic, noxious droplets.

They said good-bye. Idina swung on her heels and tripped off in the direction of the Brighton train.

Through the smoke, Euan could see Rosita Forbes waiting on the platform.

Chapter 12

Idina's two weeks to decide slid through her fingers. She left Euan on Friday, 22 November. Five days later she sneaked up to London on the day before Avie's wedding to see her mother and sister. She admired Avie's dress, examined the wedding presents on display, and slipped away back to Brighton. She would not be returning the next day. A sister who had just left her husband—particularly when he was the best man—was not auspicious at a wedding.

As Idina retreated from her own family, Euan slipped further into its bosom. An hour after Idina had gone he arrived for the bride's "reception to view presents."[1] He took Stewart out to the Ritz and then went straight on to the Albert Hall, where a Victory Ball was being held and where he had a rendezvous with the chief bridesmaid for the next day—Dickie. They danced until two-thirty in the morning.

Twelve hours later Euan was best man at Idina's sister's wedding. The two celebrations could not have been more different. While Idina and Euan had wed in a tiny church tucked away in a Mayfair backstreet, the church in which Avie and Stewart had chosen to marry, St. Martin-in-the-Fields, towered over the northeastern corner of Trafalgar Square. The pews were packed and the central aisle was lined on each side by men of the 2nd

Life Guards. Just after two-thirty in the afternoon Avie appeared. Idina had worn a traditional traveling dress in which to leap on a train and vanish on honeymoon. Avie wore a silver-and-white brocade, medieval-style gown. She wore a wreath of orange blossom over her veil and carried a bouquet of mauve orchids. Beside her walked Buck, his able seaman's uniform aggressively plain against the red and gold of the Cavalry officers and troopers lining the center aisle. Then came Dickie and four others dressed in "ruby chiffon velvet with bronze Dutch caps and gold shoes."[2] They were also carrying orchids—an even more colorful combination of red, white, and purple. "Felt rather like crying," wrote Euan. That night he cohosted a dance "to console the bridesmaids." He again stayed until two-thirty in the morning, when he took Dickie home. Two weeks later, Idina's deadline passed. Euan was back at Idina's mother's house, Old Lodge: "am Stewart and Ave's first guest, apart from my own children, who are here permanently," he wrote. Stewart and Avie's second guest was Dickie. And within a day of returning from this pleasant foursome weekend, Euan had instructed his solicitors to file for divorce in Scotland.

The following weekend he again visited David and Gee at Old Lodge, where he had "a strenuous time playing 'bears' with the children." On Sunday, Buck set off to see Idina in Brighton. Euan was willing, even now, to stop the divorce. But Buck "came back at 7:15 with no news." Idina had still not made up her mind.

Late the next evening she rang Euan in London. He had come back to Connaught Place with Stewart, Avie, and Dickie after the theater. The four of them were drinking, dancing, chatting about the play they had seen. But it was to Stewart that Idina spoke on the telephone; she would, she said, meet him for lunch at the Ritz the following day.

Whereas the Ritz in Paris slithered back in long passageways from a snippet of the Place Vendôme, the London Ritz was, and still is, a palace stretching an entire block along Piccadilly at the corner of Green Park. That day its cavernous atria echoed with jangling chandeliers, their lights reflecting off mirrors and white walls. Even in December the dining room was light and airy, overlooking the manicured lawns and almost neatly leafless trees in the park below. Idina sat across the table from Stewart. Fifteen months earlier they had been sharing a table at the Ritz in Paris. There had still been a war on. She and Euan had still had a marriage.

Had it been the war that had worn away their marriage? So much of their time had been spent apart, neither of them sure whether they would see the other again. Even their times together had been abnormal, driven by a frenzied obligation to enjoy themselves as much as they could. Perhaps they had forgotten how to be married in any other way.

From Idina's twenty-five-year-old perspective her marriage to Euan was not recoverable. She was not coming back. She was, she told Stewart, going to move on and make herself a new life instead.[3]

She stood up, the folds of her day dress shimmying around her, kissed Stewart good-bye, and left.

Euan had been lunching at White's Club, just around the corner from the Ritz and close enough for Stewart to call in were he to effect a reconciliation. After Idina left, Stewart called for him. Euan strode over. Stewart was brief. There was not much he could say. After a short while Euan returned to Connaught Place, where he spent "the rest of the day completing packing and moving kit to Grosvenor Street, paying off servants, etc." His life in Connaught Place was over. Euan was moving into the same street as his mother.

Two days after this, following a large dinner at the Ritz and the usual play, Euan and Barbie slipped away together alone. "Went to Combes' dance." They stayed two hours. "We just danced together all the time." Long, lean, beautiful Barbie, swinging around him, curling up on his shoulder.

Poor Dickie was ill at home in bed.

ON SATURDAY, 1 MARCH 1919, Euan walked from Edinburgh's New Club, where he had stayed the night before, to the Court of Sessions with his solicitor. His petition for divorce was

Euan and his sons after Idina's departure, Old Lodge, April 1919

second on the court list. At ten-thirty he was called into the witness box. The questions were short. Within less than half an hour both he and two witnesses had given evidence and the presiding judge, Lord Blackburn, had stopped the case and granted Euan his divorce.

Twenty-four hours later, back in London, Euan collapsed with a soaring temperature. "Teddie came round to see me and said I had got flu." Over the past twelve months Spanish flu had killed twenty-five million people around the world, a quarter of a million of them in Britain. "No visitors allowed." It took him two long, lonely days to decide to see a doctor, who then told him that the tonsillectomy he had had five years earlier was "badly bungled and my septic tonsils have grown again rather worse than before." Euan needed another operation but at least he could have visitors.

Barbie was the first to arrive.

It would be two weeks at least before the infection had subsided enough to make it possible to operate. Euan's throat was on fire, his temperature pistoned up and down. He couldn't go out of the house and, when friends came to visit him, which they did in droves, he could barely talk. After a week he was allowed to be driven down to Old Lodge to see the children, as it was now his responsibility to do. Gerard, now three and a half, had an infernal cough and it dawned upon Euan that, however ill he himself might feel, if he didn't arrange for his son to see a doctor, nobody else would.

Euan summoned the grandest doctor he could find for Gerard, then, having had the remains of his tonsils dug out, decided to go abroad himself. It was customary, having been involved in a scandal, to vanish for twelve months. Stewart had offered him a job in America as part of an ambassadorial mission from the then secretary of state for war, Winston Churchill. The aim of the mission was to establish an alliance between Britain, France, and America. The political advantages of such a relationship were to be presented by the former foreign secretary Lord Reading. The military point of view would be put forward by the war veteran and general Sir Hugh Keppel Bethell. Euan was to propose that Britain and America should exchange intelligence and counterespionage information. He drove down to Eastbourne, found the boys some lodgings by the sea, hired a governess to look after them, not Idina's Rowie but a Miss Jeffreys, and left for America for a year.

Unfortunately, despite his efforts to keep the divorce out of the press, it had made the front page of the *Washington Post*.

DIVORCE RUNS IN FAMILY, ran the headline.[4] The article raked over not just Euan and Idina's divorce but also Muriel's divorce from Gilbert and Gilbert's subsequent divorce from his second wife. It was not a good beginning to Euan's task in Washington.

Meanwhile, on the last Thursday in March, Idina married Charles Gordon at the Chelsea Register Office. It was a small wedding. She had three witnesses: a friend called Rosa Wood, the future collector of Surrealist art Charles de Noailles, and Rosita Forbes.

Within a week the newlyweds had sailed for Kenya.

Idina had bolted.

BOOK TWO

KENYA—HAPPY VALLEY

Chapter 13

In April 1919 Idina and Charles crossed to France and took the train south to Marseille, where they boarded a boat for Mombasa in search of a new life and adventure. Their plan was to buy a farm, build a home, and create a rural idyll on the other side of the world. Where Idina was going was new. Her husband was new. She, however, was as battle-scarred as the Europe she was trying to leave behind. She had neither fallen sufficiently out of love with her old husband, nor sufficiently in love with her new one. And she had had to give up her children.

Mombasa was achingly hot when Idina and Charles arrived. The turrets of thick purple baobabs bulged at them along the seafront, their outlines blurred by the clouds of dust. Oxen, with their sleepy lamplike eyes and wing-mirror horns, loomed around the corners as silent motorcars. Idina and Charles rattled along the streets on the town's trolleys: a bench for two balanced between an awning and a platform on tramlined wheels, pushed by barefoot Africans.

On the slopes leading down to the seafront the trolleys careered off, building up enough speed for a longed-for rush of air to blast away both the heat and the stench of dried shark curling up from the boats below.

Down on the ocean's edge they drank at the Mombasa Club

with its white plaster walls and greenish tin roof, the blood-stained sandstone walls of Fort Jesus and its inmates at their elbow and an endless sea ahead. They lolled on the upper floor's veranda, catching the sea breeze, ice-laden gin and tonics at their fingertips. Soon it would cool down, when the rains came.

Mombasa was a frontier town: shops on the ground floor and living accommodation girdled by dark-wood verandas on the first. It was the entrance to the British East Africa Protectorate, an area that stretched a couple of hundred miles north up the coast and six hundred miles inland. Sixty years earlier a British explorer, John Hanning Speke, had walked that far through the German-controlled land to the south and discovered the great gleaming Lake Victoria in Uganda. The lands around the lake were promisingly fertile and Lake Victoria was also the source of the River Nile. The British government saw control of both the Nile and Egypt as vital to keeping open the Suez Canal, which was the gateway to its empire to the east, and so decided to create its own route there. The area north of the German territory had so far been untouched in the scramble for Africa by European states: the tribes were inhospitable, much of the area was desert, and the air was thick with disease-bearing insects. The British were undaunted. The route in was through the port of Mombasa.

The British way into a new land was Church and trade: the missionaries wandered in with their Bibles and the Imperial British East Africa Company (IBEAC) was set up to bring the business in. Neither, however, made much progress. The tsetse fly was so prevalent in this part of East Africa that it proved impossible to use animals to transport supplies inland. By the 1890s the IBEAC was heading toward insolvency. In 1895 the British government took direct control of the region, in the process bringing a solution to the problem of transport. It would build a railway stretching the whole six hundred miles from Mombasa to Lake Victoria: the tsetse fly would be overcome. Five years and 5.5 million pounds later, the railway was complete. The pride of British East Africa was just under six hundred miles of gleaming iron, single track and a long, round, smooth monster of an engine, gulping wood and belching smoke. This was the Uganda Railway, called the Iron Snake by the Masai cattle herders through whose homelands it slunk. Before the rains came, Idina and Charles boarded the noon train. Their compartment was a square loose box with no link to its neighbors, the windows were dark with stifling mosquito screens, the pinpricks of ventilation choked with red dust. And off they went through the palm trees and slowly up, up, up to grassy highlands as scrub-ridden and green as a British hill. At teatime the train paused for toast and rhubarb jam and, as the sun set at an equatorial six sharp, the white-tipped Mount Kilimanjaro hovered beyond the screens. At dinnertime they stopped for a curry and were besieged by insects, while their beds were made up with crisp linen sheets. At dawn jugs of condensed engine steam for shaving and cups of tea appeared beside the line in the hands of waiters in white suits and red fezzes.

They clambered out of the Iron Snake at Nairobi. The town had started as a tented camp at Mile 327 of the planned Uganda track. By the time the railway line had reached it, in May 1899, many of those who had built it were too ill to travel further. A few miles ahead the earth split into the Rift Valley, a great crack in the earth's surface running the length of Africa. It was a vast plain of flat-bottomed canyon, channeled out of the highlands and framed on either side by vertical cliffs thousands of feet high. To build a railway down the escarpment was, to say the least, challenging, even for those who were well. The railhead paused. Headquarters were established. The Railhead Club, colonialism on wheels, pegged its guy ropes to the ground. Tents and shacks spread over the plains. In the rains groundsheets sank into a black-soil malarial swamp. In the dry season the earth cracked, its debris flying up at the touch of a heel or hoof, coating every inch of flesh and fabric in a second skin of African dust. Eventually the railway builders moved on. The town, however, stayed.

Once Idina and Charles's car had been rolled off its wagon at the back, its earth-covered canvas peeled off, engine tinkered with and recoiled until it was purring again in a haphazard way, they drove a couple of miles out of the center of town to a newish

Idina's second husband, Charles Gordon, in Kenya

club, the Muthaiga Country Club. It had opened only a few months before the war had begun and real time had halted. Muthaiga was long, low, and colonial. Its external plaster walls were painted a desert pink and surrounded by a garden at first glance classically English. The grass, however, was just a little broader, the flowers brighter, and the vegetation as lush as any in the greenhouses at Kew. Inside, dark-wood floors and window frames enclosed floral-print English armchairs and African hunting spoils, including an entire stuffed lion.

Before Muthaiga opened, the British and European gentry abroad had stayed at the Norfolk Hotel, in the center of town. When Muthaiga arrived, all those who were members of suitably exclusive gentlemen's clubs "back Home" migrated to the welcoming restrictions of the new establishment. There were rooms in the main building surrounded by a lush garden, perfect for newlyweds with nowhere else to go.

Idina and Charles did not, as yet, have a farm, a *shamba* as they called it there. They hoped to be allotted one in the British government's land raffle to be held in a few weeks' time. The Uganda Railway had created a secondary industry of farming alongside its tracks, from where those legendary three African harvests a year could be rolled downhill, onto the Iron Snake, and taken straight to a waiting steamship in Mombasa, for delivery to a hungry Europe. All that was needed was farmers, and a great many of them, for no fewer than two and a half million acres needed tending to. When the war had ended, Britain had started to overflow with trained soldiers in search of a new life. The British government, in the manner of a parish church fête, decided to hold a lottery to distribute farms in the East African Protectorate to these war veterans; given the unwillingness of the indigenous people to surrender their lands, all the better, went the thinking, that the territory should be occupied by men who knew how to handle a rifle. Anyone who had served six months in the armed forces could enter. That included Charles Gordon.

The farms being handed out ranged from 160-acre plots, which were free of charge, to larger farms of 3,000 acres for which payment was to be made. Each was numbered and applicants had to list these in order of preference. When a man's, or indeed a woman's, name was drawn, they would be allotted the farm highest on their list that was still available. The raffle was set for the middle of June, after the long rains. That gave Idina and Charles two long, wet months to draw up their choices. The rains had already started in Nairobi and in the farmlands up-country, and the mud tracks leading down from the farms to the railroad had dissolved into deltas. The best research would be here, in town: in the wood-paneled bar of Muthaiga, where the chaps were gentlemen, or ought to be, and in the glitzier environs of the Norfolk bar, open from eleven in the morning, where even the faster sort of fellows could ply their trade. Those piling out of Europe in search of the new had been both mentally and physically toughened by the war. Some had come here to find farmwork, either on their own land or as crop experts or cattle herders. Others, all too familiar with handling a gun, came to be hunters—men who could lead tourists on long safaris into the bush.

SEVERAL LONG, BAR-FUELED WEEKS LATER Idina and Charles followed the crowds into Nairobi's Theatre Royal, a parapeted and colonnaded stone building that functioned as a meeting room as well as a music hall. On the stage two large tin drums turned, containing the name of each raffle entrant. There were two thousand names and fewer than fourteen hundred farms. Name by name the would-be farmers were drawn out and their list of choices produced. Idina was lucky. Charles was called, and he was called early. They had won one of the three-thousand-acre farms. It was up in the Highlands, on the edge of the Aberdares, a range of high, rolling hills overlooking the grassy, antelope-covered plains of the Rift Valley and teeming with wildlife themselves. At the foot of the hills, as the slopes softened into a plateau, was rich, thick farming soil.

Idina and Charles hired a Somali head servant to run their home, packed tents, tables, chairs, cooking equipment, lamps, candles, and matches, and loaded them, along with a couple of horses, onto the next train heading west. At nightfall they tumbled off the train at Gilgil, a cowboy town on the edge of the Rift Valley escarpment halfway between Nairobi and Lake Victoria. A few low-built shacks and corrugated-tin huts lined a railway siding, surrounded by a crowd of local Kikuyu and Masai tribesmen who had gathered from hill and valley to meet the train. The head servant hired a guide, porters, hut builders, and a team of general servants, and pitched camp for the night. The following morning Idina and Charles's belongings were tied onto a couple of carts and oxen were harnessed at the front. They mounted horses and set off uphill. By nightfall they had reached their land. Ahead of them the Aberdare Hills rolled dark green in the setting sun; from them fell ice-cold brooks, swollen by the recent rains. Below these their virgin farmland glowed with luminescent grass and thick, red soil. This was Idina's new home.

Twenty miles from the Equator, the land northeast of Gilgil should have been arid, yellowed and browned by the sun until the grass crackled and the mud powdered. But eight thousand feet above sea level the rules of climate—for a start—changed. The altitude took the land right up to the freezing fingertips of the clouds. At night, when it was cool, it was very cool, those cloudy fingertips wrapping themselves around each blade of grass. At dawn the sun arrived to chase off the cold, damp night air and evaporate the freezing dew into a chilly mist. By midday the heavy African sun had illuminated the sky a quivering blue. Its glare bent the air and seared napes and noses, cheekbones and wrists. Then, when it had coaxed the flowers out of their buds but before it had sucked every inch of moisture from them, the sun started to dip below the horizon and those fingers of cold air and all their soggy, green-tinged moisture worked their way back in.

It was an earthly paradise. The landscape was genuinely familiar, indeed almost Scottish. Lumpy green grass spread over gentle slopes. The air hummed with the persistent buzz of insects. A burn of a slender river—the Wanjohi—gurgled and danced over flat stones. Bushes burst from the ground in a profusion of pale, paper-thin leaves and dark, rubbery plants. Tall, gray-barked trunks rose bare to a high crown of shortening branches covered in thousands of tiny leaves. Bristling bushes spiked up in between.

Yet, in a very un-Scottish way, every growth was magnified in color, size, and even intensity. Each bush throbbed with creatures large and small. Elephant, giraffe, and antelope rustled through, breaking out and swaying across open land. Leopard and monkey hung from trees reverberating with birdsong. The insect hum was deeper, lower, and more menacing than back Home. And rather than the vague, sweet scent of rolled lawn, the air was filled with a pungent but compelling smell of animal dung mixed with freshly picked herbs. At night, when Idina and Charles sat outside, they were surrounded by lookouts watching for wandering elephant, big cats, or buffalo—whose long, curved horns were the most lethal of all.

Idina fell in love with the landscape, dazzled by its beauty and the sense of adventure it offered. This was to become her longest love affair. British East Africa (shortly to be renamed Kenya) would be "her adopted country"[1] and she would "muster wholesome fury against those who she thought were trying to damage the land."[2] Time and time again she would return to make a new life here, until she simply stayed.

At first they lived under canvas, sleeping with at least two dogs, a shotgun, and a rifle beside them. The first buildings to go up were grass *bandas*—huts walled with tree trunks and roofed with grass—and mud *rondavels* which rose from dried cow-dung floors. In the meantime they wriggled out into the six o'clock dawn and damp morning mist, washing in a tent thrown up for the purpose and slipping behind another for the lavatory. Then they pulled themselves up onto their horses, saddled and waiting. By the time they returned to their camp for breakfast a couple of hours later, the large sun rising steadily through the sky had burnt the clouds and dew away, leaving a lush landscape in a kaleidoscope of green, each leaf, each blade of grass, so vibrant that it looked as though it had a light inside it.

By day they walked and rode around their farm, or stopped and bent double on their hands and knees, clearing the land for crops and grazing. They decided which breeds to order from England. They plotted and planned how to re-create up here, thousands of miles from home, the Edwardian agricultural dream of their childhoods. And, once their farm plans were under way, they went on safari with friends. For a month at a time, half a dozen white men and women clad in cotton suits the color of sand walked and rode through head-high grass harboring unseen beasts. Behind them trotted ten times their number of barefoot porters, balancing swaying bundles upon their heads. At night they sat cross-legged around the fire, flames licking their toes, hearts racing with the excitement of danger. Out there they were as hunted as they were hunters. A single rogue elephant, buffalo, big cat, or invisible snake could end their lives as rapidly as they could pull a trigger, and their ears pricked at the sound of a heavy rustle. But once they had emptied their glasses—whisky safer than water—fears dissolved and fingers stretching toward well-oiled rifles relaxed.

Idina and Charles came back to their farmland and started to build a single-story house. A hybrid between a villa and a mountain lodge, it would be small and charming. There they would settle down into their rural life. And, on a fraction of the scale of both the houses and the lifestyle she had tried to maintain with Euan, life with Charles would surely be sweeter, simpler, and more likely to last. It was an idyllic existence. Or, rather, it would have been.

For, within a few months of Idina's arrival in Kenya, her second marriage started to go wrong.

Given the circumstances in which Idina had married Charles Gordon, this was not altogether surprising. She had lost her husband's love, and her children, and had rushed into Charles's arms and run off to Africa.

Idina, like Euan, was driven, busy, a doer. Too busy. The laid-back Charles had presented a welcome change. But here in Africa, as the months passed and the list of daily tasks on the farm lengthened, Charles was too relaxed. He did not have a fraction of her or Euan's drive—in any sense. "Idina was a nymphomaniac," he later complained to his third wife.[3]

Before, Idina had taken lovers while her husband had been away. Now she needed them, it appeared, even when he was around.

Charles, it turned out, took a different view of marriage. Moreover, British East Africa was a small place. When the settlers rebounded from their farms and into the colony's towns and cities they packed themselves tightly into the few bars they frequented. The stories spread.

Charles was, by nature, a saver of lost souls.[4] Later in life he would recklessly hand over money he couldn't spare to people who said they needed it and come home to his waiting (third) wife and child empty-handed. "He couldn't stop himself," his daughter said, "even when we really needed the money too."[5] He had found a lost Idina in Oggie's flat and must have thought he had saved her.

But, as the gossip made its way around, it became evident that, far from being saved, Idina was falling further—and taking their marriage down with her.

In February 1920, after ten months of marriage, Idina took the curious step of leaving sun-drenched Africa for an England still in the throes of winter. It took three weeks to travel home, and in March, a year after her divorce and remarriage, her twelve-month exile abroad after creating a scandal would be over.

It is unlikely that Idina cared much about whether or not she would be partly accepted back into society. Her demimondaine friends were not the type to be bothered. Euan's friends, however, were quite different. And Idina knew all too well how much he cared about his social life. A year after their divorce, his exile was over, too, and Idina surely suspected—she may even have known for certain—that he would be returning to England.

Can Idina have been so foolish as to think that it was not too late to turn the clock back and return to both Euan and her children? It is still extraordinary today to divorce a second husband and go back to the first. But some people have done it. And Idina—who would notch up five divorces by the end of the Second World War—was hardly bound by any conventional view of marriage. If anyone could contemplate such a scheme, it was she.

STILL SINGLE, EUAN HAD BEEN both socially and romantically busy during his year abroad. He had spent the first few months at Washington evening swimming parties with the young Franklin Roosevelt, weekend house parties at the Joe Leiters' with Mrs. Woodrow Wilson, the Loews, the Dukes, and a Vanderbilt or two. He had stormed up and down the East Coast on its grand railcars with drawing rooms as well as sleeping cabins, with his batman (and likely inspiration for the name of P. G. Wodehouse's famous fictional creation) Wooster in tow. He had golfed in Atlantic City; sailed in Newport, Rhode Island, with the Cushings; spent weekends on farms stocked with endless ponies; dined with Teddy Roosevelt on Long Island; and nearly had to propose after he had driven a girl home, the tires on his Buick two-seater had burst, and he had been stuck there, unchaperoned, for the night. Eventually, in late September, the Americans agreed to allow a single British agent to remain in Washington as a liaison officer. According to Euan's diary: "We got the scheme nearly all fixed up over some whiskey."[6]

When he'd done that, Euan had been sent to New York to organize the Prince of Wales's visit that autumn. He'd found a showgirl named Dolores onstage in the Ziegfeld Midnight Frolic, a "tophole show." She was quite "the loveliest thing you ever saw." Then he'd left her for Ottawa and its Governor-General, the Duke of Devonshire, who needed another aide-de-camp. Euan had moved into an apartment in Government House. The air was flush with engagements. The future British prime minister Harold Macmillan, who was ADC-ing there, too, had just proposed to the duke's daughter Dorothy. "Macmillan and Dorothy Cavendish are very much in love: this was obvious to us all last week: we think it is all OK and really settled." Euan took Harold back to New York, where he "helped choose [an] engagement ring." Euan focused his attentions on Dorothy's eighteen-year-old cousin Alix but found himself summoned to see the duchess for "an interview . . . which was very interesting as showing the difference in people's points of view." Whatever the size of his bank balance, Euan was still a divorcé. Marriage to a duke's eighteen-year-old niece was out of the question.

Euan landed in Liverpool on 22 March. Idina had skipped off the boat at Marseille, taken the train north through France, and gone straight on to London, to stay with Olga Lynn, who was still at the center of a social whirl that Idina again needed. But, if Idina had plans to rebuild her old life, she was already too late. Less than a week after returning to England, Euan was engaged.

He had arrived back in the country on a Monday. Barbie had come round that first evening. By Friday he had proposed. On Sunday, after "a long and serious discussion," Barbie accepted. Euan was ecstatic: "so happy I nearly burst." Avie helped the two of them choose a ring and Barbie imparted the news to her previous fiancé, "the heartbroken Christopher," as Euan called him in his diary.

Little did Euan realize that it was a heartbroken Barbie, too.

Six weeks later, on the eve of her wedding to Euan, Barbie would sit up all night crying because she was, said her sister, "still in love with another man."[7] Christopher, however, did not have all those millions of pounds.

Euan took Barbie down to Eastbourne for lunch to break the news to the boys that their aunt Avie's great friend would be their new mother. The two of them then went back to London to sort out their living arrangements. At the very least, Barbie insisted upon living in a house other than Idina's in London. Kildonan was not, however, a house she could abandon—yet.

On 9 April 1920, "Barbs and I went all over Connaught Place in the morning with Mrs Milne & Maple's head man, despatching furniture to Scotland," wrote Euan.

After this day, in the remaining twenty volumes of his diary (which, once Barbie and not Idina was buying them for him, changed from a sleek blue to an imperial red), he never made another reference to his life with Idina.

It is one thing to close a door behind you. It is quite another to have somebody else lock it shut from the other side. Particularly if the person wielding the key is the woman with whom your husband fell in love when he was married to you. To aggravate the situation, Idina would be expected to be grateful to Barbie for agreeing to bring up her sons, while Idina had adventures abroad. And now that her boys had a new mother there could be no question of Idina maintaining any contact with them whatsoever. To do so would be regarded as destabilizing to the children, selfish of Idina, and unfair to Barbie, who had to establish her own relationship with them.

Idina went back to Africa. She had to salvage what she could of her life with Charles Gordon.

THE BRITISH EAST AFRICA Protectorate had become the Crown Colony of Kenya, named after the towering Mount Kenya. The settlers had held the first elections to their Legislative Council. As a state, Kenya was booming. The farming industry, however, was not. In 1919, when Idina and Charles had bought their farm, both the aftermath of war and excessive flooding early in the year had inflated food prices to exceptionally high levels, making it appear easy to run a farm at a profit. However, by 1920, more normal weather conditions and the influx of new farmers had collapsed the market for crops to a level at which farmers were unable to earn even the cost of production. Idina and Charles's dreamt-of farm had been all that was still holding their marriage together. And as the farm failed, Idina and Charles's marriage went with it.

Idina remained in Kenya with Charles for another year. She kept herself busy going on safari after safari. But by the summer of 1921 the marriage was well and truly over. She and Charles parted amicably, and decided to make their own ways back to Europe.

That autumn Idina organized a farewell safari: "an all-woman hunting and exploring expedi-

Euan Wallace and Barbie Lutyens on their wedding day, 10 May 1920, in the architect Sir Edwin Lutyens's house in Mansfield Street, London

tion."[8] Among her guests was the Countess of Drogheda, born Kathleen Moore in Scotland. Kathleen was a woman of many talents. A "dashing automobilist," she was "one of the best known sportswomen in society." She had played tennis in the Wimbledon Championships and "flown over Trafalgar Square in an airship" in 1918. She had also "attracted attention at Deauville . . . by her daring at the Baccarat table." But her crowning exploit, according to *The New York Times* later on, was nonetheless "to go on a big game shooting expedition in East Africa with Lady Idina Gordon."[9]

But not even the companionship of Kathleen, who, like Idina, was heading for the social stigma of divorce,[10] could disguise the fact that Idina had given up her children, husband, and homes for a life that had quickly fallen apart. And now she was quite alone. She would not forget how it felt. Years later, she wrote to her son David: "I . . . know the feeling of loss and utter loneliness."[11]

The expedition over, in November 1921 Idina sailed from Mombasa. In her arms was a serval cat that had replaced the late Satan.

On her finger was the large pearl ring that Euan had bought for her in Paris.

Chapter 14

I dina returned to London in 1921 with no other apparent plan than to stay a step ahead of loneliness. At twenty-five she had had everything. Now, three years later, she did not even have a place of her own to live in. In search of company, she again moved into Olga Lynn's house in Catherine Street. London had become a city in frantic pursuit of the new. Its pleasure-seekers had not, after the mayhem of the war, returned to the stately pace of Edwardian fine living. Instead, in noisy motorcars driven full pelt around London's narrow streets, they chased the latest fashion, the latest restaurant, the latest dance craze, and the latest nightclub. Nightclubs were the new venue for dancing. The sons of the families living in the private palaces lining London's parks had been decimated in France and these houses were being sold and demolished, their ballrooms and vast drawing rooms with them. And, having lived independently as soldiers, nurses, and Land Girls during the war, the surviving young were moving out of their parents' homes into flats as soon as they could afford to. These became places for smaller impromptu gatherings where friends drank vast amounts of alcohol and experimented with morphine and cocaine and played the gramophone to learn the latest dance steps before hitting the floor at Ciro's, the Café de Paris, the Savoy, and the archetype of them all, the Embassy.

Here, in the same groups that had gathered to dine at the Ritz and Claridge's during the war, the young, rich, and beautiful turned up to dance and push the boundaries of behavior as far as they dared in front of tables packed with the young trying to be old and the old trying to be young.

This desire to overturn every previous code of behavior overflowed into all areas of both the public and the private domain. In restaurants the young crowd was louder, attempted to drink more champagne than anyone had before, and danced on the tables, the women sometimes wearing nothing under floating skirts. Nudity was all the rage. Women appeared in transparent dresses. A fashion began, perhaps led by Idina, for receiving guests while still in the bath and then openly and slowly dressing in front of them. One hostess, Mary Mond Pearson, waited one evening until all her guests had arrived at her Belgrave Square mansion and then descended the curving staircase wearing nothing but a famous string of family pearls which reached her pubic hair.

Oggie's had become the Piccadilly Circus of the artistic and louche. Actresses, dancers, and musicians, passing through London and either preferring the ceaseless company of the Catherine Street house or lacking the means to pay for a hotel, moved in. One of them, the actress Gladys Cooper—at one point the most photographed woman in Britain and, like Idina, very publicly divorced—stayed when her performances ended too late to return to her children and their hordes of nannies, whom she had housed in Surrey.

These houseguests were followed through the door by their admirers. Between lunchtime and dawn the front door at Oggie's opened and closed, glasses clinked, cigarette lighters flared. Dinners were thrown for twenty at a time, the guests having to prove their worth with witty epigrams or outrageous stunts designed to entertain the others. Artists and impresarios chatted and argued, fell in and out of love, and in and out of bed. Lovers were no longer hidden, as they had been during the war, but flaunted. Nor did all girls wait until they were married. In 1921 Marie Stopes published *Wise Parenthood,* a book that made available to anyone

rand opera, prima dona; Willem van den Andel, Dutch pianist; Elsa Louise Roner, Polish violinist; eberg, Commander Albert Hoyt Taylor, inventor of radio broadcast apparatus.

CAT OR SNAKE—EACH TO HER TASTE.

Miss Eric Doty, a member of the Reptile Study Society, introduces a new style in spring millinery. Observe the snake coiled around her hat.

SECRET TURK PACT OF ITALY RESENTED

Britain Fears Supposedly Economic Terms May Include Political Accord.

ROME FOLLOWS PARIS LEAD

Lloyd George's Policy of Settling Near East Issue Jointly Now Virtually Blocked.

By SIDNEY THATCHER.
(Special Cable Dispatch.)
London, May 2.—The British government has told Italy in unmistak-

Lady Idina Gordon of London, with the wild Serval African cat, which she brought back from the jungles. It is only a kitten as yet and not as ferocious as it looks.

Idina in the newspapers with the serval cat that replaced her pet Pekinese, Satan, May 1922

who could afford and dared to buy it the contraceptive secrets that had hitherto been confined to quiet whispers between educated women. If that didn't work, again those women who could afford to—the rest had to rely on haphazard backstreet fumblings—slipped over to nursing homes in France on the pretext of nervous exhaustion. The only social crime here was dullness.

By the time Idina returned to London, being divorced was no longer an insurmountable scandal. Before the war, England and Wales had witnessed about five hundred divorces a year. In 1920, the year before Idina's return, this number had leapt to more than three thousand as war-damaged marriages were officially brought to an end. Several society marriages had finished this way: those of Idina's friends Rosita Forbes and Dorry Kennard and Gladys Cooper among them. Divorce was still seen as destabilizing a class system already ravaged by the war but, in these difficult times, making a single mistake by marrying the wrong person was forgivable.

But Idina's mistake was in having left Euan, not in having married him. Unlike Dorry's husband, Euan was not considered to have behaved badly. He had neither abandoned Idina nor moved in with another woman. She had been ill; he had entertained himself. He was still popular, handsome, and extremely rich. Idina appeared to have behaved utterly irrationally. Now it was obvious to all and sundry that her marriage to Charles Gordon was also over, and it would be only a matter of time before he, too, divorced her.

As the year passed, the rate of divorces continued to rise (it would peak at 3,500) and Idina appeared to be making a very direct personal contribution to this unwelcome wave of change. She had shown herself to be not a woman who had erred once but an errant woman. She had crossed a threshold that separated her from her once-only divorced friends and she was left off aristocratic invitation lists and avoided in public. Years later she wrote to her son David, describing herself as an "out-law" but adding, "I, myself, feel no wrong—I wonder why it is?"[1] From now on, social exile was where Idina would feel at home, and she made the most of it. Michael Arlen, whose best-selling 1920s novel *The Green Hat* portrays Idina as the tragic heroine Iris Storm, was a member of Oggie's set. In the book he, too, describes Iris as having "outlawed herself."[2]

Iris Storm is a tawny-haired, shingled-headed, big-blue-eyed aristocrat who was a fictionalization principally of Idina.[3] This was so widely acknowledged that another member of the crowd, the poet Frédéric de Janzé, refers to Idina as "the Green Hat" in his later roman à clef about Kenyan life, *Vertical Land—for Horizontal People*.[4] But Arlen himself seals the link between fiction and reality with the use of Idina's initials, I.S., for Iris Storm—at one time a common way of identifying the real individuals on whom fictional characters were based. Arlen portrays himself even more simply: as a nameless narrator who happens to be an author, and who meets and has an affair with Iris Storm. He writes that, having very publicly "kicked through every restraint of caste and chastity, there's the whole world open to her to play the mischief in, there's every invention in the world to help her indulge her intolerable little lusts."[5]

Idina decided she might as well be as bad as she could. Like her mother and grandmother before her, she was pushing at boundaries. She had her hair shingled to razor-thin shortness at the back and painted her fingernails green. With her new pet, the serval cat, on a leash, she stayed out all night and slept all day. She flitted to and from Paris at an indecent pace. In July the demimonde went south to the Riviera. Idina went with them. At the end of August they moved on to Venice, where Oggie took a palazzo for a month. They sunbathed on the Lido and drifted along the canals by night, stripping and leaping into the water, their naked bodies glistening in the moonlight.

Back in England, and still in possession of some of the ten thousand pounds her mother had given her on her marriage to Euan, Idina bought herself a Hispano-Suiza (Iris Storm's was canary yellow) with a vast bonnet and a silver stork on the front and careered around London in it, sober, drunk, or somewhere in between.

And there were the men. They came and went. Both physically and emotionally, Idina needed somebody in bed with her.[6] Each new body provided not only some degree of sexual satisfaction but also a physical reassurance that she was not alone—at least not for those hours. Craving love, she made the age-old mistake of confusing sexual company for it. And time and time again she was disappointed. She kept moving on.

But moving on to where? Unlike her mother and grandmother, Idina had no clear aim in sight. Her grandmother Annie's voyages had had a beginning and an end and her passionate efforts on behalf of women's suffrage had had a potential conclusion: women being allowed to vote. Idina's mother's political campaigns similarly aimed for—and succeeded in—bringing about changes in the laws of the country. All that Idina's actions appeared to be arguing for was that women could behave with the recklessness long allowed men. This could be achieved only by altering the entrenched views of the entire population: a slow transformation that would certainly take longer than her impending self-destruction. But, as long as she was occupied, or looking forward to the next amusement, she had no time to look back. "Wait until you are so free," says Iris Storm, "that you can see the four walls of your freedom and the iron-barred door that will let you out into the open air of slavery, if only there was someone to open it."[7]

"You don't know," says Arlen's I.S., "the bodyache for a child, the ache that destroys a body."[8] "I am not the proud adventuress who touches men for pleasure, the silly lady who misbehaves for fun," she tells Arlen's narrator. "I am the meanest of them all, she who destroys her body because she must."[9] Iris sleeps with the narrator on the first night she meets him. She has come looking for her brother, who lives in the apartment above him. They find her brother drunk into a stupor, and Iris comes into the narrator's apartment for "a glass of cold water!"[10] After some minutes of conversation the narrator leaves to talk to a policeman outside who is complaining that Iris's car has blocked the road. When he returns she has vanished from his sitting room. He finds her in his bedroom, where "she lay coiled on the bed,"[11] asleep. However, when he climbs in beside her, "hair that was not my own was pressed against my ear, and fingers that were not my own took the cigarette from my mouth, and teeth that were not mine bit my lip . . . and a voice as clear and strong as daylight said: 'but enough of this hell!'"[12]

The next morning Iris proffers some explanation for her behavior. "There are dreams, and there are beasts. The dreams walk glittering up and down the soiled loneliness of desire, the beasts prowl about the soiled loneliness of regret."[13] Her sexuality is the beast that haunts her life, not the desire that drives it. That desire, she says, is what they call "the desire-for-I-know-not-what. They will find it one day when we are dead and all things that live are now dead. They will find it when everything is dead but the dream we have no words for. It is not chocolate, it is not cigarettes, it is not cocaine, not opium, nor sex. It is not eating, drinking, flying, fighting, loving. It is not love's delight, it is not bearing children, though in that there are moments like jewels. There is one taste in us that is unsatisfied. I don't know what that taste is, but I know it is there. Life's best gift, hasn't someone said, is the ability to dream of a better life. . . ."[14] This was a woman, writes Arlen, who "walked, oh, impersonally, in the fires of herself."[15]

The outside world, however, saw none of the torment and only the scandal in Idina's life. As she moved from bed to bed to satisfy her cravings—all of them: not just for sex but for company, affection, and perhaps in the hope that this new liaison might be "the one" who would change her life again—her reputation as a seductress spread. She was "reputed to have had lovers without number"[16] and be an expert on the erotic use of lingerie, teaching at least one man how to touch four strategic points on a skirt that would make a pair of stockings slide to the floor.[17] And her name became a byword for disreputable behavior. Only those who cared little for their own reputation would wish to be seen "in the company of such dubious figures . . . as Lady Idina Gordon."[18]

The worse a woman behaves, the better she needs to look in order to hold her head high. Idina looked immaculate. In a dramatic contrast to the stories circulating about her, Idina made sure that she dressed at the leading edge of fashion: she had her clothes made for her by a new designer, an Irishman called Molyneux (pronounced *Molynukes*). She bound her bosom, flattening it into the androgynous style of the moment, and wore the wraparound dresses that he designed for her, making her look long, thin, serpentine, and almost tall.[19] Over these she wore the furs she had been given as wedding presents, remodeled, and the jewelry she had been given both then and by Euan. On her hand, she still wore that pearl ring.

That ring plays a part of its own in *The Green Hat*. Arlen disguised it as an emerald. It was not the only part of Idina's story he had to change a degree or two: much of the truth was too shocking to write literally, even when Arlen put pen to paper at the end of 1923. The divorce law had just changed, at long last allowing a wife to divorce her husband for infidelity, but public morality had not yet caught up. Instead of being twice divorced, Iris Storm is twice widowed.

Iris's ring was given to her by her second husband because it was, like her, "beautiful but loose."[20] The ring will stay upon her finger only so long as she remembers to curl it. If she becomes distracted and forgets the ring, and her husband, it will fall to the floor as she herself will be falling from grace. For, as her husband tells her: "that is the sort of woman you are."[21] Shortly after Iris loses the ring, she dies.

Idina wore the pearl Euan had given her until, long after Arlen had written, she, too, died.

AT THE BEGINNING OF 1923 a new twenty-year-old American actress moved into Oggie's house. She had arrived in London to star in a show called *The Dancers*. One evening she appeared on the stage at the beginning of the play with long hair but by the

Tallulah Bankhead

final act had bobbed it to the microlength of the day. Within weeks she had gained herself a large following of female cockney fans, many of whom sheared their own hair during the performance, throwing locks onto the stage. Her name was Tallulah Bankhead.

Tallulah was one of Oggie's new finds. She was exuberant and wild, inclined to shock given half a chance and certainly not dull but, compared with the practiced sophistication of the European women by whom she was now surrounded, an ingénue. Oggie and Idina took her under their wing. They taught her about food and wine, showed her how to diet off her puppy fat, took her to Molyneux for her clothes and taught her how to be decadent with style. And then either Idina or Tallulah taught the other (for they both became known for doing this) how to empty several crates of champagne into a bath and climb in—with somebody else to keep them company.

Bathing in champagne was not the only way in which Idina's and Tallulah's lives became entwined. In *The Green Hat* Arlen borrows the name of a boyfriend of Tallulah's for the subject of the thirty-year-old Iris's fatal romance with a younger man. The man in question, Napier, is starting his career in the Foreign Office and is being lined up to marry a debutante. Napier was the name of the 3rd Baron Alington and the owner of eighteen thousand acres of Dorset, with whom Tallulah had an on-off affair. Tallulah loved the story and played the part of Iris on the London stage (Garbo took the role in the movie[22]). Indeed, as Tallulah's Napier did, Arlen's Napier ends up marrying the suitable young debutante who had been lined up for him. For, in order to keep his heroine within the bounds of acceptability, Arlen has Iris demonstrate her overwhelming love—"if people died of love I must be risen from the dead to be driving this car now"[23]—by taking her own life, freeing her lover to marry his debutante, instead of ruining him by taking him herself.

But just before Arlen wrote, the now thirty-year-old Idina had done quite the opposite. She had at last found that "better life" in the form of one of Britain's most eligible, albeit penniless, bachelors. He was a tall, blond twenty-two-year-old just starting

on his career in the Foreign Office. His name was Josslyn Hay
and he would one day inherit Scotland's leading earldom. Idina
amicably divorced Charles Gordon, who wished to marry a
friend of hers, and married the young Josslyn. She then took him
away from the debutantes, away from the Foreign Office, and
back to Kenya. "I have done with England," says Iris Storm, "and
England has done with me."[24]

Chapter 15

Idina didn't have to marry Joss. She could simply have continued as his lover. Doing so would have been less shocking than taking a third husband. Idina's greatest sin was not her need for new sexual excitement but that "she insisted upon marrying her boyfriends," as her brother and others said,[1] thus shaking the traditional social structure grounded on lifelong marriages.

There were, however, several reasons to make Idina want to marry again. In part, she may have wished to play up her role as a socially outlawed femme fatale. For, to the outside world, her third marriage, to a man eight years younger than herself, was truly shocking. And the carousel of life at Oggie's was no replacement for the security of marriage, a security which Idina, needing ever more strongly to be loved, yearned for.

More important, Idina was clearly smitten with Joss. Her infatuation smothered any hesitation she might have had about embarking on a third marriage. In any case, as Idina neither expected nor hoped for fidelity from Joss,[2] being married was a way to hold on to him. For "Idina, fragile and frail,"[3] the obvious solution was to marry Joss, but to have an open marriage.[4] Each of them could then have sex with whomever they felt like without their marriage being destroyed. And, after two years of living at Oggie's, Idina had become used to having a variety of sexual partners. For this to work, nothing could be allowed to become too serious. It was the well-tried and tested formula for upper-class marriage that they had grown up with.

Having, for over two years, lived from party to party, looking no further than the next pair of arms, Idina now started to plan her life. She would return to Kenya with Joss. They would buy a farm, raise a house, and build themselves a life out there and, this time, she would make it work.

The odds on this marriage being a success were, however, not in Idina's favor. As well as her own less-than-encouraging track record there was the large age gap between her and Joss to contend with. Idina chose not to ignore this. Strangely, she appears to have mothered Joss at the same time as being his lover: "the child," she calls him throughout her only surviving letter to his parents.[5] At two-thirds Idina's age, Joss appears to have been filling not just the gap left by Euan but also the one left by her children.

Joss was serially unfaithful from the start. Idina professed not to mind.[6] She had, in any case, started off by sharing him. She had met him at the same time as another woman, an American named Alice Silverthorne, who was married to the young French Count Frédéric de Janzé, a sometime racing driver, sometime politician, poet, and member of Paris's literati crowd of Marcel Proust, Maurice Barrès, Gertrude Stein, and James Joyce as well, of course, as being a friend of Oggie's.

Alice was a beauty. She was raven-haired and porcelain-skinned, with violet eyes in a wide face. An orphan, she had inherited more money from an American meatpacking fortune than she knew what to do with and, as if bending under the weight of her riches, she appeared both fragile and almost frighteningly unpredictable. Joss and Alice yo-yoed in and out of bed with each other. Sometimes he went off with her for a few hours, sometimes a few days. But he always came back to Idina. Idina began to rely on Alice to return Joss to her, and Alice relied on Idina's acquiescence whenever she and Joss had a fling. Gradually the two women became friends, waiting together for him to return from whichever third bed he had slipped off to.

Golden-maned, with strong, aquiline features carved on a languid and slightly weak-chinned face, Joss had a direct gaze and thick, wide lips that he curled up and down into grins and sneers—whichever, for that woman, would do the trick. At twenty-one he had the confidence of the women twice his age with whom he had been sleeping since he was a teenager. His grandfather was the Earl of Erroll, the hereditary Lord High Constable of Scotland; his father was Lord Kilmarnock; as they died, Joss would climb the aristocratic tree. The only hitch was that there would not be a penny for him to inherit. The family had lost all its money, his father worked in the Foreign Office, and, shortly before Joss married Idina, even the ancestral Erroll home, Slains Castle, was more or less taken apart and sold for scrap. Although his parents could still afford to give him an allowance, it was not enough to live on. Joss would either have to work for a living or marry a woman who would support him. Idina could.

Although not as rich as Alice, Idina still had some of her ten thousand pounds, a generous mother, and an allowance from her brother, who had inherited a large amount of money in 1919 when their uncle, Tom Brassey, had been knocked down by a London taxi. And eventually Idina should receive a share of the great Brassey fortune outright from her mother. In the meantime, she certainly had enough to live well, as they planned, in Kenya. At least for a while.

Joss's career had so far pursued a curious path. At the age of fifteen he had been expelled from Eton for being caught having sex with a housemaid twice his age. He had then joined his parents in Le Havre, where his father was based, and finished his education there. At eighteen he had slipped straight into the Foreign Office and a posting as private secretary to the British ambassador in Berlin—where his father, Victor, Lord Kilmarnock, had just been posted as chargé d'affaires. Three years later, in 1923, he again followed his father, this time to the Inter-Allied Rhineland High Commission, situated in the picturesque German town of Koblenz. Idina, not quite divorced, had followed him there.

The TATLER

Vol. LXXXIX. No. 1159
London, September 12, 1923

POSTAGE
Inland, 2d.; Canada and New-
foundland, 1½d.; Foreign, 4½d.

Price
One Shilling

LADY IDINA GORDON AND THE HON. JOSSLYN HAY

A snapshot recently taken at a well-known Italian resort. Lady Idina Gordon is the Earl of De la Warr's sister, and the Hon. Josslyn Hay is a son of Lord Kilmarnock and a grandson of the Earl of Erroll. The engagement of Lady Idina Gordon and Mr. Josslyn Hay was announced a short time ago

Idina and her third husband, Joss, shortly after their engagement
in September 1923. Joss became the 22nd Earl of Erroll.

Victor Kilmarnock was now the British High Commissioner in Koblenz and Joss lived with his parents in the British Residence. This was an appropriately imposing creeper-clad, stone-walled, and fish-scale-tile-roofed building, surrounded by tall trees on the banks of the Rhine. Around it stood half a dozen similar edifices belonging to the French, Dutch, Belgian, and American embassies, whose inhabitants had turned the town into a hive of international social activity: there were boats to row, horses to bet on, a theater with a kaleidoscopic program that made it worth visiting at least once, if not twice, a week, and endless parties.

Idina's arrival shocked the staff at the Residence.[7] Not only was she much older than Joss but her hair was cut in a boyish "Eton crop"[8] and "Her figure resembled that of a boy, too, very very slim," said one of the other guests at the Residence at the time, who thought that Idina and Joss "seemed like brother and sister; there was something alike in them."[9]

And Joss's behavior went haywire. One evening, while the household was bathing and changing before a reception for Monsieur Tirade, the French High Commissioner, Idina and Joss sneaked downstairs and strung up a line of their own carefully prepared bunting—a long row of bras and knickers dyed red, white, and blue into an enormous tricolor flag. Joss's father was deeply embarrassed.[10] He "begged Joss not to marry Idina, even making him promise."[11] At least, Victor Kilmarnock must have comforted himself, Idina would not be around for long. She was openly planning to return to Africa and make a home there.[12] In Koblenz she spent her days hunting down antiques and linens for the house in Kenya and even ordering a vast bath made from green onyx. What Victor Kilmarnock did not realize was that, regardless of promises, she was going to take his son with her.

Idina and Joss announced their engagement in Venice at the beginning of September. They were staying at the Palazzo Barzizza on the Grand Canal with Oggie, who had rented the house for her usual end-of-summer gathering. The photographers followed them. A picture of the two of them, walking barefoot along the Lido, the thirty-year-old, twice-divorced Idina in a

Idina and Joss on their wedding day

Grecian-style tunic and the twenty-one-year-old Joss wearing a pair of brightly colored silk pajamas that were the fashion of the day, was the front cover of the *Tatler* the following week. Both of them were grinning—a wide-mouthed, lips pressed, smirking sort of grin at the small storm of scandal they had whipped up between them. "A snapshot recently taken at a well-known Italian resort . . ." ran the caption. ". . . The engagement of Lady Idina Gordon and Mr. Josslyn Hay was announced a short time ago."[13]

Ten days later, on 22 September, they married in the Kensington Register Office in London. Idina wore a cloche hat and a knee-length brocade coat trimmed with fur. As a final gesture flying in the face of tradition, she had had her outfit made in the traditionally unluckiest color for brides—green. It was a tiny wedding and only half a dozen guests followed them across town to the Savoy Grill. They included Joss's best man, Philip Carey, and Idina's brother, Buck, but not his young wife, Diana, either Muriel or Avie, or anyone from Joss's family. The society hostess Brenda Dufferin was there and a "Prince George of Russia,"[14] together with a young couple who had been with Idina and

Joss at Oggie's house party in Venice when their engagement was announced. Their names were Sir Oswald and Lady Mosley, known to their friends as Tom and Cimmie.

At this stage of his political career Tom Mosley was a young Conservative Member of Parliament, on his way to his first transformation into a Communist. He shared with Idina a similar level of sexual appetite and, even amid the flush of her engagement to Joss, the two of them were instantly attracted to each other.

Cimmie was someone Idina had known far longer. Before she married she had been Cimmie Curzon, Avie and Barbie's best friend. She was still Barbie's bosom pal, and Tom and Cimmie were frequent guests at the new house that Idina had poured so much into but had never seen: Kildonan. Perhaps with a tinge of guilt, Cimmie gave Idina an extravagantly generous present. It was a gilt and crystal-encrusted Cartier dressing-table set, engraved with Idina's new initials.

FOR THE NEXT THREE MONTHS Idina and Joss cavorted around London and Paris as the latest scandal of the day. Their ignominy blossomed thanks to the added misbehavior of both Idina's siblings. Stewart and Avie's marriage had not been a success. After a couple of misplaced hopes, Avie had not become pregnant. Gradually the two of them had started to wander. Stewart had an affair with Barbie's younger sister Ursula, whom he had met staying at Kildonan in August 1921. The affair had started a year later and Ursula had wanted Stewart to divorce Avie and marry her—mirroring Euan's path from Idina to Barbie. Stewart had refused and after a year the affair fizzled out and Ursula married another man. Avie, however, had found out about it and begun to console herself with a string of lovers whom she failed to conceal. While Stewart sat at his desk in Whitehall, Avie, extremely publicly, rushed around the country with a succession of different men, but Stewart remained resolutely married to her.

The tide of change that was sweeping across the world in the aftermath of the war was bringing uncertainty as well as excitement. Hard hit both financially and by loss of life, the upper classes felt vulnerable. In repeatedly divorcing, Idina was regarded as a class traitor—just like Muriel, who was still financially and vocally supporting George Lansbury and his Socialist causes. And then Buck caused the greatest stir when, at the start of 1924, he became the first member of the House of Lords to accept an appointment as a minister in Ramsay MacDonald's Socialist government. As far as British society was concerned, the Sackvilles were out to destroy it.

In February of that year, Idina and Joss went back to Koblenz to see his parents. Victor Kilmarnock had exploded with anger when he heard of the wedding. Idina and Joss had given him three months to calm down. Now they had come to say good-bye before leaving for Kenya. Faced with a farewell for what might be several years, Joss's parents brought themselves to make some sort of peace with the couple. Idina charmed them, promising to take care of their precious "child" in Africa. By the time she and Joss left a few days later, she was on good enough terms with her parents-in-law to call them darlings when she later wrote to them.[15] The affection was clearly returned. As a tribute to the happy couple, when Idina and Joss walked out of the Residence, fur-stoled and buttoned up against the biting January cold, Victor gave them a traditional Scottish exit for newlyweds and had them piped out by his tartan-clad sentry.

Within weeks Idina and Joss had crossed France to Marseille and boarded a boat for the two-and-a-half-week passage to Mombasa.

At first the journey was a novelty for Joss. On board he and Idina were surrounded by colonial officials and farmers, big-game hunters and missionaries, all dutifully studying the local lingo before they arrived. But by the end of the first week Joss was bored. While Idina was having a drink before dinner in the ship's cocktail bar, he slipped into a female passenger's cabin. Her husband, like Idina, had already changed and gone for a drink. The woman deftly unbuttoned Joss's trousers and fell to her knees. Her husband returned to the cabin door to ask why she was taking so long to change for dinner. Equally deftly, the woman pulled Joss into the bathroom with her and locked it, calling through the door that she would be along just as soon as she had finished.[16]

Joss laughed about the incident with Idina, who, in turn, made light of it.[17] While her husband openly stalked other women, Idina recounted the story to show how little she cared. It was her fault, she said, and, as if in an attempt to regain power over the situation, claimed that she had taught him to behave like that.[18] But the open marriage to Joss was already steadily heading out of her control.

The couple reached Mombasa in May and took the train straight up to Nairobi, the Hispano-Suiza they had brought with them from Europe strapped onto an open carriage. Once they had reached the capital they checked into Muthaiga and started putting the word out that they wanted to buy a farm. By the time the long spring rains had dried up, they were back up-country at Gilgil. Idina had found two thousand acres of grazing and forestland a few miles northwest of her old farm. This new property was, however, at a slightly higher altitude and right at the foot of the steep slopes of the Aberdares, twenty-five miles from Gilgil.

The *shamba* was called Lion Island, "because the lions used to breed there," wrote Joss to his mother in Koblenz.[19] He and Idina had not bought the farm outright but had leased it "at a very reasonable price, 15 shillings [three-fourths of a pound sterling] an acre on terms over ten years."[20] Idina and Joss's aim was "to be entirely self-supporting; killing our own sheep, beef etc. growing our own maize, wheat oats, barley etc, and to make money in dairy farming."[21] They bumped the Hispano-Suiza across the countryside and up to the highest flat spot on their new land, immediately hiring 150 local adult "boys" to help them clear it and raise a long, grass-roofed *banda* to live in until their house was built. It was hard work: "We neither of us have a vestige of a tummy left."[22] And at night when they fell into bed it was in the privacy of their own canvas tent, along with both dogs and guns to fend off any returning lion or adventurous leopards.

By the end of June they had dug the foundations for a low,

*Idina and Joss clearing ground: "We neither of us have a
vestige of a tummy left."*

single-story house, with a short stretch of veranda-fronted main
rooms flanked on either side by bedrooms and—as was always
the case in Kenya—a separate building for the frequently fire-
ridden kitchen. The predominant feature of the house was its
roof—vaulted to keep the rooms cool, eaves protruding over the
windows to provide shade. The walls were bricked and white-
washed to the top of these windows, and above that were cedar-
shingled up to the roof, which was of corrugated iron. It had
English cottage bay and casement windows and the simple lay-
out of a French villa. It was almost quaint, and deeply unpreten-
tious. It was, at last for Idina, a home. Joss insisted that they call
the house Slains after his family's recently sold ancestral castle.

Idina filled the house with furniture shipped to Mombasa, transferred onto the Iron Snake and offloaded at Gilgil onto heaving oxcarts that nearly toppled as they swayed their way up to the house. Their cargo was an eclectic combination of rustic pieces, the antiques Idina had bought in Koblenz, a few more that she had found in Naples on the boat journey down, and Sackville family furniture. There were sixteenth-century painted dressers, gleaming Napoleonic tables with intricately carved feet, studded Zanzibar chests, Persian carpets, and high-winged sofas that her grandfather had taken from Knole when his brother had moved into the house. At one end of the main living room sat a wide fireplace, a pair of buffalo horns twisting up the wall above. At the other, she covered the walls, floor to ceiling, in bookshelves. Week by week the latest novels arrived from England. Idina turned the pages until she shut down the generator at ten-thirty each night. She filled the rooms with fresh flowers, paintings, photographs, and a large mirror, its frame carved and colored with flowers. Idina fixed it to the ceiling above her bed: "So," she explained to one of the house's later occupants, "I could see all the different positions."[23]

Around the house rough grassland was mown into gently sloping English lawns. A path led down to them from the veranda through an explosion of pansies, roses, and petunias. Cedars encircled the grass and, at their roots, daffodil bulbs were scattered. At first sight, it could have been an English hillside, until the nettles, looming over a man's head, trembled with an unseen animal's roar. Or the ground shook with the giant gray pads of a rogue elephant pounding its way across the grass.

A hundred yards down the hill they built a red-brick dairy. "Dairying," wrote Joss to his mother, "is apparently going to be a very paying thing here, and we seem to have come at the right moment, the beginning of the boom."[24] A large "creamery combine" was being started at Gilgil. Idina and Joss's neighbor, Sir John "Chops" Ramsden, who owned seventy thousand acres, was planning on milking a thousand head of cattle.

Muriel sent them half a dozen of her prize Kerry cattle as a wedding present. They bought another fifty local cattle "to grade with Friesian bulls"[25] and started building up a dairy herd, sending the churns back down the hill to Gilgil. Encouraged by their early success with cattle, Idina and Joss had a flock of sheep shipped over from Scotland but, once installed, they started to die. Trying to work out what was so different in this otherwise Scottish landscape, Idina concluded that it was the strength of the sun. The Europeans in Kenya were fanatically sun-shy. Children wore not just wide-brimmed hats but thick spine pads under their clothes to stop the sunlight harming their backs. Idina wrote to her brother and asked him to send down a hundred knitted wool sun hats. She made holes for the sheep's ears and dressed each sheep. Still, the animals continued to die—from an unseen African parasite.

The Kerries remained a success, however. Idina took farming immensely seriously. The writer Elspeth Huxley later praised the work that the couple had done at Slains: "They enhanced rather than damaged the natural charms of their valley, by leaving native trees alone and . . . by paddocking green pastures."[26] In the era in which Idina had grown up, landowners had thrown themselves into farming with gusto. Many knew every inch of their land, every detail of their livestock, and made a hobby of trying to improve both—vying ferociously with one another at local agricultural shows. Muriel had done just this, both in building Old Lodge and in breeding her rare Kerry cattle.

Now, instead of being "so free that you can see the four walls of your freedom,"[27] Idina was busy from dawn to dusk: turning virgin equatorial soil and its thick-rooted weeds into good land for both grazing and growing cattle fodder was hard work. There were no tractors. Teams of oxen were harnessed to plows and driven slowly through the clodded and tangled earth. At every turn a new obstacle was encountered: a plowshare that twisted, an ox that stumbled and failed to rise. Idina spent her days walking and riding around her *shamba*. When the irrigation failed, when her dairy cows calved with difficulty, she was there. She designed herself workwear—an open-necked man's shirt and corduroy trousers that she had run up by the tailor in Gilgil. Idina rapidly became so at ease with her new environment that,

Idina and Joss's house, Slains, nearing the end of its construction, with the grass banda *(hut) they had been using in front*

like the local Kikuyu tribesmen and much to their amazement, she both walked and rode barefoot, the stirrups and thorns tearing into her flesh. When one friend was helping her apply a "scalding poultice" to a "very swollen and obviously painful" foot afterward, Idina "never flinched." The friend "asked if she was afraid of anything. 'Yes, one thing—old age,' " Idina replied.[28]

It was not, however, a life of unceasing toil. Idina taught her *watu* (her staff—it means "people" in Swahili) how to mow and weed. A Mr. Pidcock ran the farm. Marie, Idina's French housekeeper, ran the house and directed the *mpishi* (cook) and his *totos* (kitchen boys). This left plenty of time free for nonagricultural pursuits. As she and Charles had done, she and Joss rose at dawn to horses saddled up and waiting and galloped across the balmy, dewy hills for two hours before breakfast. They marked out polo pitches on the grasslands below Slains and employed a soldier-settler, Captain Lawrence, to school their polo ponies and racehorses. They went off on safari for days or even weeks at a time, walking or riding through eye-level grass—the excitement of being surrounded by so much unseen danger sending adrenaline pumping around their veins.

In the Kenyan hills, Idina had created a mix of rural idyll and raw adventure with which she could be truly happy. Photographs of her around the farm and bent double pulling weeds out of the mud show a radiant woman. She had a cozy home with breathtaking views, a busy farm with its constant cycle of life, and a husband whom she adored. But there was one thing that neither Joss nor she could do without: sexual adventure.

New bed companions were not, at first, easy to find. The average white farmer in Kenya, unlike Idina, would have been appalled by the prospect of bed-hopping. For the most part, Idina and Joss needed to find like-minded "Edwardians" among the Muthaiga Club set of landed gentry in exile. This was a growing group. Safaris had become an established tourist activity before the war, bringing the moneyed classes to what was then the East Africa Protectorate in droves in search of big game.

Dazzled by the landscape, wildlife, and sense of virgin territory, some stayed. Others, disheartened by a Europe ravaged by war, had returned since 1918: the number of whites in the country had more than doubled since 1914. Many of these were younger sons of peers who could afford in Africa the thousands of acres and dozens of servants that their elder siblings had acquired in England by birthright. Prominent among these aristocrats (although an elder son himself) was Lord Delamere, known as D, who had been an early settler and now owned tens of thousands of acres on the far side of Gilgil from Slains, around Lake Elmenteita in the Rift Valley. He had started as the unofficial head of the settlers and was now leader of the eleven elected members of Kenya's Legislative Council. D had been followed by his two brothers-in-law, Berkeley and Galbraith Cole, sons of the Earl of Enniskillen, and a rush followed. This included Denys Finch Hatton, the magnetic and enigmatic younger son of the Earl of Winchilsea. Finch Hatton had first come to the East Africa Protectorate before the war and had tried his hand at both shop-owning—he bought a chain of *dukas* (small shops)—and mine-owning before becoming a prominent hunter who led visitors to Kenya deep into the bush for weeks on end. In between these expeditions he was the lover of the pilot Beryl Markham and, more famously, of the writer Karen Blixen—

the affair immortalized in the film *Out of Africa.*

Regardless of each individual's private practice, all had been brought up to regard marital fidelity as infra dig and extramarital sex a normal course of behavior. The key distinction between good and bad behavior was discretion and remaining tight-lipped about others. When not at Muthaiga, however, it was hard for any settlers to talk about anything to anyone. They were spread out across several hundred square miles of the area known as the White Highlands. This was the rich farming territory on the high-altitude lands in the center of Kenya which, after a great deal of gun-toting and foot-stamping by some of the white settlers in 1920, had

Idina with her Hispano-Suiza in Kenya

been officially reserved for colonization by whites only, thereby excluding not only the native Africans, but also the fast-growing new Indian population.

The roads in the Highlands, where they existed, were no more than dirt tracks. They were regularly graded and, just after grading, could provide hard, fast racetracks along which to rattle. Rain, however, reduced them to rivers that hardened into a mudscape of peaks and gullies. The going in the racing Bugattis, solid Model T Fords, or even Idina's Hispano-Suiza, its silver stork splattered with liquid orange earth, was slow. A visit to a lover was likely to be a full morning or afternoon's drive each way, the adventure of even a short African journey spilling over into the meeting. And, with only an equatorial twelve hours' daylight for traveling in, a single encounter could take a day or two at a time. This was a day or two away for which an excuse—such as needing to look at some potential livestock—would be politely, if barely plausibly, concocted, and equally politely, if incredulously, accepted.

In between these episodes, Idina and Joss might go for several long days at a stretch, wandering around the vast expanse of their farm without seeing any of their *mzungu*—white—neighbors. Only a trip down to the *dukas* in Gilgil to buy provisions and order more pairs of corduroys to replace those ripped to shreds on fast rides through the bush presented an opportunity for social interaction.

Even then they would be lucky to turn up there at the same time as one of their crowd.

This all changed on livestock auction days, held regularly at Gilgil and the neighboring towns of Naivasha and Nakuru. These were true double-entendre cattle markets. An assortment of both hands-on and veranda farmers—so-called because they directed their farm employees from the veranda rather than working in the fields themselves—would roll up in gleaming cars a couple of hours after dawn, having driven down from the hills the day before and stayed nearby. Out they stepped into the thick red dust, suited, hatted, their wives dressed to the nines, cigarettes tipping out of long, black holders slid between gray-gloved fingers, and their eyes just glimpsed through the veils hanging over the top half of their faces. As the animals were herded through the ring in lots, bids rising, these men and women leant over the rails and eyed their neighbors. After weeks of the stark, staring, monotonous claustrophobia of sitting across the dining table from the same single face, an army of servants catering to their every possible need, even some of the industrious, God-fearing, buttoned-up types found a frustrated desire for fresh human contact overwhelming.

Auction days, and even the odd day's horse racing organized in the towns, were, however, thin pickings compared with Race Week in Nairobi. The proportionally idler, richer, and grander

Kenyan farmers all drove to Nairobi and booked into Muthaiga for the duration. The club was packed. Rooms were fought for, and then their inhabitants fought over. Instead of a maximum of a few hours around a bullring in which to operate, the promiscuous had a full seven days in which to identify, catch, and devour their prey. It was not hard. Race Week presented a rare and precious period in which to spend time with somebody other than the person you were married to and saw almost every night of the year. Emotions soared and fell with horses and the bets placed on them. Heavy drinking began at noon with pink gins next to the course or in Muthaiga's bars. Gin fizzes saw out the afternoon until teatime, when sundowners of ferocious spirit blends kicked in. Every evening there was a ball, for which the female guests had to wear a different outfit each night—and they dressed to kill, glittering with Paris silks and family jewels from some of the grandest houses in Europe. One night Joss poked fun at the absurdly overdone attire by appearing in a sequined black evening gown borrowed from a larger female friend and Idina's pearls strung around his neck. "Pearls must be worn!" he squeaked in a falsetto, as around him, intoxicated and unsatiated, new bedfellows tried to disappear to the club's bedrooms together, everyone else turning a studiously blinkered eye.

The months stretched in between Race Weeks. Idina and Joss alternately muttered that they had to see a friend or a chap about a cow and slipped off for a day or two. Idina was certain that she would return. Slains was her self-contained paradise, a house, garden, even cattle that she seems to have mothered in place of her children. And she was, despite her varied sexual appetite, smitten with Joss: "My darling Lion," she called him.[29] However, even this name carried the suggestion that Idina understood he might wander off periodically as male lions do. Her other name for him, "the child," connoted a more permanent separation: that one day he might simply grow up and leave for good. As if to encourage him to stay as long as possible, Idina made life on the farm as much fun and as irresistible as she could.

Guests were invited for weekends—and came—driving six or seven hours each way. Insect-bitten and dust-coated, they arrived

A Happy Valley picnic

at bath time on Saturday. As they drew up at the house, half a
dozen men in fezzes and long white robes started appearing from
all directions. The cars were emptied of bags and these were
whisked away as the guests were ushered through into bedrooms
scattered with tapestries and antiques, each with its own bathroom, fed by a tank, heated by a bonfire outside, that filled a bath
within minutes. When they hauled themselves out of the tub,
glowing, steam-cleaned, hair swept back or brushed down, their
bags had been unpacked and put away. On the linen pillowcase
lay a pair of patterned silk pajamas—a present from Idina, and
still the rage back in Europe. Beside them lay a bottle of whisky.

The weekend—or Saturday-to-Monday—house parties varied. There were the staid ones, when Idina and Joss invited people they knew less well, or those who were well behaved. These included European grandees in more conventional marriages, such as the writer Elspeth Huxley's parents, Jos and Nellie Grant; Lord and Lady Delamere; unattached men such as Gilbert Colvile and Berkeley Cole, and the odd colonial official or district commissioner.

The evenings began with cocktails: White Ladies, Whisky Sours, Bronxes, and gins in varying colors and effervescences. Eight thousand feet up, in that thin air, the alcohol hit hard and fast and the conversation quickened.[30] Dinner was at a long, polished table laid with a platoon of silver knives and forks and crystal glasses, linen napkins folded around each. Back in England few of even the grandest houses raised their culinary threshold above English suet. Here, halfway across the world, up in the skies, Idina and Marie coaxed four-course French meals out of a shack of an outdoor kitchen. All that was missing were copious clarets and Burgundies. Wine was harder to come by than in Europe. It was there, somewhere. But even if brought out it didn't mix well with the spirits before and after. Instead they drank more whisky—and ice cold beer.

Conversation, just as on landed estates back in England, centered on farming methods: the latest ones attempted; the old ones discarded. They talked of gardens, what would and wouldn't grow, how to manage their lawns, irrigate ponds. And they talked about books. With no cinema around the corner and the only theater a day's journey away in Nairobi, books, which could be posted, carried, lent, and exchanged, formed the cultural currency. Like one vast, loosely arranged reading group, the Kenyans strove to read what everyone else was reading—and talking about. In their half-pioneer, half-prisoner lives, the latest published theories and stories were their peephole to the rest of the world. And Idina, her shelves overflowing, with a view on each one and compulsively recommending and lending the latest she had enjoyed, was the Kenyan queen of books: "No-one knew more about contemporary literature than Idina."[31] She could devour a novel a day, falling into the characters' emotions, living their adventures vicariously from her deep sofa halfway up an African mountain.

And, halfway up that mountain, Idina threw different sorts of parties too. To these, she and Joss invited more carefully chosen friends and acquaintances. These had usually spent some time in London and Paris since the war. They had been to parties where the hostess turned up naked, they had joined in the after-dinner stunts designed to shock, they had drunk too much, ended up group-skinny-dipping at midnight (years of boarding-school dormitories had whittled away any sense of body-shyness), and, just as many of their parents had done, they had fallen in and out of bed with their friends. Having a good time meant going as far as they dared. And then a little beyond that.

Idina and Joss's friends arrived, bathed, slipped into their pajamas, were handed a cocktail, and were ushered through into the memsahib's bathroom. There Idina lay simmering in green onyx, ever-present cigarette holder and crystal tumbler on standby, welcoming them in. She chattered as she washed, climbed out, dried herself, and dressed. They drank and talked some more and the pace quickened as the alcohol flowed through their veins. A gramophone would be brought in, its handle wound, a record put on—the latest jazz arrived from England with Idina's pile of books—and off they went, dancing in paja-mas almost as soon as the sun had set. Formality broke into the evening with dinner. The same four-course French feast, washed down by whisky. Cocktails again. The alcohol and altitude together sent them as high as kites, with almost no need for the odd line of cocaine.

Frédéric de Janzé, who was a frequent guest of Idina's, describes the after-dinner scene at Slains in *Vertical Land,* named after the hillside rising sharply up behind the house. "The dark all around"[32]—only the firelight would be flickering. Idina would stand "with her back to the fire, gold hair aflame," wear-ing not pajamas but Kenyan tribal dress—a "red and gold kekoi" that matched both the flames and the color of her hair. Naked underneath, she had tied the long cloth around her and over her breasts. Her face was "framed by the dull beam, topped by buffalo horns. Like a weird lily swaying on a Japanese screen, she alone is living in that room." Her guests, burning with alcohol and physical frustration, sprawl around her—"sunk in chairs, legs crossed on the floor, propped up against the wall, our eyes hang fascinated on that slight figure . . . always the same power. Men leave their ploughs, their horses are laid to rest, and, wonderingly, they follow her never to forget. . . . The flames flicker; her half-closed eyes awaken to our mute appeal. As ever, desire and long drawn tobacco smoke weave around her ankles, slowly entwining that slight frame; around her neck it curls; a shudder, eyes close." And then she started the games.

One short Saturday-to-Monday with no chance of surreptitious lunches and teas in between compressed the time available

Idina and Joss, in red and gold kekoi and
pajamas, on their Kenyan farm, Slains, 1924

to select a new bed companion. Games—British after-dinner games with a twist—were a way to move matters on. Back in London, at Oggie's, at everywhere broad-minded enough to invite Idina, they had "stunted" after dinner. Here these games were Idina's stunts. They had another purpose too. Games with Idina as master of ceremonies were a way for her to exercise some control over who Joss would sleep with—or to appear to do so.

Joss did not drink alcohol. He said, quite openly, that he did not want "to impair my performance."[33] Instead he circled the room filling the glasses, while Idina decided upon the game for that evening. They started with word games, such as which was the real first line to which book, then charades, a bit of acting, singing, dancing, then more dancing to the gramophone. Happy swing, soulful jazz, blues that hollowed out a listener's insides. More alcohol. Then back to Idina, standing in front of the fire, long, black cigarette holder at her lips. The tension around her mounted.

The bedrooms were locked, and Idina held the keys. She spread these out on a table and with a roll of dice, the turn of a card, the blow of a feather across a sheet stretched between trembling hands, the keys were allocated and each guest would win a partner for the night.

AND THEN, EXACTLY ONE YEAR after Idina had brought Joss to Kenya, after just about the length of time her marriage to Charles Gordon had lasted there, Idina discovered she was pregnant.

Chapter 16

Rumors were rife that Idina's baby was not her husband's. She had made as many enemies as friends in Kenya. Stories of the wild parties at Slains were hotly debated—though the debates often genteelly avoided the racier details. Those outside Idina and Joss's charmed circle of invitees were split. Some, especially those who had been received more conventionally by Idina, refused to believe that such an elegant and intelligent woman might behave in this way—or that they could have failed to spot the signs of such salacious activity. Others nursed grudges over being left off the invitation list—even if events were a little too fast for their taste.

Idina's neighbors, whom she barely knew, found themselves being quizzed as to the goings-on up at the Hays'. One, Mrs. Case, was so embarrassed at her ignorance that she sent her *watu* up to Slains to talk to the servants. Tales of confusion over whom the laundry collected from each bedroom should be returned to raced back down the hill and were widely disseminated. These were fueled by Joss's bragging about his conquests at Muthaiga, dividing the women he had slept with into "droopers, boopers and superboopers."[1] And Kenya's chattering classes began to worry.

Just as the upper classes back in Britain feared the publicity of divorces among their ranks, so the middle-class settler farmers and the more prudish émigré aristocrats feared that the Hays' misdemeanors undermined the settlers' cause. The farmers were ceaselessly at loggerheads with the colonial government over how much control they themselves could have over the colony and the extent to which their interests should be balanced against those of the native Kenyans and the other immigrant population, flooding in from India. The settler farmers' argument was that they had worked extremely hard to turn virgin land into good farming soil and that they had therefore earned some legal and physical protection for their interests. If the settlers were seen to be a bunch of wife-swapping sybarites and in any sense "going native," they would lose their moral authority and appear less safe as leaders of the British colony.

British colonial authority, like class divisions back Home, had long been based upon notional differences between groups. And these differences must, the colonial ethos went, be adhered to. Whatever the greater comfort of the native way of life, the Englishman abroad must not succumb. British hours must be kept—no siesta—British food must be served, and British standards of dress must be adhered to, however burning the sun. For men this was either suits or colonial white shirts, shorts, and stockings. For women, skirts or dresses. These must suggest a life of propriety and hard work. It was also vital that sun hats be worn at every opportunity to emphasize the superior fragility of white skin. These were the rules. And, in addition to the persistent stories that Idina was "going native" sexually (many of the native Kenyan men had several wives, and her rumored bed-hopping was seen to mirror this), she flaunted the sartorial norms: she wore trousers every day, just like a man. When she started to wear shorts it was, however, too much for one settler's wife.

Lady Eileen Scott was the wife of Lord Francis Scott, the younger son of the Duke of Buccleuch. Francis had come out in 1919 on the same soldier-settler scheme as Charles Gordon, but Eileen and Idina could hardly have been more different. In the words of the Kenyan writer Elspeth Huxley: "Eileen Scott lingers

in my memory draped in chiffon scarves, clasping a French novel
and possibly a small yappy dog, and uttering at intervals bird-
like cries of 'Oh François! François!' "[2]

Eileen was a daughter of the Earl of Minto, former Viceroy of
India, and had been brought up to believe in the Englishman's
divine right and duty to rule. Eileen could not stand Idina,
whom she regarded as undermining this principle at every turn:
"Most of the women," she wrote in her diary in despair, "wear
shorts, a fashion inaugurated by Lady Idina who has done a lot of
harm in this country. It is very ugly and unnecessary."[3]

Yet, whatever Idina wore, she could please neither Eileen Scott
nor her like-minded white Kenyan farmers. Dressing to the nines
met with as little approbation as wearing shorts. For glad rags
gave the equally damaging impression that Kenyan life was frivolous. After a day's racing at Nakuru, Eileen wrote: "Lady Idina
was there in an Ascot gown with a lovely brown ostrich feather
hat. Why she didn't die of sunstroke I can't conceive."

Idina's nonchalance in the heat and dust appeared worryingly
un-British. The settlers were besieged by sun, dust, and insects
and were offered little in the way of physical comfort as relief.
While many women struggled to make themselves presentable,
Idina appeared unperturbed. This drove Eileen to a fury: "Most
of the women in this country, except Lady Idina, are burnt brick-
red. . . . I wonder how Idina will enjoy trying to eat this type of
food and washing out of a cracked old tin basin. . . . Everything
is so intensely dry, it splits the face and hair."

But Idina cared as little about these things as she did about
whether other people knew whom she had slept with the night
before. She simply lived by an entirely different set of rules: "she
was somehow outside the comic, squalid, sometimes almost fine
laws by which we judge as to what is and what is not conventional."[4] Most settlers regarded sitting down to dinner late (thus
failing to keep British hours) and keeping their servants up as
flagrant mistreatment—whereas flogging for cleaning the family
silver with scouring powder was par for the course. Idina did
the opposite. Her predinner drinks occasionally dragged on, but
she didn't flog her *watu.* Instead, they regarded her with awe as

she walked barefoot around the farm with them. Her excess of unworn shoes hardly endeared Idina to the Lady Eileens of Kenya, who couldn't bring themselves to recount the rumors that Somali drivers had left Idina's employ out of fear of being asked to sleep with her. But when the long-dreaded native Kenyan uprising did come and these other settlers found their houses being razed to the ground, Idina's was left standing.

FOR ALL HER NONCHALANCE — photographs show her lolling on the lawn, a book balanced on her bump—the pregnant Idina's life was full of, as the Kenyans called them, *shauries* (worries). However active she remained, when the baby arrived, shortly after Christmas, she would be forced to lie low for several weeks, leaving Joss unattended to. And Joss, it had become clear, needed constant female attention. As long as he returned from his liaisons, that was fine. But he might not. Especially if he found a wealthy woman willing to pay for his lifestyle. Idina and Joss had been vastly outspending the allowances that she received from her brother and he from his parents. Idina's other income had vanished, as any capital not plowed into the farm had been spent, and the shortfall had been made up in loans taken out against it. Suggesting that they rein in their expenses might be precisely the trigger to send Joss careering off for good. If she did not, however, they would end up bankrupt and then, however much she loved him, he would certainly leave her. But Idina's most immediate worry was that she needed to keep Joss occupied around the birth of their child. She sent a letter to Paris, asking friends to come out and join her for a couple of months. The friends were Alice and Frédéric, known as Fred, de Janzé.

In her four years of marriage Alice had produced two daughters, and the prospect of visiting one of his wife's old lovers did not bother Fred. He agreed to go. In December 1925 the de Janzés arrived at Slains and were immediately captivated by Kenya's wide, open sky and the promise of danger rustling in the undergrowth. Alice and Joss resumed their affair. For Idina this was a relief. Joss was happily busy and would not stray any far-

Idina, Raymond de Trafford, Alice de Janzé, Joss

ther. And Alice would never take him from her: Alice was much too neurotic for Joss ever to want to marry her. Alice and Idina had what was, in matters of infidelity, known as "an understanding." Asked whether she minded that her husband was openly sleeping with Alice, Idina replied, "But Alice is my best friend."[5]

Just before Christmas, the four of them bumped their way up the roads to Nairobi to wait for the birth of Idina's baby. They checked into Muthaiga, where a series of Christmas parties were in full swing. By day, Idina sat around while the other three played in the fiercely competitive and permanently ongoing club squash tournament. On Christmas Day they drove out of Nairobi to picnic "with Denys Finch Hatton, in the Ngong Hills," as Joss wrote to his mother while he waited to become a father. "I hope it will be over soon, this waiting is nerve-racking."[6] The baby was late. New Year passed. And then, four days later, Idina went into labor.

Idina gave birth to a girl. Both Idina and Joss were delighted. Joss had no need of a male heir. There were no ancestral estates to take over, simply a name. And that name was so ridiculously grand that, like very, very few other British titles, it could be inherited by a woman. They called her Diana Denyse. The first name, Diana, was after Idina's brother Buck's wife, just as Idina had been named after the wife of her uncle, Tom Brassey. The second name was an almost taunting feminization of fellow Kenyan Denys Finch Hatton's first.

Denys Finch Hatton was at this time the lover of Karen Blixen, who would later write the autobiographical book *Out of Africa*. She was known to her friends as Tania. When Diana was born, Tania was in her native Denmark, where she'd been for the previous ten months, leaving Denys to wander in Kenya. There was no love lost between the author and Idina. One of Idina's closest friends, Cockie Birkbeck, had been having an affair with Tania's husband, Bror Blixen, for over five years.

Bright-brown-eyed Cockie was just a few months older than Idina and a frequent guest at her more intimate, and wild, gatherings. Both she and Idina had both first arrived in Kenya with soldier-settler husbands in 1919. Like Idina, too, Cockie had a perpetually girlish air. (Her final gesture would be an explicit request to be late for her own funeral and that the reading should be the story of Jesus's turning water into wine.) However, Idina's girlishness was one of irrepressible naughtiness, whereas Cockie's was a beguiling, though utterly misplaced, air of innocence. When on safari with the Prince of Wales she so charmed him with her fascination with his Crichton ice-making machine— never before seen in Kenya—that he asked her, even though she had never fired a shot in her life, to take a gun. When he returned to England he sent her an ice-making machine.

Within a few months of arriving in Kenya with her husband, Ben Birkbeck, Cockie had gone with him on one of Bror Blixen's safaris. Bror, like many white hunters, made a habit of trying to seduce the women he led into the bush, especially those trembling on their first safari, feeling a hairbreadth from mortal danger at every turn. His reassuring air of experience and control proved almost irresistible. Cockie fell out of her husband's arms and into Bror's, where she had been ever since. Bror had insisted that Tania divorce him a couple of years earlier so that he might marry Cockie. Tania had agreed, believing that Denys Finch Hatton would marry her. He had not so far done so. The fact that Bror and Cockie had been equally slow to reach the altar—or rather the register office, being divorcés—provided Tania with little consolation. Cockie was still there, always about to marry Bror and become the next Baroness Blixen in Tania's place.

Idina's ex-husband Charles Gordon and his new wife, Honor, had meanwhile moved to a farm next to Tania's coffee plantation at the foot of the Ngong Hills. The three of them had become firm friends, and Charles and Honor had made Tania godmother to their daughter, Lukyn. However, Idina had also remained close to Charles and when, a year after Diana Denyse's birth, she and Joss visited the Gordons' farm around the same time that Tania's mother was visiting from Denmark, Tania wrote, "European standards of behavior are so quickly forgotten out here, and I do take so much delight in having Mother get to know the people I know and associate with here, but when we invite ourselves to tea with Charles and Honor Gordon and then hear that Idina and her current husband are staying there I am obliged to try to recall my civilized way of thinking and out of consideration for the dignity of an elderly, distinguished Danish lady, to postpone the visit."[7]

The baby Diana was, however, clearly Joss's, although the hard evidence only produced itself several decades later when Diana's eldest son, Merlin, grew into the spitting image of his grandfather.

Idina did not remain in bed for a moment longer than necessary after the birth of her daughter. In her experience, marriages did not wear bedridden brides well, and even with Alice and Fred to keep him company, Joss was tapping his heels. Within a few weeks of Diana's birth, Idina went on safari with Joss, Alice, and Fred. They rose at dawn and walked through the bush, ears pricked for both predators and prey, until the sun was at its height. Then they ate and rested in the shade until the early afternoon, when they continued. They pitched camp at teatime, sipping hot drinks to cool themselves down as their innumerable porters raised tents. Before dark each had taken his or her turn in the hand-pumped shower tent or, occasionally, a tin bath filled with fire-heated water. As the sun set at six, they crawled into their tents and dressed for dinner.

At seven they gathered around the campfire, cocktails in hand, and started an evening of stories and word games. They dealt poker hands to see who should begin with the standard line: "Once upon a time, Kenya was not Kenya but British East Africa . . ." And they composed poems. It was a long month. Fred accepted Alice's affair with Joss, but spending an isolated month in such a jagged foursome was not undiluted pleasure. In Paris, Fred had been used to playing these word games with literati. Here he had to listen to Joss, whom he called "the Boyfriend,"[8] reciting limericks along the lines of

> There was a young lady from Nyeri
> Whose lusts were considered quite eerie,
> On the night that she came,
> And we both did the same,
> It was fun, until I said, "Kwaheri" {good-bye}.

Even Idina wanted to move the conversation on. "Let's be jolly," she would interrupt, "and think of Paris tonight."[9]

The party returned to Slains before the spring rains turned the dirt roads to mud, and settled down to long, cozy evenings together. They were joined by two other Kenya-based friends, Michael Lafone and Beryl Purves, better known by her later name of Markham. Then, in the last week of April, Joss started running a high temperature. At first Idina and the Janzés put it down to a side effect of a cure he was taking for malaria. However, after five days "he got so bad and his heads so terrific," wrote Idina to his parents, "that the Dr was sent for."[10]

The rains had set in, making "the roads almost impassable," and the doctor eventually reached them at eleven-thirty at night. He took one look at Joss, diagnosed malaria, and bundled him into his car to drive him straight to the nearest hospital, in Nakuru. Idina and Beryl went with the two men.

Joss was critically ill. Nakuru was, in the dry season, two and a half hours' drive. The doctor's car swam slowly along the sodden roads, Idina in the back with a barely alive Joss in her arms. The journey took seven hours. The party reached the hospital shortly after dawn. Joss was still alive—just. Shortly before dusk, Beryl, who had slipped away earlier, returned to find Idina at Joss's bedside. Beryl had found a tent and pitched camp for the two of them on the Nakuru racecourse. For the next ten days Idina spent the daylight hours with Joss and the nights curled up with Beryl. Joss was "terribly and gravely ill, darlings,"[11] wrote Idina. He was running a temperature of between 103 and 105 degrees Fahrenheit and was "at times very delirious—in fact he is never quite right in his mind."[12]

The principal risk was that he might start bleeding internally. The doctors told Idina that the immediate danger period would last two weeks, and after that Joss would not be allowed to leave the hospital until he had been "normal" for ten days. Idina was finding it tough watching Joss slip in and out of consciousness. "It is all too awful," she wrote, "& I am nearly off my head . . . nothing matters at the moment except to get the child well."[13]

Joss was, at least, a "wonderfully good patient (partly because he is terrified poor darling, it is too pathetic)."[14] Eventually his temperature subsided, taking him out of danger, but he was kept in the hospital for observation. Idina drove back up to Slains to check on her baby daughter, her houseguests, and the farm. There she discovered a whole new set of *shauries.*

All was in chaos at Slains. Being trapped indoors during the long rains had been too much for Diana's nanny, who said that "she hates the place," wrote Idina to Joss's parents, "and God knows where I am going to find a replacement."[15] The farm accounts, which Joss had taken over since the birth of Diana, were in dire straits. Finally, a rogue bull elephant had wandered across the lawns and Michael Lafone and Fred de Janzé had foolhardily chased it off but it had turned and charged them: "it picked up Fred, threw him and went off—only breaking one rib—can't think why he wasn't killed."[16] Having calmed the situation down as far as she could, Idina returned to her camp on the Nakuru racecourse.

Joss was still unwell: "he hasn't even the strength to cut his nails," she wrote. "It breaks my heart to see him—just like a pathetic frightened child."[17] In June, he came home for Idina to nurse him back to health. The return of the two of them to Slains was met by some good news. The neighboring Wanjohi Farm was up for sale. It sat slightly lower than Slains, about five miles away. Rather than standing proud on the mountainside, the farm buildings were down on the banks of the ice-cold Wanjohi River, in reality a large stream barely six feet wide. There the house and its occupants were sheltered in a haven of bobbly green slopes, rough grasses, and twisted mountain trees and bushes.

Alice and Fred had visited Wanjohi Farm, fallen in love with it on the spot, and set in motion the arrangements to buy it. Shortly afterward they left for France, promising to return to their new Kenyan home by the start of winter. Idina waved good-bye to her friends. In the few months before they returned she could focus her attention on the fast-recovering Joss to make sure that he was fully entertained and did not wander off somewhere for good. She was, however, already too late.

Chapter 17

Despite all Idina's efforts, Joss had already met the woman for whom he would leave her. While Idina had been in the hospital after the birth of Diana, Joss had driven back to Slains with only his Kenyan valet, Waweru, leaving Fred and Alice behind. On the way they had stopped at the water-splash in the Kedong Valley where drivers refilled their engines with water and piled a couple of spare canisters in the boot before grinding their way up the two-thousand-foot Rift Valley escarpment. While Joss and Waweru were waiting another European turned up with his gun-bearer. The newcomer's name was Cyril Ramsay-Hill. He was a thirty-five-year-old former Cavalry officer turned rancher, who had spent his youth in Spain, British Guiana, and a minor English public school. Ramsay-Hill had just moved into a house he had built on the shores of Lake Naivasha. The two men struck up a conversation and, boasting with pleasure over the new home he had built for his second wife, Ramsay-Hill invited Joss to stay the night there. Already aware that a vast new house was being built on the spot and intrigued by Ramsay-Hill's descriptions of the place, Joss accepted.

He was not disappointed. The house was a sprawling, white-washed, Arabesque palace, modeled on Ramsay-Hill's Spanish grandmother's house in Seville. The roof rose and fell in a series of Moorish domes. A fountain-filled courtyard was surrounded by wisp-thin white-marble pillars. The floors and walls were teak, and both wood and marble had been carved into a myriad of fine decorative features by Punjabi craftsmen from among Kenya's fifty thousand Indians. Inside, the house was equally extraordinary. The main fireplace was large enough to have seats inside it and the house was filled with fifteenth- and sixteenth-century Spanish furniture, pictures, and tapestries, its ceilings painted. Ramsay-Hill's wife, Molly, had decorated the main bedroom with a lighter touch, filling it with French furniture but then adding a sunken bath surrounded by black-and-gold mosaics. Water was pumped up from the lake to a reservoir above the house to provide a decent pressure for this and the other baths and showers. The house's treasure trove, however, lay in a small room entered through a heavy door beside the library and kept firmly locked. Here was a collection of eighteenth-century French pornography consisting of both books and erotic pictures by which Boucher, Fragonard, and Watteau had supplemented their income.

Joss fell in love with the house on the spot. Ramsay-Hill had given it the name Oserian after the Masai name for the land it stood on. "Oserian" meant "place of peace," but it was more a place of drama. Ramsay-Hill's house eclipsed Slains in every dimension. Even its setting, on the balmy shores of the hippo-filled lake, mountains hovering in the distance, reeked of indolent pleasure, as opposed to the hillside-farming routine of Joss's life with Idina. And when, that evening, he met Molly, he clearly made up his mind to spend as much time as he could at the house.

Molly Ramsay-Hill was born Mary Maude in London in 1893. Her father worked at the Crystal Palace, but by the time she was fifteen he had been sacked and bankrupted for embezzling season-ticket funds. Acutely aware that she had to fend for herself, Molly discovered that her greatest asset was her looks. By sixteen she was pregnant with the child of a twenty-eight-year-old boyfriend, Guy Hughes. Both sets of parents forced a marriage in July 1910 and Hughes took the outbreak of war as his path to

Oserian

freedom, joining up on the spot. When he returned in 1918 they separated, Molly exchanging an allowance of 425 pounds a year for her son. Four years later she surfaced in Cairo, apparently in possession of a fortune, which she claimed came from the well-known and extensive British chain of pharmacies named Boots. There she met the already married Ramsay-Hill. Two years later, having divorced their respective spouses, they married in London and then set off for Kenya.

Molly was, like Idina, petite, fair-skinned, and, although eight months younger than Idina, still several years older than the twenty-four-year-old Joss. Her white skin, green eyes, Titian hair, and strong jaw gave her a classical beauty, unlike Idina. Dark red lipstick and nail varnish also lent Molly the air of an exotic who took an equal pleasure in her husband's esoteric artistic tastes. It was widely believed in Kenya that she had a fortune of thirty thousand pounds from which she derived an extraordinarily efficient income of eight thousand pounds.

Joss commented that, after three years, a lover becomes "a drain on one's vitality."[1] He and Idina had been married for two years and lovers for three. Since they had built Slains they had been examining a variety of sexual positions in the mirror they had put in the ceiling above their bed.[2] Having just given birth, Idina cannot have been at her best sexually. And Joss might just as well have been referring to financial as to sexual vitality.

Molly Ramsay-Hill

Joss knew that the rate at which he and Idina were living was not sustainable. The Brassey inheritance was not immediately forthcoming: Muriel was only in her fifties and siphoning cash at a rate of knots into her joint passions of Theosophy and George Lansbury's political career.

Molly, on the other hand, offered novel sexual pursuits, a new supply of funds, and, if things were carefully finessed, one of the most beautiful houses he had ever seen.

Joss made Cyril Ramsay-Hill his new greatest and closest friend. Each time he passed on the way to and from Nairobi or made a trip to Naivasha, he dropped in at Oserian. He had plenty of cover for this. At Slains Alice and Fred had been replaced by another American girlfriend of Idina's, Kiki Preston, and her banker husband, Gerry. Kiki had slept with Rudolph Valentino and been a lover of the Prince of Wales. She was now an overt morphine addict and chartered her own plane and pilot to take off from the lawns at Slains in search of supplies. When the airplane returned, bearing fruit, she rolled up her sleeve mid-conversation and injected herself with a silver syringe.

Joss at Gilgil with Gerry and Kiki Preston and friend

Kiki and Gerry were building a Dutch-style house just along from Oserian on the shores of Naivasha. While Kiki was lolling in a stupor on the Slains lawns and Gerry fretting around her, Joss could offer to go down and take a look at the building works.

When Joss's absences at Naivasha grew more protracted, Idina, perhaps to remind her husband that he was not the only one of them who could disappear from the marriage, started looking for sexual company.

Caswell Long, known as "Boy," was, alongside Joss, the other leading glamour boy of the Highlands. On auction days Joss wore his tartan kilt; Boy wore "brilliantly coloured corduroys, a flame coloured Somali shawl and large pirate earrings with a huge sombrero shading his handsome face," remembers one young woman.[3] Another, Elspeth Huxley, remembers him with "dark, curly hair, a ruddy complexion, lively dark eyes and [looking] like an English country squire with a dash of the cowboy. . . . Women adored him."[4]

Boy was married. But his wife, Genesta, was off and away trying to make a name for herself as a travel writer. She and Idina loathed each other. In her memoirs Genesta cannot bring herself to mention Idina by name, simply referring to "the hostess" and "one of Her Parties." When, later, Genesta married Lord Claud Hamilton, Idina remarked: "Some women will do anything to get a coronet on their knickers."[5]

Idina and Boy began an intense affair. It took Idina several hours to drive down to Lake Elmenteita to reach Boy. His job as a cattle rancher on Lord Delamere's vast estate meant that his days were spent traveling around that part of the Rift Valley. He met Idina in deserted *rondavels* on the edge of the lake thick with pink flamingos, or in the long grass. The scent of danger added to the thrill. Sometimes their rendezvous were planned. At other times Idina simply drove down and along the miles of flat, white soda-ash tracks that crisscrossed the Elmenteita estate until she found him.

In theory, having her own affair while Joss chased Molly should have rebalanced Idina's relationship with her husband— that, after all, was part of the point of agreeing to have an open marriage. At best it would have reminded him that he could not take Idina for granted and needed to turn his attentions to home to keep his wife. Joss obviously did not see it this way. If anything, Idina's preoccupation appears to have reassured him that she was quite happy while he was away, giving him more room to pursue his own interests down in Naivasha. Idina in turn spent more time with Boy.

IN LATE 1926 JOSS WAS BROUGHT homeward not by any jealousy over Idina's behavior but by the arrival of Fred and Alice de Janzé at their new house in the Wanjohi Valley. The de Janzés threw themselves into Highlands life. They farmed a bit and rode a lot. They competed with Idina and Joss for the fastest time from the Wanjohi Valley down to Muthaiga for Race Weeks, each in their own cloud of dust. Idina and Alice concocted a new fashion for wearing long velvet trousers to combat the cold mountain nights. The de Janzés spent almost every other weekend up at Slains, with Idina and Joss coming down to

Wanjohi in between. The four of them went off on monthlong safaris. And Alice and Joss took up their affair again. It was erratic and intense. They would suddenly disappear for a couple of days at a time, leaving Idina and Fred by themselves in their respective farms. It appeared rather unstylish for one abandoned spouse to ride over to the other, but Idina and Fred did, occasionally and probably out of sheer loneliness, end up in bed together at the end of a party. Fred describes their halfhearted liaisons in *Vertical Land*:

> She sits by my side laughing up at the boy. Amber liqueur; amber glass; pink nails; white skin; cream silk shirt and red kekoi.
> Her warmth by my side tingles my skin. . . .
> Her hand creeps around my waist but she smiles up at another.
> Someone begins to hum the tune and we all throb to it. The melody of the corn crakes rises in the room. The buffalo horns shine and bow, the rhythm twisting about them. Smoke hangs around the backs of the chairs. Her foot nods to the time. Her nails sere [sic] my flesh. A turn of her head, a breath of a word: "tonight!"[6]

Joss's resumption of his affair with Alice was, however, reassuring. Joss and Alice's comings and goings were a safe, established pattern. And Alice was Idina's best friend. Alice was the neurotic, Idina the steadying hand. Alice needed Idina possibly more than she enjoyed Joss's company. Idina was her rock, Joss her addiction. And in return Alice provided Idina with a soul mate during Joss's continuing trips to Naivasha to see Molly Ramsay-Hill. The two of them wandered around the garden at Slains hand in hand, waiting for him to return. Kiki, with silver syringe ever at the ready, kept them company. Visitors to Kenya started to return to Europe with tales of wild parties, abundant narcotics, and strange ménages of approved infidelities and potentially Sapphic bonds, all occurring within the Wanjohi

Valley. The gossip columnists seized upon the stories, reprinting them, as was the practice then, with clear descriptions but no precise names, and rechristening the place Happy Valley.

Idina and her inner set found this faintly amusing. The other white settlers, together with the colonial administration, were appalled. Both wanted to build up Kenya's reputation and political backing as a country, and the colonial administration was, in the eyes of the British government, responsible for all the goings-on. Meanwhile Idina—and Idina was very much regarded as the chief organizer of the Happy Valley crowd—was earning the country an international reputation as a "love colony."[7] Back in England, the joke "Are you married, or do you live in Kenya?" was doing the rounds.

A COUPLE OF MONTHS after their arrival the de Janzés took their turn hosting an annual party—a custom that was growing up among Idina and Joss's friends. Each couple would invite the twenty or so friends in their group to camp on their lawns. These consisted of the half-dozen-odd core members of the inner set: Idina and Joss, undisputed King and Queen of Happy Valley; Kiki and Gerry Preston; Fred and Alice de Janzé; Boy Long—when Genesta was away on her travels; Michael Lafone, a general womanizer; and Jack Soames—a louche Old Etonian with a penchant for voyeurism.[8] As well as these harder partiers were the inner set's houseguests, John "Chops" Ramsden, who owned a large estate over toward the Kipipiri mountain; the farmers Pat and Derek Fisher; and the newcomers Cyril and Molly Ramsay-Hill—Cyril, as it turned out, oblivious to what being a member of the inner set included, but Molly quite well aware.

In theory, the annual party was one big night and the morning after (although in practice stragglers would remain for up to a week at a time) with not a soul rising before ten-thirty and so allowing the servants ample time to clear up and prepare a cold brunch of salad, Bromo-Seltzer, and prairie oysters. These hangover remedies were needed. The custom became for the hosts to supply the food but the guests to bring the alcohol. This resulted in innovative and near-lethal concoctions, the principal being

Idina and Alice in Idina's garden in Kenya

Black Velvet—a beguilingly drinkable mixture of champagne and stout. To add to the excitement, by the time of their very first annual party, in effect their housewarming in 1926, the de Janzés had acquired a substitute for the children they had left behind in France. This was a lion cub they had found, survivor of a pride which had made its home on their farm. When they found him, Alice and Fred carried him back to the house and named him Samson.

Samson was not small when he arrived. By the time of the party he was even less so. And somehow—although that somehow had two likely coconspirators—before dinner Samson managed to find his way under Molly's chair, where he lay unseen. Dinner began. The guests were enthused by the cocktails, and the noise of conversation rose to pound off the walls and corrugated-iron roof of the farmhouse.

As the fish course was being served, one of the houseboys let out a shriek and dropped a bowl of mayonnaise down Molly's back. He had tripped over Samson's just extended paw, and as Molly herself rose to dab the egg paste off her, she too stumbled over the cub, being caught by her neighbor "just in time to prevent a heavy fall. . . . The good lady took a lot of pacifying," as Fred wrote.[9]

The party moved onto the veranda. There they played the gramophone while "plying bottles far into the night."[10] They stunted and drank, they drank and stunted, "until no one cared whether they were good or bad, even if they existed or were just illusions"[11] and eventually, at six o'clock, just as dawn was breaking, all fell into bed.

These few months, with Joss, the husband whom she adored, their tiny child, and her best friend, Alice, all with her in Kenya, were one of the high points of Idina's life. It was indeed that better life which she had worked so hard to create.

But it was all too brief and fleeting. Almost as soon as Idina had pulled these strands of her life together, they unraveled. Having herself bolted twice, Idina would now find out what it felt like to be bolted from.

Chapter 18

Toward the end of 1926 Cyril Ramsay-Hill left for Europe on a long shopping and hunting expedition. Although he took with him two Somali servants—whom he outfitted in Savile Row suits[1]—he did not take Molly. She was therefore left completely free for Joss's attentions. To make matters worse, the unsuspecting Ramsay-Hill asked Joss, his so-called good friend, to keep an eye on his wife. As Fred de Janzé put it, "her husband told him to go up and see her as often as he could: 'Do her good not to be always alone.' "[2] On the pretext of taking "a month's shooting leave,"[3] Joss left Slains, only to pitch camp on the shores of Lake Naivasha, in Molly's garden.

Even when Idina heard that her husband's safari was a purely sexual adventure, she had little choice but to accept it, but she could console herself that Cyril Ramsay-Hill was returning after Christmas. His reappearance should put an end to Joss's expedition. And despite his involvement with Molly, Joss saw Alice's presence in Kenya as hard to resist and he kept popping back to the Wanjohi Valley.

It was a far from satisfactory situation for Idina, and there were immediate practical ramifications: "bad debts that he had run up in her name with the Indian merchants" and prolonged absences that threatened to "disrupt her social programme."[4] Not to mention that she was relying on a friend's sexual attractions to keep her husband home.

SHORTLY BEFORE CHRISTMAS an old friend of Idina's arrived in Kenya. Idina had known Raymond de Trafford and his brothers for many years. And, however badly Idina had behaved, Raymond had outstripped her. He gambled away any money that passed through his hands. He drank himself into violent outbursts of temper. And, as it became clear, he appeared not to give a damn about the happiness of anyone around him.[5] Since the end of the war he had "stunted" all over London and Paris and now that the Kenyan Highlands' reputation for its Happy Valley was spreading in Europe it was almost inevitable that Raymond should end up there. His deeply Catholic family in Britain were pleased enough to see him go that they gave him some money with which to set himself up with a farm. As well as Idina, Raymond knew Lord Delamere's eldest son, Tom Cholmondeley: like the Delameres, the de Traffords were a Cheshire landowning family. Raymond therefore turned up at Muthaiga and immediately headed off on safari before returning to spend the Christmas period between the Delamere ranch down at Elmenteita and Slains, up in the hills. And there, at Slains, was Alice.

The attraction was both mutual and immediate. They sprawled on the lawns in the afternoon sun. A photograph taken at this time shows them sitting on the grass, Alice's eyes half closed, the pair of them flirting and teasing. And when, shortly afterward, Fred left on a short hunting expedition, Alice and Raymond vanished together.

Fred returned to discover that they had gone. A few days later they came back, but Raymond's volatility and the suddenness of his temporary elopement with Alice shook Fred. Whereas Alice's affair with Joss had become a predictable part of the establishment and would never lead to anything, Raymond was obviously different. Fred took Alice away to Paris immediately.

Alice and Fred's departure was a serious blow to Idina. She not only lost her closest friend, it also marked the end of the happily extended Hay–de Janzé ménage.

Joss, however, was not going to leave with Molly yet. He had fallen in love with Molly's house at least as much as he had fallen for her—and that remained firmly in the ownership of Cyril Ramsay-Hill. Living, or rather camping, with Molly at Oserian was evidently a delight. However, leaving the comforts of Slains for nowhere in particular was less appealing. When Cyril returned to Kenya shortly after Alice and Fred's departure, Joss slid back home to Idina. They had a beautiful home, each other, and a child. Idina had converted a guest bedroom at one end of the house into a nursery wing for Diana and a new English nanny. Now a year old, Diana was making her first tottering steps across the lawn at Slains

and struggling to utter the three long syllables of her name: Di-an-a, ending up with "Dinan"—a name that stuck. Photographs show Idina dancing around the garden, Dinan in her arms, as she twirled her daughter round and showed her off to friends. It was at least the appearance of domestic bliss.

It lasted for two months after Joss's return. Then, at the end of March, appalling news reached them from Paris. Alice had shot both Raymond and herself.

Raymond de Trafford and Alice de Janzé on the lawn at Idina's house

WHEN THE DE JANZÉS HAD ARRIVED in Paris, Alice had told Fred that she wanted a divorce in order to marry Raymond. She then promptly moved out of the family apartment and into one lent for the purpose by Fred's American mother, who perhaps was trying to do what she could to keep the marriage together. Raymond, however, simply moved in with Alice.

Fred then capitulated—not even a change of scene as dramatic as that from Kenya to Paris had shaken his wife's resolve to leave him. He set in motion the exclusive divorce open only to Europe's grandest Catholic families: a papal annulment. In theory this should avoid the inconvenience of either party being classed as a divorcé. When a marriage is annulled, it is as though neither had been married in the first place.

In the third week of March 1927 Raymond returned to England to speak to his family about marrying Alice. On the twenty-fifth he arrived back in Paris and went straight to Alice's apartment. There he told her that, divorce or annulment, his strictly Catholic family had forbidden him to marry her and that he had to end the relationship, or they would cut him off.

Alice begged him to stay with her. He refused. "I immediately," said Alice later, "determined upon suicide."[6] The next day "we took a last luncheon together," she said.[7] She again asked Raymond to stay with her. Again he refused, telling her that he was leaving Paris by train within a couple of hours.

Alice offered to see Raymond off but told him that she needed to visit an armorer's that afternoon. Together they went shopping. Alice bought a pistol and a round of bullets. "Raymond's phlegmatic English type suspected nothing in this incident, evidently thinking that I was doing an errand for my husband," she would say later in her statement to the investigating judge.[8] Raymond stood beside her and bought himself a pair of hunting knives. They then took a taxi to the Gare du Nord. There Alice disappeared into the station lavatories, where she "had an opportunity to load the weapon,"[9] and emerged to say good-bye. "It was during the anguish of the last moment's separation as we embraced that I suddenly acted on impulse. Slipping the revolver between us, I fired upon him and then upon myself," Alice testified.

The first bullet hit Raymond in the chest, narrowly missing his heart and lodging itself in his kidney. Alice's second bullet hit her in the "lower abdomen."[10] The story made headlines the world over. "AMERICAN COUNTESS SHOOTS ENGLISHMAN AND SELF IN PARIS," shouted the front page of *The New York Times*.[11]

When the news reached Idina she packed her bags. It was clear that Alice needed her in Europe—that is, if she was still alive when Idina reached her, for both she and Raymond had been severely wounded. The single glimmer of light on this otherwise bleak horizon was that Joss agreed to come too.

During the two months he had been back at Slains, Joss had been going off by himself from time to time. It was unlikely that he had genuinely ended the affair with Molly as abruptly as he had appeared to when Cyril returned from Europe, but his willingness to rush away for several months—even given that it was to Alice's bedside—suggested that it had cooled considerably.

IDINA AND JOSS LEFT at the start of the April rains and reached England in May. They took Dinan to stay with Buck and his wife, Diana, Dinan's namesake, at their house on the De La Warr estate, the relatively modest Fisher's Gate. The pretty, dark-red-brick and white-windowed farmhouse, even if generously sized, was more appropriate for a minister in a Socialist government than the ancestral home of Buckhurst. After two sons, Buck and Diana, too, had had a girl in the past year, providing a playmate for Dinan. And having installed their daughter in the Fisher's Gate nursery, Idina and Joss could dash over to Paris to see Alice.

By then both Alice and Raymond were out of danger, but Alice, once she had recovered sufficiently, had been charged with Raymond's attempted murder and had been moved to the women's hospital section of the Saint-Lazare Prison—where she was much in need of visitors. Raymond, on the other hand, had been flown back to England to convalesce. From there he was making statements to the press that suggested the love affair was far from over. " 'I told her,' he said, 'that all was over between us but this decision is not irrevocable.' "[12]

Joss and Idina followed Raymond back to England and scooped up Dinan to take her over to Koblenz to see his parents. By the middle of May, Alice was out of prison, albeit temporarily. She was allowed to retire to the French country estate of Fred's still surprisingly understanding mother, "until in sufficiently good health to appear in court."[13] A month later Fred obtained a straightforward divorce in the Paris courts. He was granted custody of their two daughters. Meanwhile Alice remained at his mother's house, where her friends could visit her until she stood trial.

With Alice and Fred settled, Idina and Joss returned to London. For a couple of months they had a chance to wind back the clock to their old pre-Kenyan days. There they could dash around town together visiting friends, spend evening after evening in the theater, and go out dancing at their old haunts. It appeared to be very much a family visit. Joss's grandfather died in July, which gathered everyone together for the funeral and brought a couple of changes to their lives. The first was that Joss's parents became the new Earl and Countess of Erroll and he and Idina stepped into their shoes as Lord and Lady Kilmarnock. The second was that Joss came into the modest but not negligible sum of three hundred pounds a year of his own.

Although this eased the financial strain on their lives back at Slains, it also gave Joss a potentially dangerous sense of independence. He was no longer reliant on his parents' approval for money—and they had clearly come to approve of Idina. What Idina did not realize was that Molly Ramsay-Hill was in London too.

Instead of Joss's needing to drive for several hours to find her, never sure when Cyril might be in, in London Molly was just a few minutes' cab ride away. At some point during these months, Joss and Molly settled upon a plan to marry and live in Oserian together.

Idina and Joss returned to Kenya in September. Molly remained in London for a further month, arriving at Oserian in

November. It was vital for the scheme that she and Joss had concocted that no suspicion of their affair should reach Cyril's ears.

Once back at Naivasha, Molly started entertaining lavishly at Oserian, her houseboys dispensing liquor from a specially designed, hand-painted bar underneath one of the house's domes. Cyril was becoming annoyed with the Happy Valley crowd using his house as a watering hole and an incessant flow of "unwelcome guests who began drinking immediately after breakfast," as he later wrote,[14] and he failed to see through the cover that it provided for his wife's affair. The parties continued for six weeks. Then, on 17 December 1927, Molly took her husband into Nairobi to visit their solicitor, Walter Shapley of Shapley, Schwartze and Barratt. There, perhaps now slightly less enamoured of the house, he signed over "an undivided half share and interest" in Oserian for which, "in consideration of the Vendor's natural love and affection for his wife," he accepted the nominal sum of just ten shillings.[15] Molly had her half share of the house and she and Joss were now ready to elope.

But within less than a week, Alice stalled Joss's departure. On 23 December she stood trial in Paris for the attempted murder of Raymond. Alice's impassivity flummoxed the judge, "who seemed to think the pretty young woman did not quite realize the nature of her offense"[16] and chastised her for leaving her children. "To leave one's husband is perhaps understandable, but really, Madame, one has no right to leave one's children like that."[17] Alice's response was that "I was carried away by passion."[18] The judge was charmed. Alice was given a six-month suspended sentence for having committed a *crime passionnel* and fined four dollars for carrying a firearm without a license. The verdict made as many headlines as the shooting: "Countess Who Shot Lover and Self Gets Off with $4 Fine in French Court."[19] And, having again shocked the world, Alice immediately and publicly set off to return to Kenya. Joss waited for her to arrive.

Alice reached Kenya in January 1928 to what must have been Idina's great relief. Idina's antennae were more finely tuned than Cyril Ramsay-Hill's and, even if she did not know the details of the transfer of the half share of Oserian, she knew that Molly was clearly far more than a passing infatuation for Joss. It must have been becoming abundantly clear to Idina that it was only a matter of time before her "child" left home for good.

Alice's reappearance, however, meant Joss and Alice started careering around the country together. Far from upsetting Idina, her husband's disappearance with her best friend was just as she had hoped. According to the old Edwardian morality to which Idina still clung, extramarital affairs were acceptable as long as they did not become "serious" and hence threatening either to the other spouse's primary position or to the marriage itself. This of course worked for men and women alike. Idina believed, correctly, that unlike Joss's entanglement with Molly, his affair with Alice would never become serious. In the meantime she was free to pursue her own "not serious" liaisons. With luck Joss would forget Molly, inevitably tire of Alice, and then return to Idina. It was a far from ideal situation but Idina was still very much in love with Joss and it may have appeared her best chance of saving her marriage—at least from the claws of Molly Ramsay-Hill.

ON ONE OF HIS TRIPS at the end of February 1928, Joss bumped into Tania Blixen in Nairobi. Less than a year earlier she had avoided his company and referred to "Idina and her current husband."[20] Now she seemed only too eager to see him and invited him out to her house for "a bottle" that afternoon. Joss asked whether he could bring the notorious Alice. Tania readily agreed "and thereby acquired a tea-party that was really so comical that I lay in my bed that night laughing about it."[21]

Shortly before Joss and Alice were due to arrive, another car pulled up. This contained a pair of prurient Government House types and, wrote Blixen, "two really huge and corpulent old American ladies" from a cruise ship moored in Mombasa. They had come up-country "in the hope of seeing a lion" but, squeezed into Tania's chairs, they immediately "started to discuss all the dreadfully immoral people there were in Kenya . . . and as the worst one of all, they mentioned Alice." Blixen, mischievously, let the group chatter in "great detail about it." Five minutes later Joss and Alice arrived. "I don't think the Devil himself could have had a greater effect if he had walked in; it was undoubtedly better than the biggest lion."[22]

Not all of Kenya was as thrilled as Idina and Tania at Alice's return. Lady Grigg, the wife of the then governor, Sir Edward Grigg, was particularly horrified.[23] Having made headlines for almost a year, Alice was still being followed in the world's press with ongoing speculation as to whether, having shot Raymond, she was now going to marry him.[24] Her choice of Kenya as her refuge and her extremely public parading with Joss reinforced the London view that the country was little more than a love colony. Lady Grigg persuaded her husband to issue an order for Alice's deportation.[25] In March 1928 Alice was sent back to Europe. Within days Joss had decided that he, too, was going. A few weeks before, on 20 February, his father had died suddenly at the age of fifty-two. Joss was still cavorting with Alice in Nairobi over a week later. However, now that Alice had gone, his mother's shock at his father's death—she was apparently ill enough to be unable to attend the memorial service in St. Margaret's, Westminster[26]—gave him a pretext, if not a need, to leave Kenya.

Idina was not included in the plans for the trip.[27] It is not clear where she was on the day Joss disappeared from Slains, or whether he had even told her that he was leaving. But it is possible that he avoided seeing Idina face-to-face. If so, she would not have heard that her husband had finally left her until the scandal that was about to erupt had broken.

Joss left Slains, drove down to Gilgil, and boarded the train for Nairobi and then Mombasa. The train stopped at Naivasha, a long stop, for a meal. Joss slipped off the train and went to fetch Molly. Shortly afterward the two of them slipped back on board. Molly was clutching a suitcase and a pair of first-class tickets for Marseille.

At about exactly the moment that Molly was boarding the train just a few miles away, Cyril Ramsay-Hill returned to Oserian early from a hunting trip to find his wife gone. One of his servants explained to him that his wife had just left to board the train with Joss. Furious, Ramsay-Hill grabbed a pistol and raced to the station to discover that the train had already left. Calculating that he could still beat it to Nairobi station, he turned straight onto the Nairobi road and put his foot down on the gas pedal. By the time Joss and Molly's train reached the city, Ramsay-Hill was there. As the train drew in, he ran onto the platform but dropped the pistol. "I had thought of killing him," Ramsay-Hill later wrote, "but a friend advised me that losing a wife was preferable to losing one's life by hanging."[28] Instead he grabbed a rhino-hide whip from a waiting horse and carriage, asking, as he took it: "May I borrow your *kiboko* a moment? I've got to whip a dog."

As Joss descended, Ramsay-Hill collared his trusted friend and "in full view of the other passengers"[29] whipped him. Then he let the man who had cuckolded him go. Bruised and bleeding, Joss rejoined Molly to continue their journey to London.

This was a far greater scandal for the Kenyan administration than just another irritating story of adultery and elopement. A crucial sociopolitical boundary of colonial power had been broken. A large crowd of native Kenyans, all rooted to the spot by the spectacle on the station platform, had seen a white man humiliated.[30]

YEARS LATER, WHEN SLAINS had fallen into other hands, Idina returned for lunch and asked if she could spend an hour or two alone in her and Joss's old bedroom "to remember the old times." She went in and shut the door. When she came out, glowing, she declared it "Heaven, darling," and sauntered away.[31] But back in March 1928, at the moment Joss left in such a thick cloud of scandal, Idina had a hard truth to face. She was thirty-five years old and, for the second time in her life, a husband she loved had fallen for another woman. And this time she had been the one abandoned. The Wanjohi Valley without Joss, without Alice, without Fred, and without any prospect that they might return, was suddenly a lonely enough place for Idina, too, to decide to leave. Three weeks later, just before she would be trapped by the onset of the long April rains, Idina sailed for England, taking Dinan with her.

Chapter 19

In London Idina was very openly a deserted wife. The story of Joss's horsewhipping was doing the rounds in England, to great delight. Determined to hold her head high, Idina went straight to Buck's house, Fisher's Gate, parked Dinan with her cousins, and headed up to the fray in the capital, showing the world that she was still alive and kicking.

She moved into Oggie's new house in Glebe Place, a Chelsea street buzzing with artists' studios, and within days she had rounded up a host of admirers and had embarked on a raging affair with one of the most sexually attractive—and active—men in London.

Tom Mosley was in England what Joss was in Kenya: physically magnetic and a renowned philanderer. His wife, Euan and Barbie's old friend Cimmie Curzon, professed not to mind. Tom, Cimmie knew, would always come back to her. He was wealthy in his own right and lived in a dreamy, rambling Tudor manor house, Savehay Farm, in Denham, Buckinghamshire. Tom was very much part of Oggie's crowd—he and Cimmie had been at Idina and Joss's wedding—and, having been first elected a Conservative Member of Parliament, he was now a Labour MP and a close colleague of Buck's; both were regarded by fellow members of the upper classes as Communists. And in both cases the sense of danger this came with increased their appeal to the opposite sex—which they manipulated to their advantage.

It was almost inevitable that, at some point in their wide-ranging sexual careers, Idina and Tom should sleep together. In any case, Idina owed little to Cimmie.

On Saturday, 26 May 1928, Idina drove down to the Mosleys' for the extended bank holiday weekend of Saturday to Tuesday. The need for discretion had subsided. Divorce had become common and some marriages, such as that of Tom and Cimmie, even seemed to have found a certain strength in their open acceptance of sexual infidelity—if adultery wasn't treated as serious, it somehow remained not serious.

Even though Idina had already found a new admirer, she was not yet confident enough to turn up alone. She also knew that, given Tom's reputation, it was unlikely that she would be the only flirtation he had lined up for the weekend. She arrived with Ivan Hay, Joss's uncle.

One of Idina's rivals who was slinking into Tom's sight lines was the twenty-three-year-old Georgia Sitwell, wife of the writer Sacheverell Sitwell and now sister-in-law to the writers Edith and Osbert. Inspired by the literary circles into which she had married, Georgia kept a detailed and opinion-rich diary. When she arrived at Savehay that Saturday afternoon to discover Idina, her hackles rose: "Lady E [Idina was now Lady Erroll[1]] has been married 4 [sic] times and is reputed to have had lovers without number . . . a fair heavily made-up face covered with blue-white powder, chic, empty; dissipated, hungry-looking spoilt and vicious. She has dyed hair and no chin but with all looks like a pretty chicken, the same colour, the same contours, the same consistency."[2] Fair or foul, it was, however, Idina, twelve years older than Georgia and with the experience behind her of all those husbands and lovers without number, who won the battle for Tom.

On Sunday morning the dozen or so guests arose to the first baking-hot day of the year. After breakfast Cimmie Curzon produced an array of bathing suits. They changed with alacrity: "Tom evidently fancies himself very much in bathing shorts &

displays with pride a sunburnt muscular torso," Georgia wrote, whereas another guest, the photographer Cecil Beaton, looked "dangerously thin in a bathing suit which hung off him in folds." As for Ivan Hay, whom Georgia could not stand (partly due to his arrival with Idina and his subsequent failure to keep her occupied and away from Tom), he displayed an "enormous pot belly." The party leapt into the river at the end of the garden and "shot the weir on rubber mattresses, very good fun."

Then, just as Georgia was emerging from the water, Idina appeared. She had risen neither for breakfast nor for the swimming expedition, thus implying that she had needed to recover from an active night before. Now, "she sauntered down elegantly at about 11:30, very chic in black and white chiffon." Tom, parading his pecs and biceps, gave her his full attention until midday, when another car rattled up to the house and out stepped Irene Curzon. She had inherited the title of Lady Ravensdale and with it the nickname Raveners. With her was Edith Baker, newly married to a scion of a banking dynasty known as Pop d'Erlanger. Edith Baker was "very pretty and so young looking." Tom started "trying it on with her" straightaway, wrote Georgia. This was a situation Idina could handle. She threaded her arm through Tom's and chattered, giving "him as little opportunity as possible" to pursue Edith. Edith was not, however, as much the ingénue as she looked. At twenty-eight she reckoned she could hold her own against Idina (poor Georgia Sitwell was now very much on the sidelines), and after lunch Edith sat down at the piano and played. One guest sat "enthralled for hours." It wasn't Tom, but it was a male admirer, and one was all it took to raise Tom's competitive hackles. At the end of the afternoon some guests suggested an expedition to the boat club at Bray for cocktails. Idina announced that she would like to go, too, and Tom started to follow her automatically, but as he did so Edith piped up that she needed to wait behind for her husband to arrive. "Tom was torn between the two," wrote Georgia, who "heard Cimmie in an aside say that she really could not choose between them for him." In the end he stayed. So Idina remained too. And when the cocktail expedition finally returned at 9 p.m.,

Tom seated himself between the two women at dinner. As Tom flirted with Edith, her new husband, Pop, sitting opposite, grew "angrier and angrier." Pop could not cope with either Tom's flirtation with Edith or the crowd of friends. He found Cecil Beaton mystifying, asking in an extraordinarily loud voice: "Is C.B. a fairy?" Eventually Pop insisted upon driving Edith back home that evening instead of staying the night. The way was open for Idina.

The following evening the house party was joined by the poet Stephen Spender, who "arrived from London looking beautiful." Cimmie served cocktails as her guests unpacked the dresses her mother had worn as Vicereine of India before she had died, twenty-two years earlier. They were "gorgeous beyond words being Edwardian, being for the Indian court, being for a Vicereine, & being for Lord Curzon's wife. Yards of brocade, gold tissue, embroidery, tulle & every exquisite material imaginable."

Cimmie had planned that her guests should wear them at dinner that night. The waists were, however, only nineteen inches around. Georgia Sitwell alone managed to do one up properly: "It was torture but well worth it." The rest of the guests, men included, each chose a dress and clambered into it as they could. Cecil Beaton and Stephen Spender were "at their best in these fantastic dresses. Stephen had a wreath of artificial flowers in his hair & Cecil had picked every blossom from Cimmie's lilac walk & stuck it either in his 'bosom' or on his head." Tom abstained from the cross-dressing. Instead he matched the level of decoration by appearing "as a sort of toreador." At dinner he sat again beside Idina but, Edith Baker having been whisked away, Georgia found herself promoted to his other side. As the meal ended, neither woman moved. The three of them sat there discussing "young men" until Stephen and Cecil rose, resplendent in their vicereinal attire, and "went through all their stunts" until 3:30 a.m. The next morning Georgia left with her husband. Idina stayed on with Tom.

Neither Idina nor her sexual appeal had diminished. However, the fallout of her split from Joss was far from over.

While Cyril Ramsay-Hill finally divorced Molly, citing her

adultery with Joss, Idina stayed in London, at Oggie's, until the end of July, making occasional trips to Fisher's Gate to see Dinan. Joss, too, was in England, checking into hotels with Molly under the pseudonym Mr. and Mrs. Hay. On 23 November he sailed for New York on the United States Lines' *Leviathan,* also under the name of Hay instead of the now ignominiously whipped Erroll, and alone. On 24 November Molly followed on the Cunard liner *Aquitania.* Six weeks later, at the beginning of January 1929, Idina's bankers in Kenya foreclosed on Slains. She did not return. Every brick and stick of furniture there had been put together for a life with Joss. That was over. Slains was put up for auction.

The same month the *Daily Express* printed a lead article headlined "EARL'S WIFE AS MANNEQUIN."[3] It claimed that Idina was about to leave London for the French Riviera, where the winter season was in full flow, to work as a mannequin for Molyneux. Her job would be to parade clothes up and down the catwalk at his morning and afternoon *défilés* for customers. This was no surprise, the *Daily Express* continued, as Idina had "a much-envied gift for wearing clothes attractively. It has been remarked of her that the simplest gown becomes distinguished when she puts it on, and a Paris dressmaker once offered to dress her for nothing if she would only wear his creations." It would be only "a minor excitement in a life . . . little hampered by convention."[4]

In 1929 the suggestion that Idina was about to become a leading model was far from flattering. Instead it implied that she had become so penniless that she needed to earn a living and that she was going to do so by displaying her body. The allegation was that she was selling herself—akin to calling her a prostitute today. Idina, a woman who did not usually give a damn about what the papers said about her, sued.

Joss then asked for a divorce so that he might marry Molly. Idina instigated proceedings. And, for the next six months, she was in and out of the law courts. It was during this time that Beaton photographed her (see page 301). Idina, quite literally, sat on a mirrored floor. Her knees are bent, one foot tucked under her, the other extended to the side, her shoe pulling at the footstrap of her silk jodhpurs. Her arms fall by her sides, her hands, hidden in long chiffon sleeves, steadying her balance. Under her chiffon jacket she wears a sequin-embroidered vest, a single string of thick pearls around her neck. Her hair is short, coiffed in lacquered waves over her ears, around her face, and across her forehead. She is looking to the side, and far into the distance, not even the glimmer of a smile on her lips.

On 25 June 1929 Idina obtained a decree nisi from Joss "on the ground of his adultery with Mrs. Edith Mildred Mary Agnes Ramsay-Hill at an address in Sloane-street in April, 1928." After a decade of exuberance Idina had reached a nadir. The sole comfort—apart from Dinan—was the settlement from the *Express* a fortnight later, which at least provided her with some money. In the summer of 1929 any money at all, it was felt, could be turned into a small fortune.

For the past ten years, while the flappers had danced until dawn in city nightclubs and on country-house lawns, the stock market had climbed. All one needed, it was said, was a little capital and guts and nothing could go wrong. But two months after Idina's life had hit this new bottom, the world's stock markets, too, began to tremble, and in late October 1929 Wall Street crashed. The Roaring Twenties, all their excess of money, music, and mollifying liquor, and Idina's Kenyan dream with them, had been reduced to a whimper.

Chapter 20

Even after three failed marriages, Idina still yearned to marry again. Marriage, in theory, would provide her with a guarantee of the companionship and affection that she yearned for. Without this and, unlike her mother and grandmother, lacking any vision to pursue, her life felt empty. And she still believed that she might find the right husband with whom she could make a life. If anything, brokenhearted as Idina certainly was by Joss's departure with Molly, her marriage to him had shown that it was possible to have a dream life even if only for a short time. But 1930 did not start well for Idina. In February Joss married Molly in London and the two of them returned to Kenya to live in Oserian—Ramsay-Hill gave up his share in the house. Six months later Idina's mother, Muriel, died of tuberculosis at the age of fifty-eight. A few years earlier, she had moved every stick of furniture at Old Lodge onto its lawns and held a public sale of her possessions to raise funds for the Labour Party. She had then sold Old Lodge, donated that money as well, and moved to a house in the London suburb of Wimbledon. Although she shared the house with the American Mary Dodge, it was a lonely life and death despite its achievements. Loneliness was what Idina feared and longed to avoid. As she later wrote to her son David: "Nobody knows better than I how bloody difficult marriage is! Yet I still think it is probably the only real solution to happiness—the whole thing [is] one has to be so damned intelligent and subtle about it all."[1]

Muriel had kept some money to live off and left most of her remaining funds to the politically active Buck, "knowing he will make good and wise use of same"[2] in his own pursuit of Labour politics. Avie, who had originally been left ten thousand pounds, now found herself cut out of Muriel's will, perhaps because she had recently left Stewart Menzies and eloped with a country squire called Frank Spicer, who had inherited a substantial sum himself. Idina was left some money—not outright but as an interest in a Brassey family trust. The amount itself was five thousand pounds—not a fortune—and Idina could not even touch the capital but was entitled only to the income. Muriel had left more money, however, to Dinan—twenty thousand pounds of the trust and the income from this to be used for her upkeep until she married, when the capital would become hers. Charles Gordon and Joss had eaten their way through the ten thousand pounds of Brassey capital that Muriel had already given Idina. Giving the money to Dinan instead was a device that would prevent any future husband Idina might take from spending the rest.

In the interim Idina and Dinan could together live well, especially if they went back to Kenya and started farming. Idina had no desire to live a single life on a farm several miles from her nearest neighbors, and three months after her mother's death she married for the fourth time. Unlike her previous three husbands, all Scotsmen, Donald Haldeman, sometimes known as "Squashy," was the English-born son of an American shirt manufacturer. Divorced himself, he had been a "white hunter" leading safaris in Kenya for several years and, like Idina, adored the country.

On 22 November 1930 they wed in the register office in the small Sussex town of Steyning. Buck gave his sister away for the second, if not third, time and witnessed the marriage. The new couple then left for a honeymoon in the United States, whose press shivered with anticipation at the marriage of such an infa-

Newspaper report of Idina's fourth marriage, to American Donald Haldeman. These images and the following feature were widely syndicated across the North American continent.

mous woman to one of their own. "Idina has been the wife of two captains, an earl and now has become the bride of an American resident. All inside seventeen years and she's still young and beautiful" ran a widely syndicated story entitled "Love Failures of the Countess."[3] And after that, for the third time in just over a decade, Idina sailed to build a home in Kenya with a brand-new husband.

Idina was clearly in love with Donald. And enough in love to think that this new husband was a man to whom she could be faithful—or perhaps she had no understanding of what Donald expected from marriage. Like Joss, Donald had been educated at Eton. Unlike Joss, he was not a compulsive womanizer, ready to wander off at a moment's notice. Quite the opposite: he

Donald and Idina's wedding

was fiercely possessive of Idina. For the sexually driven Idina to marry a possessive husband was nothing short of folly.

The plot of land Idina and Donald arranged to buy was not in the Wanjohi Valley—Happy Valley—but on the far side of "Chops" Ramsden's farm. It was up on the shoulders of a mountain whose peak rose between two broad wings that appeared to flutter in the haze of sun and mist and which the Kikuyu called the Kipipiri—the Butterfly. The Kipipiri was lush, thick-forested, and higher than Slains. Tall green bush and jungle sprouted from every inch allowed it and rustled with brightly colored birds and belligerent beasts. Here the mist hung over the giant, dark-green leaves for most of the morning before the sun finally drove it off, yet, even at the height of the day, the peak of the Butterfly remained tinged with the purple stain of altitude. Idina decided to call the home she would build Clouds.

Halfway up the mountain, most of Idina's new farm was sloping, but just beyond and below Chops's house, she found a spot for a house. This consisted of a few acres that had plateaued out and clung precariously to the side of the mountain above a steep drop toward the distant, dry, yellow Rift Valley below. She decided to position the house at the back of this area, so that it could take shelter from the mountain slope behind and leave room for a sprawling expanse of lawn and garden leading to the cliff edge. This she left fringed with eucalyptus, thronging with the company of large, beautiful, humanoid colobus monkeys.

Between the trunks it was possible to glimpse a kaleidoscope of green foothill and amber valley floor, but this view little prepared a visitor for the shock of walking through the trees to suddenly stand on the edge of a mountain-forest world and look beyond to a grassland stretching almost as far as the eye could see.

Up in the hills, most of the settler farmers, even Alice and the Happy Valley set, lived in cottages with corrugated-iron roofs. The few grand houses in Kenya, like Oserian or Kiki Preston's Mundui, were confined to the shores of Lake Naivasha or the outskirts of Nairobi. Idina, however, had no intention of seeing her new husband leave her for a grander house.

Clouds was a mountain house, an African house, its single story dwarfed by its high-vaulted roof, but this roof was not, like the one at Slains, made of the standard corrugated iron but of thousands of handsome dark cedar shingles. The house itself was square and entered from the back, the mountain side. Here Idina spread a large gravel drive and surrounded it with beds of hibiscus, rose, and bougainvillea bursting with red and orange, purple and white—which distracted from the sprawl of stables and dairies to the side. And sprawl it was, as, for all that it had the traits of a pleasure palace, Clouds was a working dairy and pyrethrum farm. As Europe and the United States spiraled into the mass unemployment and bankruptcy of the Great Depression, Idina, perched on a mountain ledge thousands of feet up under the Equator, was slowly building, this time, a Jersey herd.

The entrance to the house was through an archway leading to a central grassy courtyard. Around the edge of this ran an open passageway like a cloister walk linking a series of doors. The lawn was divided into four squares by two straight paths crossing in the center, where a birdbath stood framed by four circular urns overflowing with greenery. Idina loved birds, and in the rose garden outside her bedroom a birdhouse of several stories perched on a high pole in the middle of a pond. As a consequence, Clouds was alive with Egyptian geese, crested cranes, herons, storks, guinea fowl, a peacock, and a very lazy peahen, who always laid her eggs on the thatched dairy roof, to save building her own nest. The eggs invariably rolled off. And there was Kasuku, a

Clouds, the house Idina built when married to her fourth husband, Donald Haldeman. She remained there after the marriage fell apart.

red-and-gray African parrot with a wide vocabulary. He would call out "Boy" in Idina's voice and one of the servants would come running. He also imitated the clinking of empty glasses being carried back to the pantry.

Clouds, wrote Rosita Forbes, who stayed with Idina there, and copied some of the design for her own retreat, in the Bahamas, was an "entrancing" house. "It was the last word in comfort, and it was clever too—in the way that the rooms fitted. . . . A house should be planned like a coat and skirt. . . . It should fit and suit the people who are going to live in it. Dina's low grey house on rising ground about the tawny plain fulfilled these conditions. It was welcoming and at the same time, mysterious."[4]

On either side of the courtyard ran two long bedroom wings, like the rest of the house a single room deep, and in all containing six guest bedrooms, each with its own bathroom and hot-water tank heated by a bonfire outside. Inside each there was a fireplace too; a deep, wide fireplace that shared a chimney with the adjoining room and through which—if a fire was not lit—

a guest could crawl to his neighbor. The bedrooms, indeed, the entire house, were paneled to give the same matte, dark effect that Idina had planned for Kildonan fifteen years earlier. She furnished them with four-poster beds and tapestries, each with furniture of a different period and style. At one end of these rooms were two others—a nursery for Dinan and an adjoining room for her governess, a lady called Joan Trent who had come with them from England.

The main rooms spread across the front. On the far right a dining room looked out from the corner of the house. This led into a drawing room paneled not only on the walls but on the ceiling too, giving it the air of a sixteenth-century farmhouse in some English rural retreat. Inside, Idina had put high-armed sofas around the wide fireplace and cushions over the deep window seats looking out over the lawn and Rift Valley beyond. On one side French doors led onto a terrace scattered with chairs and tables and surrounded by both Idina's plants and flowers and a great panorama of African animal scents and sounds. Back inside, a thick velvet curtain hung across the archway into the library, the walls laddered with floor-to-ceiling bookshelves, a deep white sofa piled high with cushions also facing out to the lawn.

Beyond this, in the far wall, was a door to Idina's bedroom. It was a large room, almost the size of the drawing room, but, sited on the corner of the house, it again had windows on two sides. Near the door lay an enormous bed covered in a rug of wildcat skins and above which hung a childhood photograph of herself, Avie, and Buck (pictured on page 35). Beyond its sleeping area was another "room," space for a writing desk and chair, another sofa even, all looking out to the view beyond. The door was left propped open by a tortoiseshell-topped elephant's foot, to allow her dogs to wander in and out. Toward the rear of the house was another door from Idina's bedroom that led into a vast bathroom. Along one wall stretched a bath, a shining lion's-head tap above it. Next to this was a mirrored wall which, when pushed, led to the water closet. To the side ran twenty feet of walk-in closets, with rails above and, below, a staircase of shoe racks containing

*Idina, right, dressed for a Rift Valley picnic with
her friend Paula Gellibrand — Cecil Beaton's
"living Modigliani" — who married Idina's
former lover, Boy Long*

Idina's dozens and dozens of barely worn shoes. In the far corner
of this room there was another door. Almost invisible in the wall
next to the bath, it led into another room.

Clouds was, for a mountain lodge, palatial. It could take a
dozen guests overnight and, remoter than Slains, it needed to;
once guests had arrived they had to stay. In the rainy season,
when the roads were impassable, its only access was by airplanes
landing on the wide, open lawn. Idina made it worth the journey.
The French housekeeper, Marie, had come back to Kenya with
Idina and again they trained up a cook and kitchen staff to pro-

duce soufflés. The familiar silk pajamas and whisky bottles lay on the pillow, fires raged in the fireplaces, hot water bucketed out of the taps, and champagne brimmed from glasses. In the evening Idina appeared in a dark blue velvet kaftan to keep out the night cold: it was colder and higher than at Slains up here. By day she wore corduroys, an open-necked white shirt and, as ever, her feet were bare.

Idina and Donald entertained from the start. Familiar faces from the twenties, and a few new ones, turned up by car, by plane, on horseback, some even on foot at the end of a planned safari to the house. The tables and sofas filled. Alice, who had eventually married Raymond and then, three tempestuous months later, separated from him, returned to Kenya from a Europe plunged into Depression. Even her and Idina's favorite clothes designers were suffering. From their hill farms the two women were now sending regular financial aid to Paris. In return they received pieces from the latest collections in which they continued to dress exquisitely, even for picnics down on the floor of the Rift Valley.

Up at Clouds the lights were kept on well past the usual ten-thirty generator shutdown. At first, even these late evenings were proper enough to invite Dinan's sequence of governesses to. (One, Joan Trent, thus met and married Boy Long's brother Dan.) But, as it became clear, Idina, whisky flowing through her veins, soon felt the old "beasts" return. Donald was tall, classically handsome, if with a hairline that receded a little far for his thirty-odd years. But Donald was not enough.

One evening Chops Ramsden went to gently warn Dinan's replacement governess, Peggy Frampton, who was already dressing for dinner, "There's a bit of a party going on in here, Peggy, you had better not join us tonight."[5] The following morning Marie calmly told Peggy that there had been an "orgy" the night before. Peggy, equally calmly, saw no signs of it and equated Marie's description to her frequent hand-wringing and exclamations: "*Cet affreux Afrique! Cet affreux Afrique!*"[6]

Donald, however, did not take Idina's infidelities in quite such a matter-of-fact way. Instead, his previously appealing protec-

Idina and her eight year-old daughter, Diana Hay, known as Dinan, in 1934

tiveness erupted into ferocious anger. When in late 1933 he returned early from a safari to witness a half-dressed man leaping into a car and skidding away, Donald swung his ever-loaded gun and fired at the departing car until Idina arrived to restrain him.

After that Idina employed a manservant to sit with a view of the road for miles down the hill and a tom-tom under his fingertips. The moment he saw the cloud of dust that marked an approaching car he was to beat the drum, giving Idina's visitors time to leave by another route before her husband returned. It wasn't enough. Whenever Donald returned, footsore and camp-tired, from leading an expedition through the bush, he would find something to make him suspect that Idina had taken a lover in his absence. Idina began to fear the outbursts of violence that accompanied his return home.

After an unpleasantly effervescent Christmas in 1933, Idina realized that his devotion had evolved into obsession. Donald was now trying, quite literally, to shoot any man he suspected might be her lover. For the first time in her life Idina had to consider that life alone was an option preferable to life—or possibly death—with a gun-toting husband. She decided to tell Donald that she was leaving.[7]

Early in the New Year Donald left on a monthlong safari. In his absence Idina made preparations to leave for Europe for several months without him. With bullets flying around the house and garden and the now eight-year-old Dinan in need at least of some company of her own age and species (wildlife wandered through the house, sometimes semi-tamed, sometimes creating a great deal of panic), Idina decided that her daughter should return to England, as her friends were doing. For the past few years Idina had organized exchanged visits with Gemma St. Maur, a young cousin of Chops Ramsden, and Robin Long, Boy and Genesta's son. Both of these children, and nearly all other European and American eight-year-olds in Kenya, were now being sent away to boarding school or back to England to be educated.

Sending children back Home from the far reaches of the British Empire was standard practice. It was regarded as Not Good to bring a child up under a raging sun. When Dinan had been small Idina had cared enough about this to dress her not only in a wide-brimmed sun hat and long sleeves but also in the thick spine-pad that helped to counter the sun. Boarding schools would take children from as young as four and even keep them over the holidays if they had no relations to visit in England. Many middle- and upper-class British children at this time conducted a purely postal relationship with their parents for years at a stretch.

Idina did not, however, have to send Dinan to boarding school. Buck's daughter, Kitty, was also eight. While Kitty's elder brothers had been sent away to school, Kitty, as was the custom among the families who could afford to, was being educated at home by a governess. Buck invited Dinan to live with them, to share lessons with Kitty and provide some company for her. He added to the generosity of his offer by allowing Idina to keep the income from Dinan's share of the capital until Dinan married, on the basis that Clouds, even if Dinan rarely managed to visit it, would remain her maternal home.

Idina bought a pair of tickets, packed her and Dinan's clothes, and waited for Donald to return from safari. She intended to tell him that their marriage was over, she was going away, and that when she returned she expected him to have left the house. In sharp contrast to the end of her previous marriages, Idina had this time decided that she would stay living at the house she had built in Kenya, even if it meant living alone. She might be moving on from Donald, but she had invested too much of herself in Clouds to let it go. It had become clear that the only way to hang on to a better life was not to stake it upon the survival of a marriage. In any case, the new craze for airplanes meant that she was just a short flight from Nairobi—the planes could land on the lawns in front of Clouds. Life alone on a Kenyan farm was no longer such a lonely prospect.

A couple of days before Donald was due back Idina began to contemplate what his reaction to her departure might be. On 11 February 1934 she sent a message to Cockie, who had by now not only married but left the incessantly faithless Bror Blixen, to come up to Clouds to give her moral support and to bring reinforcements. Cockie in turn asked Nellie Grant, Elspeth Huxley's mother, to come too. Even though Donald was, in Nellie's own words, "given to fits of violence," she decided to go. "Have just agreed to go with Cockie to Clouds tomorrow for one night only as Dina wants moral support in facing Donald," she wrote. "Anyway shall get some garden loot even if Donald does shoot us all."[8] The garden loot consisted of bundles of clippings, which Idina and Nellie had been exchanging for a decade and a half.

Thus reinforced, Idina told Donald and then left for England immediately. She reached Fisher's Gate in early March and installed Dinan in the care of Buck and his wife. After a few days she left for Paris, where, as the American newspapers reported, she ordered some new clothes: "Lady Idina Haldeman, before leaving for Cairo, ordered a peach crinkled crepe satin evening dress with peach ostrich feather cape from Molyneux. Peach chiffon covers the shoulders and the feathers begin midway between shoulder and elbow. Very pale at first they deepen into almost orange and the tips curl up like inverted question marks."[9] Idina went on to Egypt for Easter at the beginning of April and, toward the end of the month, returned to London. She would spend three months in England catching up with old friends and then return to Kenya to live, as she had settled upon, without a husband.

It seemed as though at last, as she entered her forties, Idina had found confidence in herself. She was showing an emotional stability that she had not displayed since her early marriage to Euan. But, in the first few days of May, amid the mêlée of cocktail and dinner parties that marked the beginning of the London social season, Idina received a note from a friend that would turn this new state of affairs on its head.

The name of the friend was Sheila Milbanke. Sheila was a glamorous society beauty, generally described as "quite the nicest thing ever to have come out of Australia."[10] She had arrived in England in her late teens and made an early marriage. Like Idina, she had divorced, and was now married to the considerably older Sir John Milbanke, known as Buffles and a military hero who had won Britain's greatest award for bravery, the Victoria Cross. Being Australian, Sheila was engagingly unconcerned by some of the rules of British society and approached life and the people around her in a straightforward, matter-of-fact way. As Cockie had done on safari in Kenya, Sheila had thus entranced the Prince of Wales and made herself a name as a Court favorite.

In the note Sheila asked to meet up with Idina. When they met, Sheila was characteristically direct. Sheila and Buffles were extremely close friends of Euan and Barbie's. They spent a great deal of time staying with them and Sheila had therefore spent a great deal of time with Idina's two sons, David and Gerard, who were now nineteen and eighteen, together with their three much younger half brothers, Barbie's children.

Idina, in contrast, had not been allowed to see her sons since she had first left for Kenya with Charles Gordon. Barbie had become mother to Idina's children, too, leaving Idina with no right to see them herself.

But right or no right, Sheila told Idina, David now needed to see her, his real mother.

Idina's two sons had "totally different characters," as Barbie's sister Ursula Lutyens had spotted a dozen years earlier.[11] While Gerard was "the most determined, obstinate little fellow with a will of iron," David was "affectionate" and "very easily influenced . . . you can get him to do anything by showing him a little love." Life, Ursula had predicted, "will probably be harder for him than for G."

She was right. Both David and Gee, as Gerard had become known, were extremely bright and had jumped a school year at Eton, which they had now left. Along with many of his generation, Gee's imagination had been captured by the Air Force. He sat the exam and passed into Cranwell, the training academy, in second place, winning a prize cadetship. He settled in well, was utterly content, and within a month flew solo.

David, meanwhile, sat the Oxford entrance exam. He narrowly missed a scholarship but took a place at the aggressively academic Balliol College to read Greats, consisting of Philosophy, Latin, and Ancient Greek. He had been there since the previous October and was now burning with both brilliance and anger. He scorned his parents' lifestyle as he did their politics—Euan was a Conservative MP and government minister, Barbie a political hostess—to the extent that he was no longer able to have a rational conversation with either of them. He was currently agonizing over whether or not to become a celibate "Christian Socialist" priest and, Sheila believed, he desperately needed to confide in somebody outside his parents' circle.

For fifteen years Idina had not heard her son's voice, seen his face, or touched his skin. David, Sheila said, really needed to talk to somebody who understood the "fire" he was in,[12] and who could listen.

Idina could certainly do that.

Chapter 21

David Wallace by no means kept every letter he was sent, although a few sets of intense correspondence with fellow undergraduates survived him. From Barbie, he kept very few letters, and only two from this difficult time in his life. The first was written to him on his year abroad, saying that he should stick out his time away, however miserable he felt. The second was about his passionately held political beliefs and the emotional crisis he was in. It was not a warm letter. Its coolness had so incensed him that he had picked up a pen and scrawled his own comments over it:

Mayfair 6212

19 Hill Street
Berkeley Square W1

Monday
My darling David,
    Thank you for a {"Oh!" scrawled by David} letter I got this morning. I realized all these holidays that you were going through some sort of mental change and hesitated several times whether to talk to you about the outward signs of it, which seemed to be a sort of intellectual air of

snobbery and superiority and lack of effort ["largely 'ability'" added by David] to talk or mix with anyone.

Darling, whatever you may do in the world one has to get on with one's fellow men—either you are going to lead them or you are going to serve them. In either case you have got to understand them and get on with them and even the people you may despise as frivolous, idle or anything else you like probably have something in them that is fine and lovable so try never to judge hardly. And it is the typical soldier sailor type, which you may find very antipathetic at the moment which have yet, in the past, almost more than anyone made possible the life that you and your generation enjoy. . . . You are quite right to be dissatisfied with the present capitalist system which has obviously partially failed and quite right to wish to alter some of the awful inequalities of life but please don't just say you're a communist just to startle and frighten me [underlined and "NO!" added by David]. In the first place it doesn't a bit, in the second place ["Oh!" added by David] what do you mean by it, and what are you going to do about it? If you wish to put down the present system you must replace it with a thought-out system of Communism and plan to bridge the transition stage—it is no good being mearly [sic] destructive but you must be sure of your constructive plan as well. Then do you think Communism does away with inequalities, poverty etc? Certainly conditions in Russia, which is the only country that has tried it, are far worse, specially those of the poorest.

Don't you think perhaps more could be done by trying to improve the present system under which with all its faults the standard of living has undeniably improved every 10 years.

Please if you want to be a communist or a socialist or anything be a constructive one not just a rather priggish critic of the present system, from which you've drawn every advantage [underlined and "Did I ever deny it?" added by David].

I wonder if you would like to go up to Blagdon for part of the holidays and work in some of the very poor parts round Newcastle.

I'm sure you would be harrowed and perhaps you could help. Anyway you would see a little of conditions and know more what you were talking about. I hope this letter makes sense to you but I'm not too good with the pen as you know ["I certainly do!" added by David].

With love from <u>Mother.</u>

With love from Mother. Barbie had been "Mother" to David and Gee ever since the day she appeared in Eastbourne with Euan, twisting the heavy new ring upon her finger. Euan had come down a week earlier with Aunt Avie and before that had been away for so long that the two boys could barely have remembered who he was. For a year their life had been a rotation of habitats: Granny Muriel's, where they kept their ponies; Euan's sister's, "Aunt Jean's," where they had spent a long summer bouncing through heather and tunneling through bracken; and Eastbourne. The seaside town was a place of endless damp sand and shingle, a wide, open sky and wind that required coats to be buttoned up when outside and lips when inside—an inevitably gray boardinghouse, its dining room filled with walnut faces emanating disapproval.

Then, suddenly, David and Gee had had a father again, and a mother too—although a different one from the figure who had bounded through their nursery before. She had been "Mummie."[1] Barbie was most definitely "Mother."

Then, almost as soon as they had arrived, Euan and Barbie had vanished again, taking the boys' nanny, Miss Jeffreys, with them. In her place had come Nanny Sleath. Nanny Sleath had brought up Barbie, and Barbie's brother and sisters—the entire Lutyens family—and now she was going to bring up Barbie's stepsons too.

David and Gee had stayed in Eastbourne for three more weeks. On Friday, 30 April, ten days before Euan and Barbie's wedding, Nanny Sleath and the two nursery maids who trotted behind her, each clutching a boy quite firmly, piled themselves and David and Gee onto a train for London, arriving, wrote Euan in his diary, at four-thirty. And then, as though discharging a duty before they again vanished for months, Euan and Barbie took the boys to a society doctor, who declared himself "delighted with them in every way."

Within a couple of hours Barbie and Euan had bundled the boys onto an overnight train to Scotland—"the kids went off to Kildonan by the 7:20"—leaving the newly engaged couple free to enjoy their wedding and a two-month-long trip abroad.

By lunchtime on 1 May, David and Gee were standing in front of a gleaming new building-in-progress that promised to be as large as a seaside grand hotel and staffed on the inside by columns of black-dressed and white-capped housekeepers and housemaids, footmen and bootboys, cooks and undercooks, scullery maids, and even a tweeny[2] or two. The grounds, too, were packed with an army of retainers in brown and green: gardeners and gamekeepers, woodmen and kennel keepers.

This, the Kildonan House that Idina had designed, was to be their new home. The only Wallace family staff missing were Euan's valet, Wooster, and Barbie's lady's maid, Miss Knight. They were, of course, accompanying Euan and Barbie on honeymoon.

Kildonan was heaven for little boys.[3] There was a vast amount of space to run around in and, unlike an Eastbourne boardinghouse, no wrinkled faces clearly wishing they were not there. There were lawns, with a climbing tree neatly split into two so that each of them could take a trunk and race the other as high as they could go. There was a wide river reached by climbing over a low fence and crawling through the long grass to the edge, where they could lie, dipping their hands in the water. There was other water too. A brook across the lawn and, behind the house, a burn—"a burrrrn," said MacDowell (pronounced McDool), who ran the grounds. This stream also ran along one edge of the lawn but, for the sake of a few feet of extra grass, an enticingly long, dark tunnel had been engineered over it and turf laid on top.

Up behind the tunnel and the burn were a tennis court, an

orchard—it was too early in the year for apples when they arrived—a nursery garden straight out of *Peter Rabbit* and acres and acres of a very deep, very dark wood in which they built houses "out of sticks and bracken & played Red Indians all the afternoon," wrote Barbie's sister Ursula in her diary of a visit to the house.[4]

Euan and Barbie came; and stayed. For two long months the house bulged with their friends; then in late September the household packed up, piled back on the train, and headed for their new London home. This was a Mayfair town house, filled with some of the same faces that had been at Kildonan and, of course, Nanny Sleath. From time to time Euan and Barbie wafted through their new nursery and the schoolroom in which a governess came to give them lessons. After two Christmases, Easters, and summers at Kildonan, a new mewling bundle of baby boy joined them in the nursery, and two little black Shetland ponies arrived in the stables—"too sweet for words, and the children are marvellous on them," wrote Ursula.[5] Within months, David and Gee had been sent away to boarding school: "Barbie and I chose Heatherdown," wrote Euan, "with 90 boys, as 150 is too many."

For David and Gee, leaving for boarding school had been the beginning of the rest of their boyhood: three terms a year of joshing and teasing and freezing on rugby pitches and burning on cricket fields and Latin and arithmetic and parsing and Greek with ink-stained fingers. Then it was back to Kildonan for the summer hols, to a house jammed with braying red faces and tweed bottoms for the grouse, and again at Christmas, this time for the pheasant. Too young to shoot, they instead loaded guns on the moors, tied on flies on the riverbanks and cast a line or two. When it rained they ran inside. There were 250 feet of carefully thought-out passageways on each floor, with a single corner to navigate at speed.

From now on Easter was spent with Nanny Sleath by the sea, at Bognor or Brighton or Poole or Eastbourne again, or back at Frinton, on the other side of the country. It must have seemed that whenever they came home there was a new face in the nurs-

ery: brothers one, two, and three. Johnny came first, Peter immediately after. Then there was a gap before Billy, who was not, as it
had been hoped, a girl. But very much the youngest, and the
only one not in an almost-twin pair, he was kept as spoilt as only
the baby of a family can be. At the other end of the family, David
and Gee clung to each other, inseparable: "When one of us was
punished, and kept indoors for the day, the other stayed in with
him."[6]

IT WAS IN THE SUMMER OF 1931 that David first began to
feel anger with the world. He was sixteen years old, his parents
had beautiful homes, limitless funds, and ranks of servants. He
himself was now at Eton, bound in stiff collars and ancient traditions designed to insulate him from the world outside. But he
had only to read a newspaper or open his eyes on the Windsor
streets and see humans reduced to refuse, trying to sell anything
they could with the fragments of dignity that remained to them.
For almost two years businesses had been folding, the survivors
supported only by the mercy of their lenders. Through June and
July, the lenders themselves were imploding, throwing not just
their debtors' but their own employees onto the end of the wind-
ing, ragged queues waiting for the dole, waiting for soup, waiting for change.

The halfhearted new National Government under Ramsay
MacDonald wasn't enough for David.[7] Quite the opposite. His
father was put back into the government. His parents' friends
continued to loll around drawing rooms, leaning back on the
sofas, their own or their neighbor's pearls twisted in one hand,
the stem of a champagne glass in another. Outside there was still
rampant unemployment. David did not hesitate to tell both his
parents and their bejeweled friends that he did not believe it was
right. He rapidly gained a reputation, wrote Euan, for being
"socialistic."[8]

By the end of 1931 even Euan and Barbie were beginning to
feel pinched. "World financial conditions," wrote Euan in his
diary, "resulted in the loss of 40 per cent of our income and in

October we had to make drastic household economies: everyone is in the same boat, & most people worse off than we are. All the same it is impossible to go on for many years when expenditure exceeds income by 60%." Family economies were made: the previous year the Wallaces had spent Christmas at Malaga and visited Cannes, Rome, and Vienna. In 1932, however, "we did hardly any travelling & spent more time than usual in London," wrote Euan. They paid off as many servants as they could bear (so adding to the ranks of the unemployed), leaving a "reduced staff" that "worked very well." This saved Euan "£4000 on general expenditure" alone—a sum equivalent to a couple of hundred thousand today—of which "£1000 represented no foreign expeditions," though "no foreign expeditions" still meant "a week at Corne d'Or in July" for Barbie and a "week-end at Le Touquet" in Normandy for Euan.

That year David's anger subsided a little, at least as far as Euan noticed. He "became much more sociable and less socialistic and everyone likes him enormously." It was his last year at Eton. He had been busy. A year younger than his classmates, David had still been House Captain; he had his School Certificate to sit and then the Oxford entrance exam. He left "with the most wonderful reports as to character from GWL [his housemaster] and the Headmaster." On the basis that David and Gee's "motor bikes caused no casualties" so far, at Christmas Euan "gave them a small car."

Then David had gone abroad for the rest of the academic year, until he started at Oxford. He left for Paris in January. But, within a few weeks, he felt "not very happy."[9] Barbie urged him to give it more time. He did, and then went on to Germany for another three months, which he did not enjoy either.[10] But Euan, busy with his political career—he was a junior defense minister, Civil Lord of the Admiralty, and that year, 1933, "foreign affairs (France & Germany & Japan) very awkward at times"—was too preoccupied to notice otherwise. David's sojourns abroad, he wrote, "were both very successful."

The week before David went up to Oxford, Euan left for a

two-month tour of the "China and E. Indies Stations." Barbie was busy with the younger ones, so David took himself up to Oxford alone.

OXFORD IN THE EARLY THIRTIES was a maelstrom of ideology, emotion, and beliefs that the world was broken and only an extreme course of action could mend it. And David was caught up in its currents. Oddly, nobody in the family saw him from the day he went to the day he returned home at the Christmas vac. By then wearing clothes that looked as though they hadn't been washed since he had left, he had come to his decision to live on the other side of the moral world as a temperate, sexually abstinent, Christian Socialist priest.[11]

David scrawled in the diary Gee gave him for Christmas that year—not a leather-covered Smythson's but a two-shilling, cardboard workingman's diary, one that Gee knew David would accept—that abstinence did not come easily: "Another great failure. Changing, was nude before glass and as usual, after a few games, slipped straight into bed and making bloody mess and as usual being livid with self after."[12] But, notwithstanding the difficulty of attaining his objective, the rift between David and his family broadened. When Barbie sacked a servant, Arthur, for visiting the doctor in working hours, David picked up *Equality,* by R. H. Tawney. "It is extremely interesting. Marked a few passages. The rich are all kindness until their claims are questioned, when they become like a lion. The value of the working class movement is not to adjust the present order, redistribute wealth more equally, but to substitute the standard of men for that of wealth, gain that usual respect, which is owing to them and they do not get (e.g. Mother and Arthur)."

Idina's son David Wallace

This time Euan noticed that his son was at odds with the life he had been brought up in. Within days David recorded that his father had "told all the ancestors that I am going into the Church."

David Wallace in the early 1930s

In January David returned to a university full of "ju-jitsu," being invited to dons' rooms for late-night whiskies "which I made water," and the Labour Club. He went to talks and wrote afterward in his diary: "Aneurin Bevan spoke. Repetitive and tiresome manner, demagogue and quite interesting. . . . Walked back with Crofts. Tells me he has no confidence in working class. Comes of working class, which I did not know. I must talk to him more."

But, clearly now realizing that David needed some attention, that spring term the family made an effort to visit him at Oxford.

David's first visitors were Nanny Sleath and his brothers John and Peter. They arrived at midday one Saturday in late January, stayed for lunch and a short walk, and left at three. Having observed her former charge in his student habitat, a few days later Nanny Sleath sent "another pullover from Selfridges and said send her the yellow one to wash," wrote David.

Next came his beloved brother Gee. He stayed an entire weekend: two full days alone together after their first whole year apart, since David had left school the Christmas before. It was "grand" to see Gee, "lovely having" him, he wrote.

Finally, on 19 February, on the way back from what was now widely called a "weekend" of hunting and golfing, Euan and Barbie decided to drop in, leaving their car to be driven on to London ahead of them. They lunched in David's room, the college butler Adams rustling up a "last minute" meal.

This visit ran a little less smoothly. "Mother," wrote David that evening, "wants us to call Daddy 'Father.'" "Mother" wanted a bit more than that too. In her eyes David's appearance was giving the impression that the family had, like some of their friends, slipped into financial ruin. On the train to Paddington she complained to Euan that David was a mess. Euan, perhaps seeing only what he wanted to see, wrote that night, "David seems well and happy and looks no dirtier or untidier than his colleagues!"[13]

But by the time David returned home at the Easter vacation and looked around his parents' dining-room table, packed, as ever—"Duff Coopers and Lord Titchfield there," Barbie glowering at one end—David confessed to his diary that he "felt a terrible misfit."[14]

Three weeks after that he received that first letter from Idina. Having learned his mother's surname from Sheila, David replied and, on Friday, 25 May, he wrote in his diary:

To London to see Dina, my mother, whom I had not seen for 15 years.

Chapter 22

On Friday, 25 May 1934, Idina stepped into Claridge's Hotel in Mayfair shortly before a quarter to one. Ahead of her stretched a maze of sofas and tables, chairs and kissing chairs. In the center a vast glass Medusa's head of a chandelier writhed above serpents of cigarette smoke curling up toward it. Idina sat down, lit a breakfast cigarette and ordered a cocktail. The weather was still turning in that haphazard English way and feather boas and entire dead foxes bobbed around, crisscrossing the lobby, with the odd "sorr-eh" exhaled through motionless lips. The hallway echoed with steps accelerating and hesitating across the marble floor and up the wide staircase that wrapped around the walls. Here and there a head turned back toward her with a look of surprise.

At least there was no chance of a direct confrontation. Sheila had very deliberately taken Euan and Barbie for a long lunch at the Ritz.[1] Idina had been left to face only the life she might have had.

When she saw the red carnation, she knew it was her son. He was taller than his father. Six foot two, a long, pale neck rising from a pair of shoulders strong enough for Idina to trace the blades through the back of his leather-patched jacket when he turned—and an Adam's apple that danced as he glanced this way

The foyer of Claridge's Hotel, Mayfair, where Idina met her son David in 1934

and that, swallowing. The four-year-old boy she had said good-bye to was now a grown man. It seemed that, as her youth had drained, so his had blossomed. He had her high cheekbones and thick hair, a curl or two trying to kick through the Brylcreem. There was the Sackville slope to his eyes but, in a rather charming contrast to his hair, they were, as they always had been, Euan's deep, dark brown.

Fifteen years on, however, this "Brownie" needed her.

David "loathed Claridges." It epitomized all that he abhorred: "vulgarity, servility, the abasement of men's lives before the very rich,"[2] he wrote in his diary. But as he stood in the lobby he saw a woman approaching him, wearing a haze of peach[3] and a deep, wide, intimate smile. She kept on walking, if you could call her sway walking, straight at him. Her hair was the color of corn and she barely reached his shoulder, but her bright-blue eyes were locked on to his, smiling. He "did not recognize her." But she knew him. And as she raised her face and opened her lips and started to speak, the hard edges of David's world began to melt.

She was Dina to him. That was how she had introduced herself. It had been too long for "Mummie," while "Mother" had, of course, been taken by Barbie. Sitting beneath that Medusa's head, then into the dining room for pea soup and Dover sole, and back again to the serpents, they "talked for three hours."

Three hours was long enough for Idina to tell him about her farm in Kenya, where Heaven appeared to brush the earth. There was a lot to tell: trees full of colobus and leopard; bushes full of birds and rhino; zebra and elephant; giraffe, heads swaying tens of feet above the ground; the sun hovering in the sky; and the smell of life that has existed for millennia. However, the pure-white tablecloth stretching between them, there was much about her life that could not be said.

David sat and listened, entranced. He had inevitably heard some stories about his mother as the newspapers had followed the most recent of her messy divorces and remarriages. But now here she was in front of him, the temptress Eve, describing her life in the Garden of Eden itself with such a heartfelt passion that she seemed an innocent. And she was so unlike Barbie. She was, as he put it in his diary, "very sweet." He knew already, he was quite "sure," that this was the beginning of something, and they would be "very fond of each other." He explained to her the future that he believed in. There the poor wouldn't starve, sick children would see doctors, and the self-interested capitalist class would cease to keep the workingman down. And he told her "how the church alone can meet the needs of these people."

Idina listened and tried to tell him that all is not black and white; there are shades of gray in this world. That if you burn bridges between yourself and the people you love, they are hard to rebuild.

But David's views were deeply entrenched, and not to be over-turned in a single afternoon: "She tried long and hard to per-suade me not to go into the church, but her arguments were so shallow."

Her arguments might not have worked that afternoon, but now she had found her son, Idina did not let go. This young man needed her. Now realizing just what she had forfeited by giving up being his mother, she had fifteen lost years of love to give him. He, as headstrong and emotional as she was herself, would clearly love her in return. And, unlike her husbands, he would neither fall out of that love nor leave her for another woman.

The following week she wrote to him: "Beloved Child of Mine—how I adored your note & the thought that prompted it. Those things mean so much. Yes, Sweet Friday was all heaven— I was so entirely happy we seemed to touch perfection. Surely having found those heights we can never lose them again. Such complete understanding & oneness. Darling will ring you up Tuesday morning to arrange when I can come to Oxford on adventure. Bless you dearest Heart, your own <u>Dina</u>."[4]

Two weeks later Idina arrived at Oxford and found David waiting at the station. They walked up the hill, along Broad Street and into Balliol. He showed her his room, of which he was very proud, and, as he later wrote, they "talked for hours."

The next day he walked with her around the colleges. As Idina stepped along beside her tall, handsome son, her crêpe-sleeved arm slipped through his. "Though we do not agree on much," he wrote that evening, "I find her very easy to talk to." Idina clearly hung on her son's every word.

At three o'clock David took her back to the station. She asked when she could see him again. He told her that he was off to work at a Boys' Club camp and then he would go on a religious retreat. The next night he would be free, he calculated, was three more weeks away. Idina invited him to come and dine with her in the London flat she had taken, and to stay the night, just as if they were mother and son.

David arrived in London on the morning of 9 July. It was, he later wrote, a "pleasant journey, dreadful day." He had come straight from the Boys' Club camp via a retreat at Canterbury Cathedral and had "too much to do all day." He "hurried thro streets" and, as he was dining with Idina that evening, "had to hire dinner jacket." There were several hanging in the cupboards at his parents' grand house in Mayfair's Hill Street, where the hall was dominated by a vast mural by the well-known artist Rex Whistler, whom Barbie adored to the extent that he stayed with Barbie and Euan for years. But he had not spoken or written to either Barbie or Euan since he had felt such "a terrible misfit" in the middle of April, almost three months earlier. So he went to the gentlemen's outfitters Beale & Inman, on the corner of Bond Street and Grosvenor Street. He came out clutching a suit and, as he did so, the heavens opened, soaking him. His grandmother's house was across the street. He could see the front door from where he stood. "Sad & wet & weak," as he later wrote, he rang the bell. "Afraid it was silly. Of course I found Mother there."

Barbie loomed in the hallway. David was appalled to see her: "I was frankly sorry and thought it disastrous." By some unfortunate chance Barbie had been at that moment visiting her mother-in-law, with whom she, unlike Idina, found much in common. She might not have seen David for three months, but she started by showing no sign of being pleased to see him now, as he recorded:

> She was a little cold, very surprised, thought my clothes disgraceful. I had to tell her my plans. Quickly, boringly. She did not understand. I felt she never could. . . . It is all horrible. Then I said re Dina. I saw she was hurt. So I asked her if she minded. And she said, in practice, yes. And I said how much more she was to me and how I would never see Dina again and I suddenly found myself crying and we were in each other's arms and I was glad and glad I went and I felt that a first step had been taken in healing the breach, we had come together a little though it was not over and we were divided. I must talk to her more, become intimate, and we may come to understand each other better again.

His eyes wet with tears, and having promised never again to see his real mother, Idina, David eventually prised himself from Barbie's arms. As he had arranged, he went to Idina's flat for the first, and now the last, time. Buck, Diana, and Avie were already there to see him. "Fun, nice seeing them again, they are sweet," David wrote. It was only after they all left that he could spend some time with Idina alone: "I had a long talk to her in my bedroom."

David had a chance to tell Idina what he had been up to. How at the Boys' Club camp, designed for healthy outdoor pursuits and exercise, all the boys had wanted to do was "permanently to go into Swanage and stay there late at night." How when it had rained for days on end, drenching every piece of camping equipment, he and his fellow Oxford undergraduates had tried to amuse the boys by giving "an entertainment. . . . Pain and grief it cost us to compose it and it was as flat as a pancake." How he had been on retreat, spending a week digging potatoes and studying texts, with hours of prayer at Canterbury Cathedral: "I preached my faith to her." And how he had "become far clearer in my vocation since I last saw her." And that "I now feel fundamentally that, barring some unforeseen change, I shall be ordained priest."

Then he must have told her what had happened that afternoon in Grosvenor Street.

For, when he awoke the next morning, Idina had gone.

Chapter 23

Idina had bolted back home to Kenya. She had perhaps been just as idealistic as her son in thinking she might be able to slot back into his life. But, however little Barbie might have understood David, she had made herself his mother and had no intention of allowing Idina to share him.

David was, initially, perhaps too wrapped up in himself to think anything of Idina's abrupt departure. However, Idina had shown him that the Church was not the only source of tenderness and love, and by the end of his morning alone in her flat, his religious fervor of the night before was beginning to waver. He had promised to spend a week helping in a religious order in southeast London but, as he "lunched alone at Dina's [I] wished I had not said I would go."[1] He reached the Brotherhood of the Holy Cross that evening and "from the start it was disillusioning." He spent the days walking "around the poor parts of the parish, ghastly poverty and squalor, God knows what inside, wretched children playing in alleys, nowhere else." Then he returned to help out with the chores: "every sort and kind of work, garden labour in the boiling sun, washing up, sweeping rooms, dusting, helping cook, ironing, washing, all sorts."

When, as Barbie had demanded,[2] he returned to the house his

parents were renting in Sunningdale, the contrast of what he had
seen with the luxury of his own life sent him reeling further:

> How empty, barren, rotten this home life is . . . with all
> this artificiality, selfishness, utter blindness that cannot see
> or feel the needs of others and wallows in its slough, chuck-
> ing away money that could be used to such good . . .
>
> Every day I feel the gulf widening between me and
> mother and daddy. We are poles apart. I never see them
> alone. They never make any advances to me. I have not for
> months opened my heart to them. I feel almost that I never
> could and they could not understand. . . . It is all I can do
> to be polite to their friends. I am a Christian and a Socialist.
> They are pagans, hedonists, conservatives (of what they've
> got). . . . This society is rotten to the core and I hate it.
> These people stand for everything to the fighting of which
> my whole life will be dedicated.

What made David's feelings all the more acute was that
nobody at home, unlike Idina, appeared to want to listen to him.
Three days after he arrived at Sunningdale, David decided to talk
to some people who might care about the same things he did. He
went up to London to spend a night on the Embankment with
the crowds of down-and-outs. Shortly after midnight he entered
a "Salvation Army hostel at Blackfriars, not bad, large, fairly
clean, rather smelly and hot, I hardly slept at all."

Nonetheless, on Wednesday, 25 July, he decided to join
his new rough-living friends by becoming a tramp himself. He
packed a rucksack, took a train to Gloucester and set off "on the
road":

> 16 miles to Ross on Wye; very hot. To my surprise and
> delight was approached by several chaps on the way as a
> fellow tramp and we had a few words: I talking with a
> Scots accent when I could remember and clad in old shoot-
> ing shoes, tan socks, corduroys, string, collarless blue shirt
> and P Robinson coat; having "A Sheepskin Lad" Words-

Kildonan House, Ayrshire, from the southwest

worth's selected poems given me by Chute, a handkerchief, knife and stub of pencil, a tiny crucifix, matches and a few Woodbines.

A week later Gee tracked David down to Worcester Cathedral. He fed his elder brother lunch and packed him into the car. They headed north.

They reached Kildonan at four the following afternoon, in time for a "delicious tea and dinner." David always relaxed at Kildonan. This time was no exception. He was back in the bosom of his family. Gee was there, to whom he could talk at length. With his stomach full, David's rage against injustice began to soften.

The next morning Barbie arrived to find David covered in the pullulating sores of scabies, a mite infestation of the skin.

"Spent most of morning talking to Drs," wrote Euan, "and decided to get him [David] South tonight and put him in a home, where 4 days intensive treatment ought to cure it. We can't risk keeping him at K."[3]

It was 3 August. In less than ten days' time Kildonan would come into its own with the start of the grouse season on the Glo-

Kildonan House

rious Twelfth. Before that the house would fill with fifteen of his and Barbie's guests and the servants they brought with them. If David remained at Kildonan, he would be either prowling the lawns and passageways looking like a leper or locked upstairs like the Monster of Glamis. But Euan's greatest concern that day does not appear to have been his son. The time he had spent on David's illness, he wrote, "ruined my chances of clearing up by 12 and going to lunch with Maureen and playing a round of golf after with Basil."

Barbie ordered the rear seat of one of the cars to be covered in towels and loaded David in. As she did so, "after 2 agonizing failures" David apologized and, perhaps thinking of Idina, asked if he "could begin again under a happier state of affairs."[4] Barbie looked straight at him and said "so sweetly, that all the while she had felt I was emotionally concerned with myself, self-centred, superior, uncongenial company, inverted snob, ignorant of life." David fell back into the car, and drifted in and out of sleep. The following afternoon he reached London.

A skin specialist was waiting for him in the nursing home, and confirmed it was scabies. As he left, Barbie's GP, Kirkwood, whom she called Kirkie, came in to talk to David. He "gave me a long lecture of how . . . class based on fundamental biological difference."

David was in the nursing home a week while the rest of his family chased one another around the grounds at Kildonan. The one highlight of his arrival was a "charming" nurse, Miss Fenhall. On his second day there the formidable Minnie Wallace turned up to visit David. After one glimpse of how her grandson gazed at Miss Fenhall, she had her "transferred to another floor."

David found Miss Fenhall again. On Wednesday evening he dressed and "took Miss Fenhall to the Ballets Russes; we saw Senola de Ballo, Choreastium, and Contes Russes. I thought it one of the loveliest things I have ever seen." By the time he went "North on 8 o'clock" sleeper two days later he "was quite sorry to leave the home. I am glad," he wrote, "I have met Miss Fenhall. I wonder what her Christian name is. I thought of asking her but did not dare."

David returned to spend another six weeks at Kildonan. But something in him had changed. One afternoon when everyone else was busy—"G a bad foot, Guy a cold, Mike a headache"—David picked up "a most enjoyable book 'The Legacy of Greece.' Particularly like Heath's and Burnett's and Gardner's articles and Zimmern's." The following evening another of Barbie's girl-friends engaged him: "Quite an interesting dinner conversation with Nin Ryan on Greece." By the time he finished the book two days later he was smitten. Ancient Greek was, after all, what he was reading at Oxford, not God. He could immerse himself in Greece, sink into the people and politics and philosophy and let its waters close over his head. Two days later he picked up another book: "Hall's History of the Near East. It is absolutely enthralling."

David had found a new set of beliefs and way of life for which he could "live and die fighting."

This new God Idina would be able to share.

BY THE TIME IDINA REACHED CLOUDS that summer, Donald had been gentleman enough to have moved out, and she had the house to herself. Too much to herself. Not even the eight-year-old Dinan was around, running in and out with the latest animal she had picked up to show "Mummie." With Dinan had gone the stream of twenty-something governesses to chat to over dinner. Marie, however, was still there. And there was her farm manager. But, in between dealing with whatever daily *shaurie* reared its head, doing her morning horseback barefoot rounds of the *shamba* and step-by-step trawl of the flower beds and lawns, Idina was very much alone. She had friends to stay and, in turn, went to stay with them. She went down to Muthaiga, she went to Mombasa, she went on safari. And she continued to write to David. But with nobody beside her to discuss her next plans for the farm and garden, day-to-day life felt empty, as, for Idina, living with nobody to love and, more important, nobody to love her, presented little purpose. Whereas her grandmother Annie Brassey's life had been brimming with purpose, and her mother, Muriel, had carried this political banner further, Idina had filled her life with only a search for affection. It was an aim that was bound to fail repeatedly. When, toward the end of 1934, a young pilot called Chris Langlands landed on the lawn at Clouds, Idina turned to him. Chris ran an air charter service called the Blue Bird Flying Circus and had been bringing Idina a houseguest. Chris was athletic, blond, innocently blue-eyed, and a few years younger than Idina. She invited him to remain for the weekend. He stayed for two years.

Chris's arrival perked her up. They wandered off on safari, flying from camp to camp in his plane, and when they returned to Clouds they started to work on the garden. At weekends they packed the house with their friends. Idina's letters to Dinan from "Mummie" started to include photographs of tents in the bush and the family pets beside the vast new series of ponds and waterfalls that were being dug along the edge of the lawns at Clouds, with Idina and Chris standing together—just like a married couple.

Only they weren't. Chris was the first man Idina had openly lived with without being about to marry. At the point at which she had broken up with Donald the idea of a husband had not been attractive. Living with a boyfriend had appeared the perfect way to balance her longings for adventure and domesticity, which "Idina, fragile and frail," yearned for. And, unthinkable when Idina had been born—even her father had bothered to marry again—in the mid-1930s people were beginning to live together.

However, the reality of doing so was less easy than expected. Marriage, even to the four-times-married Idina, offered the promise of permanence, of looking after each other in the dreaded old age. A boyfriend, particularly a younger one living in a home that was very much hers, was disturbingly temporary.

She suggested that they marry. Chris was far from sure that this was a good idea.[5] The role of Idina's fifth husband was not a compelling one. Donald Haldeman might have moved out of Clouds, but he remained on a trigger-happy warpath against Idina's lovers. One of Chris's former girlfriends, Eileen Scott's niece Alice, had married King George V's third son, the Duke of Gloucester. Alice turned up at the Delameres' house on her honeymoon, wandered into the drawing room, and sat down, only to be advised immediately to move to the other end of the sofa, out of range of the man with the gun in the tree outside: Haldeman, waiting to shoot one of Idina's boyfriends. Far from prolonging their affair, Idina's idea that she and Chris should marry destroyed it. At the beginning of August 1936, she wrote to David: "Chris has left me—yesterday—so forgive me for not writing more—I am completely knocked out & can register nothing but pain."[6]

It was not a good time for Idina to be alone. All around her the old Happy Valley set were sinking into a haze of drugs and alcohol. Kiki Preston had been generous with her supplies of morphine, sharing them with friends. Joss's new wife, Molly, who was desperately trying to give him a child and failing, was already racked by the addiction that would soon kill her. Idina's friend Alice de Janzé, now Alice de Trafford, but again separated from Raymond, had also taken to regularly injecting herself with a silver syringe. Initially this had been to manage the pain of an operation she had needed after the shooting. But, like Molly and Kiki, she now had a drug habit that was out of her control.

The weekend parties with the old crowd were starting to become, even for Idina, a little unhinged. The "sheet game" took a new turn. A sheet was strung up across the room. One gender would hide behind; a single representative of the other would grope, in a sort of blindman's buff, to work out which of the figures on the other side was who, and select a partner. As cocktails were sunk, the game developed further. Holes were cut into the sheet. Hands, feet, elbows, noses were stuck through for identification. More cocktails were drunk. A new sheet was pulled across the room. New holes were cut. The men unbuttoned their trousers.

At one party Derek Fisher, somewhat the worse for wear, agreed to be locked into one of Idina's wicker laundry chests. By the time he decided he wanted to escape, everyone was too deafened by the gramophone and full of alcohol to notice. Eventually a young woman sat down on the chest and started to kick her heels against it as she chattered away. Derek, like all Kenyans, had a "bushman's friend" knife attached to his belt. He drew it and thrust it through the chest's lid to attract attention. The blade went straight into the woman's bottom and she ran out of the room screaming. Idina followed her to her bedroom and gave her some lint and plaster and a looking glass with which to apply the bandage and a sleeping pill to take afterward. When, an hour or so later, Idina returned to check on her guest, she found her out for the count, a pool of blood on the floor, and the lint and plaster stuck, with great care, on the looking glass.

Idina decided she needed to find someone, anyone, to move in. Within weeks another young man, "Precious" Langmead, came to make love to Idina one afternoon and found himself staying at Clouds. Precious, as it would soon become clear, was not a man with whom Idina would fall in love. For that moment, however, he would do. And then, as if to her rescue, came Idina's old friend Rosita Forbes. In early 1937 she arrived at Clouds with her second husband, Arthur McGrath.

By that time Rosita had published several books covering her travels in North Africa and the Middle East and been made a fellow of the Royal Geographical Society. She had first made her name in 1921 when, disguised as an Arab woman, she had been only the second Westerner to reach the oasis of Kufra in the center of the Sahara. At the start of 1937 she and Arthur had decided to take advantage of the inflated London rents for the Coronation year and let their house to the Maharajah of Jaipur before setting off to stay with Idina. They brought with them a letter from the Belgian Ambassador to London, who "prided himself on having 'made the world safe for gorillas.'"[7] The letter was addressed to the Belgian authorities who controlled the Congo, instructing them to take Rosita, her husband, and their friends gorilla-watching.

Rosita, Arthur, Idina, and Precious left for Rwanda, where, as Rosita describes in her book *Appointment in the Sun*,[8] they climbed up into the forests and installed themselves in a government rest house to wait for the sighting of a gorilla. After a few evenings the news came that one had been heard crashing through the forest. They set off at dawn, much to Rosita's disquiet, unarmed apart from a single rifle that "looked suitable for peppering rooks . . . So stringent were the regulations against killing the rare gorilla that the hundreds of spear men acting as beaters were warned not to use their weapons, except as a last desperate measure in self-defence." As they scrambled deeper into the forest a Belgian official warned them not to move if a gorilla charged them, "Then he may not kill you." By the time their party had caught up with the rustling bushes, Rosita was terrified.

The expedition proved worth it. "The branches parted. Out came a delicious shaggy creature on all fours about the size of a Shetland pony. It looked kind and soft" and was followed by two babies, "exactly like nursery toys." Then, suddenly, the father appeared: "a great silver-streaked male . . . stood upright and glared at us, beating his breast." The four friends, obeying instructions, froze until, a few moments later, the silverback "dropped and shambled after his family."

After the gorillas they went deep into the Congo jungle, to meet a pygmy tribe. Finding the tribe was easy enough but the people were shy of the strangers and kept disappearing into the trees until Idina, even though deep in the jungle, somehow "produced ice out of a thermos bottle." One of the men stopped to watch. Idina gave him a fragment of ice. "He dropped it as if it had been a live coal. But when he saw that we handled it with safety, he put it very carefully between two leaves and left it in the sun." Half an hour later it had vanished. The poor man fled "gibbering, into the tree depths."

That evening, back at their government rest house, "an inn consisting of a whole family of huts, large and small" in the depths of the jungle, the party bumped into the society millionairess Edwina Mountbatten—the future Vicereine of India—and her reputedly bisexual sister-in-law, Lady Milford Haven. They were accompanied by a man known as Buns Phillips. Edwina had inherited a vast sum of money. Once married, she had embarked on a series of affairs and had now vanished with her sister-in-law for several months. "We sat upon skin rugs and talked unceasingly. Except for our trousers," wrote Rosita, "it might have been a party in London." Idina, surrounded by the other women melting and perspiring in the heat, emerged from her hut for the evening looking "as if she had just come out of tissue paper."

Precious's company on the trip, however, Rosita noted, had been "rather a nuisance mid-river upon an inadequate raft." When, on their way back to Kenya, the four travelers reached Uganda, Rosita's husband left them to fly back home across the Sahara. Idina seized the moment and "discarded Precious," enabling herself to finish the journey with just Rosita.

In 1918 Idina went to Rosita when she split up from Euan. Now, just over eighteen years later, it was with Rosita there to provide encouragement that she decided that, this time, she would not be defeated by Barbie and would try to see her "darling son" David again. She now had not seen David for almost three years and, although God had been replaced with a passion for Greek culture and history, David's desire for political revolu-

David traveling in Greece

tion had not abated. Whenever David went home he came face-to-face with a world that he believed, quite simply, to be wrong. The year before he had been arrested with two friends for shooting a policeman with an air gun. The shot had come from the windows of the student house they shared in Oxford's Beaumont Street. They were known as "rather an elite group of Socialists"[9] and the shooting appeared to be a form of protest. The policeman had been only slightly hurt and was therefore capable of telephoning for help. Within minutes, armored cars and the Oxford police force had surrounded the house and the three young men were dragged out in their pajamas at one in the morning. David saw again only too clearly that there was one law for the rich and another for the very rich: they avoided jail and, a few weeks later, he graduated from Oxford with a then extremely rare First Class degree. He then joined the academic staff of the university, winning a fellowship to go to Greece. In the late spring of 1937 he was living there. Idina obtained his address and wrote to him, suggesting that she visit him. David agreed.

Shortly after returning to Clouds from the Congo, Idina left for Europe. She boarded the Marseille boat at Mombasa, left it at Italy, crossed from Brindisi to Piraeus, and met David in Athens in early May. She bought a car for them to travel in— open-topped for the morning and evening, with a shade for the middle of the day. They clambered in and drove off.

Side by side in the car with the roof down, they made an unlikely pair. David, never out of thick-rimmed glasses, looked intently serious, and Idina, tiny, bottle-blond, and short-skirted, beside him, looking almost young enough to be his utterly inappropriate wife.

Their first stop was on the coast a few miles south of Athens, where a girlfriend of Idina's, Balasha, was living with the author Patrick Leigh Fermor, then just twenty-two years old. Their house was a single-roomed water mill and the four of them camped together on the floor. By day they walked around packed local markets, Idina's short skirt parting the crowd; by night they sat around having what Patrick described as "extremely racy conversations."[10] It was one thing for Leigh Fermor to watch his girlfriend's friend talk like that. It must have been quite another for David to watch his mother.

After a week Idina and David left the couple and set off sightseeing. But by the time they had hauled themselves around half a dozen ancient monuments, each miles from the next, in the baking sun, they were at loggerheads.[11]

David had inherited every ounce of Idina's tendency toward headstrong behavior as well as her easy charm, and at times the first could override the second. He still saw the world in stark contrasts of black and white. He refused to take any criticism of Greece and believed his point of view to be the only one viable. Idina had to bite her lip. But she was not always quick enough. The dreams of both of a perfect filial reunion began to evaporate in the heat.[12] As she later wrote to him: "I indeed know what you can be like when you get into one of your bloody moods—it's hell and there is just nothing one can do."[13]

But something in Idina had changed. Maybe, now that she was forty-four, she was old enough to realize that if she kept moving on, she would reach nowhere. And, in any case, children, unlike husbands, could not be easily replaced. (David's brother Gee had made it quite clear that he felt his loyalty lay with Barbie and his father and had not come to meet Idina in England.) Whatever it was, this time Idina did not fly away from her fallout with David. Instead she held firm. And, before she left Greece, a month later, she had persuaded her son to come and see his sister, Dinan, when he returned to England later that summer.

Dinan had not had the easiest time staying with her uncle Buck. It appeared that her parity of age with her cousin Kitty had, far from making them best friends, turned them against each other. The Christmas before, when Buck had taken the family to stay with Avie, Dinan had remained with Avie when the others returned to Fisher's Gate. The move, it appeared, had been a success. Dinan continued to make frequent trips to Fisher's Gate to see her cousins in the holidays. For the rest of the time Avie had found a young French governess, Mademoiselle Ida Bocardo, universally abbreviated to Zellée, whom Dinan adored. And, to what must have been both Idina's comfort and her torment, Avie, who did not have any children herself, was bringing Dinan up as her own daughter. At least Avie was no longer bosom buddies with Barbie, for, when Avie had left Stewart for her new husband, Frank Spicer, the two women had drifted apart.

Idina took David down to Avie's in August, in the vain hope that he and Dinan might find some bond. It was not obvious. They had met before. Euan and Buck knew each other through politics and Euan occasionally rented Fisher's Gate from Buck.

Buck had also, on two occasions while David and Gee had still been at Eton, persuaded Euan to let the boys come and stay with their cousins and sister (although clearly on the understanding that it would not be during one of Idina's visits). Buck had even sent his own car and driver to pick the boys up and ferry them back.

Dinan was now a shy eleven-year-old and David a twenty-two-year-old academic. In a group of two rather than six cousins, it was harder to see that they would get on. They had nothing in common apart from a mother they hardly knew. To David, one of five boys and educated in single-sex boarding schools from the age of eight, girls—as it was clear from his encounter in the nursing home with Miss Fenhall—were a foreign species.

Somehow, however, perhaps driven by Idina's determination now to pull her family together, or swayed by their mother's delight at seeing the two of them side by side, they managed to find a common ground. As Dinan later said, she had been "very fond" of one of her brothers.[14] And, for the precious couple of days of this visit, Idina had two of her three children with her and could pretend that her life had never kept them apart. She had made mistakes in the past and run from them. Yet here, out of that very past and those very mistakes, were David and Dinan.

AT THE END OF AUGUST, Idina left for Oggie's annual house party in Venice. She stayed for a couple of weeks and then wound her way back through Europe, reaching England again at the beginning of October. David had gone back to Greece to pursue his research fellowship, leaving Idina to spend the next few weeks visiting Dinan and both buying and equipping a car according to a list of detailed instructions that she had extracted from Rosita. And at the end of November, as the temperature in the Northern Hemisphere dropped, Idina persuaded a recently widowed girlfriend, Charlie Dawson, to accompany her, and they drove to Kenya—all the way home.

The two women reached Lisbon alone. There Idina picked up a young man called Emmanuele. After a couple of nights together she asked him whether he felt like driving through the Sahara. He asked if his identical twin might come too. There was, Idina assured him, plenty of room.

The party of four now crossed to North Africa. By the time they reached Alexandria, Emmanuele's twin had given up all hope of making the same progress with Charlie Dawson that Emmanuele had with Idina, and left. The three of them headed south, camping, as Idina had done with Euan twenty-four years earlier, beneath the emptiness of the vast night skies. And, for Idina, now, the past must have been a relatively sweet place to look back to.

When they reached Kenya, Emmanuele followed her up to Clouds.

A FEW MONTHS LATER, in the autumn of 1938, David became engaged to a fair-haired, bright-blue-eyed former actress three years older than he. She was the daughter of tin miners turned tea planters, who divided their time between Calcutta and Essex, not far from Frinton. David had, however, met her in the café at the British School at Athens. Her name was Prudence Magor, known as Pru. Expected to follow her older sisters and become a debutante, Pru had run away from home at the age of seventeen to audition for a student place at the Old Vic in London—the theater where John Gielgud and Laurence Olivier were playing their first lead roles. She won a place and called her parents from a telephone box with the news. They were horrified. But Pru was a tough negotiator. Eventually, over the course of the conversation, they agreed to support her if, for the first twelve months, she lodged at the house of a woman they knew in Bayswater— and was home by midnight.

By the time she met David, Pru had toured the world with various theater companies. The countries to which the stage hadn't taken her, she had taken herself off to—further shocking her parents by working as a salesgirl in dress shops to earn the money for her tickets. She was now living in Athens, studying to be an archaeologist.

Idina's son David at his wedding to Pru Magor,
London, January 1939

Two months after David's wedding in January 1939, Idina married for a fifth time. She then wrote to her son with some advice: "Another book I would like you to read on quite a different subject is 'Ideal Marriage' . . . as a rule I can't stand these books but this is full of sense and I think it should be read by everyone. Some of it is drawn out but that you skip—it is especially good for a man."[15]

Idina's new husband, Vincent Soltau, was an Air Force pilot known as Lynx "because he flew a Lynx airplane."[16] Idina wrote to David: "I am divinely happy—for some unknown reason Lynx worships me and we completely love and understand each other. It is what I have been searching for since Euan and I parted. Apart from love I have a feeling of absolute peace and security— that one is no longer alone in any way. The only snag is that his job takes him away a lot but there it [is] one can't have everything."[17] Lynx was away a lot, and his first wife had run off, leaving him with a daughter, Ann, aged four, and a two year-old son, Tom. He married Idina knowing she would look after them.[18]

*Idina at her fifth wedding, to Vincent Soltau
("Lynx"), Mombasa, March 1939*

For Idina this was a chance to do right what she had earlier failed to—be a good mother to two tiny children, almost exactly the ages that David and Gee had been when she left.

They married near Lynx's RAF base in Mombasa. After the ceremony they held a small lunch at the Mombasa Club and posed for their photograph on its wide, white wooden steps outside: for this moment, Idina's life appeared complete again. She had children, a husband, and a beautiful farm in the wilds of Africa—both domesticity and adventure. Lynx's children moved into the room that led off of Idina's bathroom, which they shared with her. "I can still smell that lovely horsey smell, as I sat in the bath hugging my knees every night, whilst the water from the lion's mouth poured out into the middle," remembers Ann.

Then, toward the end of 1939, six months after her marriage, as it had long been threatening to do, war came again. Nontroop travel ground to a halt. Mail sank to the ocean floor. Kenya and Europe were once again thousands of miles apart.

Chapter 24

When the war started, Idina stayed up at Clouds with Ann and Tom. The children's days followed a delightful rhythm. "I have always been grateful that my father chose her," wrote Ann, "for she was a wonderful mother to us. . . . Though I know I often gave her good cause, she never raised her sultry voice to me. She was always polite, and fair in every way—(also to all the natives)." She "taught us kindness and compassion, and nursed us through various illnesses," driving the children through the night to the hospital in Nairobi when emergencies arose.

Idina found Ann and Tom a governess, Miss O'Dell, whom they called Dellie, with whom they had breakfast and lessons each morning. Unlike Idina, she was "not a warm person." She had perhaps been chosen for the total lack of sexual threat that she posed, "being short, fat, and lame, poor soul." Every day Ann and Tom had lunch with Idina in the dining room. Idina would then take them for walks in the forest, looking for colobus monkeys, dik-dik, chameleons, and any other wildlife, and "collecting maidenhair ferns to put with her roses." She taught her stepchildren how to fish for the rainbow trout stocked behind the dams she had built to provide electricity for the farm, and play croquet and clock golf.

Sometimes the three of them would stretch out a tartan rug under a tree and play records on the windup gramophone. Idina's favorites were the mournful "Stormy Weather" and the eternally optimistic "There's a Small Hotel." These were two songs whose lyrics seemed to sum up both the men who let her down and the search for new love. "Stormy Weather" describes the emptiness that follows the end of a relationship and the fear so embedded in Idina—that of a lonely old age: "When he went away the blues walked in and met me, If he stays away old rocking chair will get me . . . keeps raining all the time."

In "There's a Small Hotel" a woman longs to be curled up in bed with her lover: "Not a sign of people—who wants people?— . . . We'll creep into our little shell. And we will thank the small hotel together."

When it rained, they stayed indoors. Idina played cards with Ann and Tom, or mah-jongg. Idina "was always very enthusiastic about our various projects," wrote Ann, "and very, very patient, and full of fun." The children ate their supper with her in the library, while she had her "drinkies" before guests arrived for dinner. During the war, the three of them would sit there listening to the six-o'clock news every evening. If nobody was coming, Idina had her dinner brought to her on a tray and ate with Ann and Tom. Each night, before Ann went to bed, Idina brushed her hair one hundred times, taking it in turns to count each stroke. She "always said, 'You start,'" wrote Ann. And when Ann and Tom went to bed, it was under covers of hyrax skins. From time to time, Idina tucked her stepchildren up in her own huge bed together with an array of pet dogs (Mickey, an Alsatian called RAF, and a dachshund called Dushka). They would all fall asleep to the night sounds wafting in through the door, propped open for the dogs.

Clouds was a children's paradise. Each June, elephants came down to the salt licks that Idina put out, and cavorted in the dams that she had built on the edge of the garden. Throughout the year Ann and Tom drove toy cars across the lawns, rode donkeys and even cows around the fields, and their own ponies across the hills. Other pets included two mongeese, who lived in the woodpiles on each side of the large fireplace in the sitting room. They were vicious to the household cats and dogs but Ann and Tom gave them Ping-Pong balls which they rolled along under their stomachs before flicking them against the wall, thinking they were eggs that would smash. One night, Idina, Ann, and Tom gave the mongeese some beer in a saucer, which they loved—too much—and "were soon rolling around in front of the fire. It was the only time we were able to touch them."

Life up on the Kipipiri was punctuated by trips down to Gilgil. "It wasn't exactly your round-the-corner trip to the grocery shop," says Ann, as the roads were ox-wagon tracks and the gorge through which they ran was often impassable in the rainy season, forcing drivers to turn back. When they did reach the town, they had to stay overnight. Back at Clouds, Idina had by now built up one of the strongest Jersey herds in Africa. She kept them breeding, calving, and being milked, sending great churns rattling down the hill to feed the troops and their support staff. During the week she ran the farm; at the weekend she entertained, trying to keep everyone jolly while the world tore itself apart.

In the middle of 1940 Lynx was moved from Mombasa to Cairo. From there back to Clouds took at least two days' flying: Cairo to Khartoum, Khartoum to Kisumu on Lake Victoria. Each flight involved waiting around for a seat that wasn't prioritized to somebody else, then for the plane itself to be working, and then for the fuel. Then, even when Lynx reached Kisumu, it was another long day's drive down to Gilgil and up the hill. And for Idina to find the spare seats to take her up to Cairo was near impossible. Lonely at weekends, Idina started to travel up to Muthaiga. The club was no longer waiting for Race Week for its parties. Every weekend there was a band and a dance, the floor packed with young officers, most of them Air Force, who had driven from Kisumu and Mombasa desperate to have a good time on what might be their last night out. But Lynx wasn't there.

Idina spent the evenings on the dance floor, careering from one pair of young arms to another, gathering up invitees for a weekend at Clouds and, at the end of the evening, tripping up the wide stone staircase, her fingers, with their dark-red nails, entwined with a younger hand.

Joss was at those parties too. He was still good friends with Idina, and Ann and Tom were taught to call him Uncle Joss—"even though he was not," says Ann, "interested in children." A couple of years earlier, in 1938, he had embarked on an affair with a woman called Phyllis Filmer. Phyllis was, like Idina, petite and large-breasted with short blond hair. She was the wife of the local managing director for Shell and lived in the company house, which was just around the corner from Muthaiga and therefore close to the bungalow opposite the club in which Joss lived. He and Molly had moved from Oserian at the start of the year for two reasons: Joss's career in the Kenyan Legislative Council, and the need for the ailing Molly to live nearer to medical care.

Drugs and alcohol killed Molly in the first few days of the war. Joss had not, however, proposed to Phyllis. He had joined the Kenya Regiment as a second lieutenant and had been rising through the military ranks. In June 1940 he had been made Staff Captain to the East Africa Force, soon becoming the Force's Assistant Military Secretary. And although he continued his affair with Phyllis, it was not an exclusive arrangement. He swanned around Muthaiga's dance floor, a widower who could make some lucky woman his third Countess of Erroll.

Phyllis, besotted with Joss, accepted her new role as the woman he was unfaithful to until a month or so before Christmas 1940, when she was suddenly replaced by a recent arrival to Kenya, Diana Delves Broughton.

The young Diana had been married to her fifty-seven-year-old husband, the wealthy Sir Jock Delves Broughton, for all of a week when they reached Kenya in November 1940. Jock came from a grand farming family in Cheshire and had acquired land in Kenya under the 1919 soldier-settler scheme. Ostensibly he had now come out to farm and produce food for the troops. Delves Broughton was Diana's second husband. Her first marriage, to a man called Vernon Motion, had been made under the mutual misconception that the other was wealthy. The union had barely lasted a fortnight and Diana had resumed work by day as a model in a London fashion house and by night at a cocktail bar just off Berkeley Square called the Blue Goose, a happy hunting ground for rich men. Diana was a woman who knew how to make the most of herself. She dyed her mousy hair a bright blond, applied her lipstick with expertise, and learnt how to walk across a room. She had started off as Delves Broughton's mistress, and he had installed her in a cottage in the grounds of the family's stately home, right under his former wife's nose.

While they looked for a house to rent, the Delves Broughtons had moved into Muthaiga. They hosted a large dinner to introduce themselves and began settling into Kenyan life. Almost immediately Joss started an affair with Diana. At first they were reasonably careful. Joss used the cover of being an old friend of Delves Broughton's. Then Diana started finding excuses to slip away from her husband for a couple of days. By early January 1941 both Joss and Diana no longer appeared to care. They clung to each other for hours at a time on Nairobi's plentiful dance floors—any venue with the space had drafted in a band to satisfy the wartime frenzy for a good time. Jock Delves Broughton, however, was not having a good time. While his new young wife danced with one of his friends, he sat to the side, drink in hand and a sad smile on his face. By the middle of January he had almost ceased to bother to go out with Diana, remaining at home.

On the morning of 24 January 1941, Joss was found slumped in the foot well of his car near a crossroads a few miles outside Nairobi. His arms and legs were tucked beneath him and there was a patch of congealed blood behind his ear, and more flecks of blood were spattered across the windscreen. He had been there some time and his corpse was beginning to stiffen.

He had been killed by a bullet that "passed inwards through the soft tissues of the neck, and passed between the first vertebra and the base of the skull, through the medulla of the brain from left to right and out of the spinal canal. . . . The bullet [was] in two parts in the ligament attaching the vertebra to the base of the skull, lying in a mass of blood clot underneath the skin."[1] Death would have been "instantaneous."[2]

Joss's body in his Buick

Joss had been murdered.

Idina was at Clouds when she heard the news. She leapt into her car and pounded up the road to Nairobi and into Joss's bungalow by Muthaiga. The week before, Diana had been wearing the exquisite Erroll family pearls. These were the only heirloom that Dinan might ever receive from her father and Idina did not trust Diana not to steal them. She walked in and searched for the necklace. It was not to be found.[3]

Idina returned to Clouds in what must have been a state of both grief and anger. She and Joss had remained friends, seeing enough of each other to keep her affection alive. And she had still been enormously fond of him.[4] Day after day, as she, Ann, and

Tom listened to the war news at six o'clock, they heard the latest details of the murder investigation. It was "the only topic of conversation" among visitors to Clouds. The six-year-old Ann asked Idina what had happened. Idina told her that Joss had been driving back from Karen, a suburb of Nairobi, when he picked up a lady in uniform. The lady claimed to suffer from car sickness in the front and asked if she could therefore sit in the back. From there, she shot Joss in the head. Ann asked Idina whether the woman had been caught. Idina replied that she had not been. So, replied Ann, "how do they know that she was carsick in the front?" Idina replied, "I don't want to talk about it anymore, darling, I am too upset." This was, of course, in Ann's view an account invented by Idina, but, she says, "it was such a huge issue that I have never forgotten it."

Idina was not alone in being upset by Joss's death. During seventeen years in Kenya, Joss had had affairs with many of the women there, nearly all of whom had retained a soft spot for him. Barely a female eye at Muthaiga was dry. Alice almost immediately again attempted suicide by taking an overdose of pills. And then, fifteen days later, when Idina had hardly had a chance to dry her eyes, she received a cable from Buck that sent her reeling yet further: Euan, too, had died—of stomach cancer.

Euan had been forty-eight—too young to die. And Joss had been even younger: thirty-nine. Unlike the relationship Idina had enjoyed with Joss, there had not been a trace of amiability between her and Euan since their divorce. Once Idina's decision to leave him was final, Euan had not wanted to hear her name mentioned again. Married to Barbie, he had started a new life.

Idina, however, had never managed to move on completely. Euan's photo still sat in her bedroom—a constant reminder of all that she had given up.

Now Euan was dead, taking with him any lingering wonder about what that life might have been. In theory, his death should have closed a chapter for Idina that had been open too long. But he and Joss had been the fathers of her children. All three of them, David, Dinan, and Gee—whom she had not seen for over twenty years—had now become fatherless within a fortnight.

Dinan in her early teens

Idina, trapped in Kenya by the war, was frustratingly and upsettingly unable to do anything to help them.

It took another month for the police to make an arrest for Joss's murder. The story continued to give rise to salacious headlines, about which, back in England, Avie and her husband were doing what they could by carefully cutting them from the newspapers before they reached Dinan at the breakfast table. But Dinan saw the news in the complete versions sitting at the counter in the village shop. And, when an arrest was made, the suspect was not some highway robber, but Diana Delves Broughton's husband, Sir Jock.

There was something particularly tragic about the idea that this sad old man might have been driven to such misery that he had murdered someone as young and vibrant as Joss. And this was the beginning of a serious decline for Idina. She was shaken enough to try to cross a war-torn Africa in search of a few days' consolation from her husband. She drove to Kisumu airfield to see if she could cadge a lift north to Cairo, and Lynx.

CAIRO WAS TO THE SECOND WORLD WAR what Paris had been to the First. It was a city held by the Allies but surrounded by battlefields. Six months earlier there had been a few thousand troops in the city. Now there were thirty-five thousand—in every Allied denomination and all in search of diversion. The shops were full, Groppi's café was still roasting its own coffee, and the white-gloved waiters at Shepheard's Hotel were filling glasses with wine and champagne. In the spring of 1941, however, when Idina arrived, the city was welcoming a new flood of immigrants from the Balkans and Greece. Accommodations, cafés, restaurants, were all straining at the seams, and the heat was steadily rising. The hot khamsin desert wind and dust were suffocating the streets. Lynx was immersed in Air Force activity. After a few lonely days in the bar at Shepheard's Idina decided to return to Kenya for Jock Delves Broughton's trial. She had in any case promised to accompany the still suicidal Alice to the court-room to watch. On her last day in the city Idina went to join the long queue in the bank to withdraw cash. As, after the best part of an hour, she reached the front, she heard the woman ahead of her give her name to the cashier: Mrs. David Wallace.[5]

Idina approached the woman. She turned to face Idina. It was David's wife, Pru, and, to what must have been Idina's great joy, she was heavily pregnant. Pru had just been evacuated from Athens, where she and David had been working in the Embassy. With barely two weeks until the birth, she had sat in a small boat rocking its way out of Piraeus harbor, clutching a white Moses basket filled with things for her unborn child. So many bombs had fallen so close to the boat that she was frankly sur-prised to have made it to Cairo alive. But she didn't yet know where David was, or whether he would reach her before the baby came. It was a big baby, she had been told. And it could arrive any day. She would tell David, when she saw him, that she had seen Idina. Then Idina watched her daughter-in-law turn firmly back to the cashier. Pru didn't suggest that they stop for a coffee or meal, or even exchange addresses in order to meet another time. She was, Idina could see, just managing to cope with sur-vival and impending childbirth in this strange, hot, dusty city. It was quite clear that she didn't need or want to deal with anyone else too.[6]

Pru certainly didn't. As she later said, she already had one tricky mother-in-law, Barbie, back in England. The last thing she wanted then was another to deal with. Especially one who had not only abandoned her husband as a child but who, as far as she could see, would now do neither him nor the child she was carrying any good whatsoever,[7] as both the murder of one of her husbands and her own dissolute lifestyle were being plastered over the world's press.

It was Idina's turn at the cashier. She walked forward, withdrew her money, and headed off to the airfield to see if she could find a flight home. Her first encounter with her daughter-in-law had not been promising. Pru's coldness can hardly have filled her with hope of seeing much of what would be, once born, her first grandchild.

Idina returned to Kenya to find not just Alice but also Phyllis Filmer in a state over Joss's death. Phyllis's husband's unsurprising inability to sympathize with her on this had finally cracked their marriage and she needed somewhere to live. Idina invited her to stay at Clouds until she had somewhere else to go.

The trial began on 26 May. Idina, Alice, and Phyllis turned up each day, dressed to the nines. They sat in the gallery and hung on every word of evidence given, their eyes burning holes in the back of Diana's neck as their lives were pored over, scribbled down by court reporters, and wired back to the London and New York press. Regardless of who had actually pulled the trigger, as far as Idina was concerned, it was Diana who had killed her darling Joss.

Six weeks later Jock was acquitted, and Joss's murder declared unsolved.[8] Alice, however, continued to decline. She started secretly labeling her possessions. To each item of furniture, each object, and each and every book, she attached a piece of paper with a name of one of the fifty people she had decided were her friends.[9] By late September she had finished. On the morning of the twenty-third she walked her dog, Minnie (Idina had the other in the pair, Mickey Mouse), across the lawn to the Wanjohi River. She pulled out a revolver and shot Minnie, burying her there. She then went back to her bedroom, where she had asked her servant to make up the bed with a set of extraordinarily ornate lace and linen sheets from her first marriage—each embroidered with the de Janzé crest. She picked up her bottle of sleeping pills and, one by one, swallowed the lot. Then she lay down and closed her eyes for the last time. The heyday of Idina's Happy Valley was now over. For Alice was, as Idina had written to David, her "greatest friend in the world."[10]

The war, however, was not over. Idina settled into being her

David at home in England, just before he left for Cairo, 1941

own land army, running the farm and, when she didn't have friends up to stay, still careering down to Gilgil and Nairobi for weekend dances. From time to time Lynx came home on leave, but the gaps in between his appearances lengthened. Idina filled the emotional vacuum that followed this cascade of painful and violent deaths of people she loved with a series of affairs; she was vulnerable enough to need to. And she became increasingly indiscriminate in her choice of lovers, as if flailing around for reassurance. Precious Langmead started walking over again in the afternoons. And, after that had ended again, came Arnold Sharp, an airman stationed at Gilgil. Arnold Sharp was, in Ann's view, "poisonous," and it was a "war sex" relationship only. The "terribly sweet and kind" Idina was "plagued by a terrible urge to get laid and have someone in bed with her." She needed, says Ann, almost desperately to be loved, both by her two stepchildren and by the men who came through her life.

IN THE SPRING OF 1943 Lynx came home with the news that he had been joined in Cairo by David. After the loss of so many young men in the First World War, the British government had been exercising a secret policy of keeping the most academically able away from the front line. David had therefore been, much to his frustration,[11] kept in barracks in Yorkshire while everyone else he knew seemed to be given the chance to fight for their country. He had spent endless evenings in the officers' mess with men too old to fight again—and who spent the time reminiscing about dancing with Idina before the last war had even begun.[12]

Eventually David had been selected to be the Foreign Office's representative in Greece and had come to Cairo on his way there. He had been asked to contact the Greek guerrilla leaders and report on SOE's (Special Operations Executive) activities there for the Foreign Office.

David had left two daughters, Idina's granddaughters, Laura and Davina, behind in England. Laura had been born in Cairo in May 1941.

Davina had been born in June 1942, in the head gardener's cottage at Lavington Park, a country estate that Barbie and Euan had bought shortly before the war. Barbie had never liked Kildonan,[13] and when Lavington, less than two hours' drive south of London, came on the market at a surprisingly reasonable price, she had snapped it up without stopping to wonder why. While David was over in Cairo, Pru and the girls were living in the cottage on the grounds, grating along beside Barbie.

Gee, too, whom Idina had still not seen since he was a boy, had married. Like David, he had fallen in love with an older woman.

This one, however, was old enough to be—and had been—the wife of one of Euan and Barbie's friends, creating a small scandal.[14] But Gee and Elizabeth had married and were spending as much time as they could together until he was posted abroad.[15]

Shortly after Lynx returned to Cairo, Gee received his orders to leave Britain for the war. And, having lost three lives close to her, Idina was now brought a new one. Gee was sent to Mombasa. With his father no longer around to be upset, and Barbie several thousand miles away, he wrote to Idina.

THEY MET AT MUTHAIGA, at one of those heaving, balloon-filled dances with couples' chests pinned to each other, legs flying out in all directions. To a newcomer the place appeared a maze of dance halls and dining rooms, sitting rooms and bars—somewhere in which was a mother Gee hadn't seen for twenty-five years. He asked a senior officer if he knew Lady Idina.

"Well," the officer replied, "everyone knows of her. She has a dreadful reputation and it wouldn't be wise for you to be seen about with her."[16]

Gee saluted, turned, and walked away.

He found her himself.

THERE WAS TOO MUCH TO SAY to know where to begin. In the years since Idina had last seen him, Gee had grown from a toddler to a great bear of a man of twenty-eight. Idina was tiny next to him. For, like David, he was tall but, unlike him, far from slender, almost round with joviality. Idina took Gee's large hand in hers and led him onto the dance floor, put her head against his chest, and let her son's thick arms wrap around her back. They "were seen dancing most amorously."[17]

Gee was good at hugs. He was a warmer, cozier character than David, able to smooth any social situation. In the latter regard, particularly, he was very like his father, Euan, extraordinarily so. As David's wife, Pru, later said of him, "You never met a lovelier man in your life. He was so funny, charming, always good-humored."[18]

Idina had never had Euan in Kenya, the country she had come

to adore. In his place had come their son: a living, breathing part of Euan who, unlike his father, had a great deal of love to show her. They swayed together for hours.[19] The war, which was wrenching so many apart, had brought the two of them together. As when she had met David at Claridge's nine years earlier, this was for Idina the beginning of a new, loving relationship. Gee was a steadying character, and now he was here to steady her.

For Gee, Idina offered something similar. The war had taken the father he loved, spread his family across the globe, and separated him from his wife. But here at last he had his mother, his real biological mother, who had borne him and cradled him in her arms. He held her tight.[20]

The next day, Gee was hauled up in front of the senior officer.

"Look here," he told Gee, "I have warned you about Lady Idina. . . . She's old enough to be your mother."

"She is my mother," was the reply.[21]

Chapter 25

And thus Idina and her second son came to know each other. For days at a stretch Gee would be down at his base at Mombasa, piloting a Catalina flying boat on sea patrols. At weekends they could meet in Nairobi or, with enough days of leave ahead of him, Gee made the long drive up to Clouds. Whenever he visited, Idina was beside herself with excitement. She was "literally ecstatic both at the mere prospect of one of his visits, and throughout his stay," says Ann. "I, too, adored him, for he played with us and gave us piggyback rides around the garden." By day, Idina showed off her mountain paradise to her "darling son."[1] In the evening, they curled up on sofas in front of a roaring fire, talking through the night.

David had offered her a headstrong and intense filial love. Theirs had been a relationship in which Idina adored and David burnt—both himself and her. Gee, on the other hand, was a rock who could give Idina the feeling that he would always be there for her. In her own son Idina had found the constant love that she had been searching for.

But, on 25 August 1943, four short months after Gee had arrived and just long enough for the sharp newness of their relationship to begin to soften into permanence, a thin line of dust appeared along the hillside road leading to Clouds. As the min-

David Wallace's wife, Pru, and Idina's two granddaughters, Davina and Laura, 1943

utes passed, the dust filled out into a cloud that eventually came to an abrupt halt at the gates. The usual small swarm of fezzes appeared. The gate was opened. The dust-covered car rattled in among the flower beds. Out climbed Dorothy Blin Stoyle. Dorothy had come to Kenya eight years earlier when her husband, Herbert, had been sent out to be Chief Mechanical Engineer on what was now called the Kenya and Uganda Railway. She had become friends with Idina. She had invited her and her current flame, whoever it was, to her parties—pointedly ignoring the raised eyebrows among the rest of her guests.[2]

Dorothy's daughter Molly was working as a nurse in Mombasa. One of Molly's friends had become Gee's "girlfriend"[3] and had invited Molly, since she knew Idina, to come and meet him for dinner. Two days earlier the two girls had gone to the air base to pick him up for the evening. When they arrived they were told that he had taken a crew out on an exercise in a Catalina that afternoon and had not yet returned. Molly and her friend decided to wait. They waited. Dinnertime passed and they continued to wait. Eventually, at around eleven o'clock in the evening, they were told that Gee had now been posted as missing.

Dorothy had come to tell Idina for, as she later said, "I couldn't think who else would."[4]

Idina drove down to Mombasa. Two days later, when she arrived, Gee had still not returned. Her "darling son," so full of life and with so much to live for, was dead.

Idina somehow found the strength to buy a plot of land in the cemetery close to the ocean. Between the great, round, purple trunks of the baobabs, she raised a stone: "To my beloved son, Wing Cmdr G E Wallace, who flew from here to the unknown, and to his crew."

She then drove back through Nairobi to Clouds. She stayed up there in the hills with Ann and Tom. She didn't come down to Nairobi for dances, not even to the club at Gilgil. She stopped eating and exercising. Surrounded by flowers continuing their relentless Kenyan bloom, Idina wilted.

As though she were cursed, the touch of her affection appeared fatal. She was "genuinely devastated," says Ann, and turned her emotions to objects that she could not kill: she lit endless ciga-rettes and watched the bottoms of bottles clear. "I should never," she said to anyone who visited, "have left Euan in the first place."[5] At the end of December that year David wrote to his wife, Pru, "Saw Lynx, in Cairo, who tells me Dina is wasting away."[6]

Throughout her turbulent life Idina had, so far, managed to bounce back. The deaths of Joss, Euan, and Alice had weakened her but she had nonetheless managed to absorb herself in a new wartime farming life. The death of her son was, however, too much for even the resilient Idina to bear. As she would shortly write: "I am not very brave any more."[7]

Idina was not the only one wasting after Gee's death. Two months beforehand, in June, David had been parachuted behind the German lines in Greece. The Foreign Office thought that what SOE was doing risked a rise of Communist power in the country. David had met up with both the Greek guerrilla leaders and Brigadier Myers, the head of the British SOE in Greece. There he had at last learnt that behavior did not come in black and white. The Greek guerrillas could be an unruly bunch, yet the other British officers were deliberately turning a blind eye in order to keep them on their side. He was obviously shocked, wrote Myers.[8] On 9 August, David, Myers, and half a dozen rep-resentatives from almost as many guerrilla factions had been picked up from a makeshift airfield and flown to Cairo. After six

*Idina's son Gerard Wallace, "Gee," at his
wedding to Elizabeth, née Lawson, who had
been married to one of Euan and Barbie's
friends, Gerard Koch de Gooreynd*

weeks with SOE, David had been convinced that Myers was not
enabling a Communist takeover of Greece. When he reached
Cairo he told the ambassador this.[9] The ambassador was furious
and spent several days trying to persuade David to change his
mind. In the middle of this, David heard that Gee had been
killed.

David gave up battling his boss. Anthony Eden ordered him
to come back to England immediately three days ahead of Myers,
in order to report on what he had seen. David saw both Eden and

Churchill. But, deeply upset by his brother's death, he ended up in an argument with Churchill "about the Greek monarchy."[10]

When he returned to Cairo he was still reeling. Perhaps due to the absence of a mother's love, he and Gee had been as close as many twins, and now this other half of him was missing. And he had gone while doing a proper, fighting job in the war. David's new job in Cairo was a desk job in the Embassy. He felt he wasn't doing anything useful, anything that counted.[11] Like Idina, he began to waste. But, instead of being "not very brave any more" he started an affair with one of the secretaries in the Embassy. And then he asked the ambassador to send him back into Greece.

Eventually the ambassador agreed. David was elated. And his misery over Gee's death swung into ebullience. Lynx saw him just before he left, reporting to Idina that he was in high spirits. But it was a reckless, dangerous high.

This time David went in by sea, from Italy. He spent the first two weeks of August observing guerrilla operations. On 14 and 15 August he sat down and wrote his report. On the 16th the group of guerrillas he was with planned an attack for the next day on a German garrison at the town of Menina. It was David's first chance to pick up a gun and fight in this war. He loved the Greeks he was with, as they both loved and appreciated him. And David, said his wife, was fearless. Just like Idina.

On 17 August the Greeks broke into Menina, where, just inside the town, they met a heavy line of German resistance fighting "from fortified houses."[12] Rifle in hand, David walked toward the center of the town. A rifle fired from one of the houses. The bullet went straight through his neck.[13]

The message was brought up to Clouds from the telegraph station at Gilgil. Telegrams in wartime rarely bring other than devastating news. It was almost exactly a year to the day since Gee had died. When she read the message inside, Idina collapsed.[14]

For several days, high up on her mountainside, Idina felt as though she, too, must surely die from grief.[15] It took a week for her to find the emotional and physical strength to scribble a short note to the woman she had met in a bank in Cairo two and a half years earlier.

She sat at her desk at the far end of her cedar-paneled bedroom, under a window looking out across her manicured lawns and hedges, framed by the dust of the Rift Valley beyond. She took a piece of transparent airmail paper, almost as fragile as she now was, and finally picked up a pencil. This time, her violin-stroke script was so light that it was barely visible:

Clouds

Sept 13th

Dearest Pru,

There is so little I can say for what are words when one has lost all one loves—thank God you have the children— I have been completely shattered since I got Buck's cable last week—I couldn't write to you before—I am afraid I am not very brave any more & this on top of G, has nearly killed me. But I do want you to know how my whole heart goes out to you—you are young and you must have planned so much together for the future & I know how he adored you & how little happiness you had together—always a turbulent unsettled life—so little peace & home happiness.

I can write no more for I am crying with you—anything you can write me about him do please—your children look so lovely. Bless you and your children are in heart broken heart {sic}.

Idina

Pru wrote back to Idina. She sent her a photograph of herself and Idina's tiny granddaughters, now two and three. She passed on what details she had of David's death and that he had been buried in the Greek village of Paramythia. She told Idina that Anthony Eden himself had written an obituary for David in the *Times,* saying that "he was destined to be one of the leaders of his generation. Had he lived to take up that political career upon which he had set his heart, no position would have been beyond his reach."[16] She enclosed a copy of the full text, and of the other tributes in the press. The Greeks had declared him the "modern Byron,"[17] saying that "a new name has been added to the pages of

Greek history" and he "died like a hero at Menina, falling in action like a true Greek."[18] On his tombstone the guerrillas had carved: "The soil of Greece is proud to offer hospitality to this hero."

To Pru, however, his death felt less than heroic.[19] David had recklessly walked straight into the line of fire. It felt even less heroic when the British Embassy at which he had been working returned all his papers, including a love letter and photograph from his mistress with "From a sleek domestic pussy" written on the back.

And then Barbie asked Pru to move out of the gardener's cottage. She needed it, she said, to lend to Pamela Churchill, Winston's daughter-in-law, who wanted somewhere for her baby son, also named Winston, to live far from the bombs falling on London.

IN KENYA, IDINA ABSORBED HERSELF in her lost sons. She ordered a copy of a new novel, *The Sea Eagle*,[20] about a man fighting with the Greek guerrillas, and curled up and read every word of what David's last days might have been like. And she began to fall apart again. The brief rally which had enabled her to write to Pru subsided and a latent frailty took hold. The then ten-year-old Ann remembers that Idina stopped eating and "she became what would now be called anorexic." One evening, Ann was alone with her, chatting before dinner, when Idina, who had been standing with her back to the fire, suddenly collapsed. Ann tried to lift her onto the sofa but wasn't strong enough and so rushed off into the bathroom where Arnold Sharp was immersed, shouting that "Dina has died!" As the two of them lifted Idina onto the sofa, she came around. It was now that she first began to talk to Ann and Tom about her past with David and Gee. "But she never divulged that she left them when they were four and three," Ann says. She simply said that "it was so tragic that she had had to be separated from them." Ann still finds it hard to believe that Idina had gone willingly, for she was "so loving and kind and compassionate"— in contrast to Ann's own mother, whom she found, when reunited with her at the age of eighteen, "a cold fish."

In February 1945, Idina began to suffer knife-sharp electric shocks running down her arms, her legs, up her neck. Her nervous system had collapsed. The doctor blamed her inability to recover on the fact that, since Gee's death, she had not descended from the high altitude of Clouds and her body was no longer able to cope with prolonged periods at eight thousand feet. If she wished to live she would have to leave her home and go down to sea level.

Idina started to pack. Her reclusive mountainside life had come to an end. She could visit Clouds, but it could no longer be her main home. She would, however, continue to come back for Ann and Tom's holidays—they were now both in boarding school. Ann was at Roedean, in South Africa. For the moment, Tom was closer—at Pembroke House in Gilgil, just down the road from Clouds. Her marriage to Lynx was, however, over. As she later wrote to Pru: "I was not in the best of form as I had my divorce against Lynx which I hated—he wants to marry someone from South Africa and it is no good hanging on. We were so happy but it is the war."[21] Nonetheless, Ann and Tom stayed on with Idina. She was, says Ann, "the only mother I ever knew until I was quite grown up." And even Ann's signature is a daughter's mimic of Idina's style.

Shortly before she moved down to the coast, Idina received another letter from Pru. It contained more photographs of Pru with David's two daughters, some newspaper clippings from his death (including Eden's obituary), and a copy of his memorial service sheet. And Pru's new address.

Idina wrote back immediately:

Clouds

February 27th
[1945]

Pru dear—

Your very wonderful letter and enclosures came yesterday—thank you so so much—I still think you are grandly brave & everything that David would want you to be but I know how unutterably lonely you must be in your heart.

I, too, would love to know you talk to you & hear so much from you. I wonder so what David would have felt about the situation in Greece—it is so hard to understand it from here—one just feels the ghastly futile & tragic waste of it all. Have you read "Sea Eagle" I thought it marvellous—one feels so terribly for those unflinching guerrillas.

I often look at the photograph of you and the children & I long to see them. I am so glad Laura liked Dinan—it is now over 6 yrs since I last saw her—it's hard to imagine her grown up. Do you see much of Elizabeth? What a terrible time she has had.

I do think Anthony's appreciation of David is lovely to have & I am so glad you have some of his diary—it must have been enthralling. You are right, he did go off gaily—Lynx saw him just before. Why is it in war the best are always taken—it seems to be inevitable, some cruel fate marks them down—as Anthony said a future leader that apart from all his sweetness that we knew. What an utter blank life must seem to you. Thank God you have the children.

Am going to the Coast to recover from a slight nervous break down followed by neuritis & the Dr says I must get down to sea level—8000 feet for 2 yrs is too long.

Bless you Pru—I often think of you & wish I could help but no one can only Time can soften the pain. My love to you & my grandchildren—

Idina

Idina moved down to the coast, into a bungalow near Mombasa, where she started to plant a tropical garden. But she never fully recovered. Nor did she ever meet either David's daughters or Gee's wife. When the war ended, with neither Gee nor any children to live for, Elizabeth committed suicide. Pru, alone and having fallen out with Barbie, took David's two little girls back to live in Greece. Eventually she would return to England and marry a Welsh squire, moving straight to his tumbledown castle and rambling estate in the hills near the Black Mountain town of Hay-on-Wye, far from Idina's orbit.

DINAN HAD SPENT her wartime teenage years continuing to live with Avie, have her lessons with Zellée, ride her ponies around, and spend her holidays with her cousins, Buck's children. Idina had sent her regular letters packed with photographs of Clouds, each with an inscription on the back, but by the end of the war Idina hadn't seen her daughter for so long that it was, as she had written, "hard to imagine her grown up."[22] Yet, grown up she had, and in 1946, before Idina could visit Britain, the now twenty-year-old Dinan became engaged to be married.

Her fiancé was a twenty-seven-year-old named Iain Moncreiffe, who was, like Dinan's father, Joss, a Scot. Iain had been a captain in the Scots Guards during the war. Since being decommissioned, also like Joss, he had spent six months as the private secretary to a British Ambassador. Iain had gone to Moscow. After half a year in the Soviet Union he had decided not to pursue a career in the diplomatic corps. When he had returned to Britain he had met Dinan.

Avie was organizing the wedding. Among the guests invited were the queen—a great girlfriend of Avie's—and the two young princesses, Elizabeth and Margaret.[23] There was no question of Idina's also being able to attend, as it was thought that neither the queen nor either of the princesses could be introduced to a woman now five times divorced.

But the presence of the Royal Family may have been more of an excuse than a reason not to invite Idina. Dinan had by now not seen her mother for eight years. She had last said good-bye to Idina as a twelve-year-old girl. Now she was a twenty-year-old—and the Countess of Erroll in her own right—and about to be a married woman. Idina had been absent for the entirety of her daughter's growing up. Dinan's mother figure had instead been Avie. Moreover, Dinan's teenage years had been spent under the shadow of Joss's murder and both of her parents' misbehavior, to the extent that there were still widely held doubts as to who her real father was. It was hardly surprising that she wanted little more to do with Idina.

Sadly, Idina understood the situation. A lunchtime guest at Clouds remembers Idina showing her around. Idina stopped by a large photograph of a young woman.

"That's my darling daughter," said Idina, "but she doesn't speak to me, she doesn't approve of me."[24]

The war had taken both Idina's sons. It had separated her from her daughter, too.

The following year, Lynx wrote to Idina to tell her that he and his new wife, Grace Sleddon, had established a proper home together. This was in southern Tanzania, hundreds of miles from Clouds across the African bush. From now on, it would be there that Ann and Tom would go during their school holidays. They never returned to Clouds, leaving their childhood possessions behind with Idina.

IDINA DID NOT GIVE UP on Dinan. However, now that Dinan had married, Idina no longer received the income from her daughter's share of Muriel's trust. Nor, as she was no longer able to run the farm at Clouds herself, was she earning much money. A trip to England had become a barely affordable undertaking. It took Idina two trips to meet her daughter again. The first time, she arrived at her brother's house, Fisher's Gate, with a new escort, a tattooed former sailor called James, or Jimmy, Bird, who managed her farm in Kenya. Idina introduced Jimmy and explained to her bemused brother that he would be very happy staying while Idina went to see her friends in houses to which it might be a little difficult to take him along. She then sashayed into the drawing room where she kicked off her shoes, curled up in a chair and asked for "a little ginnies."[25] And another. Despite the attentions of a succession of young men as well as Jimmy, Idina had not had a good time since the war. By now that "slight nervous breakdown" was joined by cancer of the womb. It took more than just one little ginnies to numb the pain.

But Dinan would not see her. And, several weeks later, having

Idina by one of her landscaped ponds in front of Clouds

visited a number of her friends (leaving Jimmy behind with her
brother each time), Idina returned to Kenya, rejected. She had
left her sons when they were small, but she had not left her
daughter. Of her three children, it was Dinan, the one from
whom she had been separated for so long by the war rather than
by her own hand, who presented the most difficult relationship
to recover.

It was 1950 before Idina saw Dinan again. This time, Buck had a plan. He knew that Dinan's husband yearned to become a writer. He therefore tempted both Iain and Dinan down to his house in Sussex with the promise of lunch with Idina's cousin, the writer Vita Sackville-West, and her publisher husband, Harold Nicholson.

Dinan and Iain arrived with their two-year-old son, Merlin, toward the beginning of August. It was twelve years since Idina had said good-bye to a twelve-year-old Dinan before the war. Idina and her daughter now stood facing each other. Both were petite, with the same eyes and hair, but Dinan, with softer, more rounded features than her mother, was as retiring as the far more glamorous bottle-blond Idina was bold. But, at last face-to-face, Idina managed to win her daughter around. Idina followed their meeting with effusive correspondence, each letter bursting with praise: "What a success my little Dinan is, and her Mummie loves her so much, with all her heart and she mustn't go out of my life again."[26]

By the time Idina left for Kenya, plans had been made for a safari the following year, and they had even slipped into a familiar mother and daughter correspondence about whom Dinan should remember to write to: "I went to see poor Row[27] yesterday . . . a letter and a snap of Merlin she would love. . . . Buck and I are going again this morning,"[28] wrote Idina. James Dunn, who thirty-five years earlier had commissioned Orpen to paint Idina, had offered to give the portrait to Dinan: "Of course I will write to him & very plain that you should do so too . . . and send him one of your most glamorous photographs."[29]

Dinan kept the letters. And when Idina announced that she was considering marrying Jimmy next, an inevitably horrified Dinan asked her not to. Instead of taking a sixth husband, why didn't Idina simply return to her maiden name of Sackville, and keep it?[30] Idina agreed, and mother and daughter appear to have exchanged promises. Dinan was pregnant with her second child and Idina asked her, if the child were a boy, to give him Euan's name.[31]

Portrait of Idina, 1922, after she had separated from Charles Gordon

Although Idina returned to Kenya under the name of Sack-ville and with a vow not to marry again, Jimmy stayed with her, becoming known in Kenya as James VI. In reality he tolerated Idina's still-wandering sexual appetite and pursued his own with the same sex.[32] It was a non-marriage of convenience. "Drunk," said one young woman who knew Idina then, "she would fre-quently end up in bed with my father."[33]

When Dinan gave birth to a boy in February, she kept her promise to her mother. She chose Peregrine for his first name, and then gave him both of Euan's: Peregrine David Euan.[34]

In 1951, just when Idina had planned her daughter's trip, a wave of violent killing broke out in Kenya. The first victims were "loyalist" Kikuyu chieftains. A gang of Kikuyu extremists, who called themselves the Mau Mau, were going around the villages demanding that the headmen take oaths of violence and murder against the white settlers. Oathing was a traditional Kikuyu form of ceremony that took the place of legal contracts in Kikuyu society, and an oath-breaker was subject to magical retribution. However, not only were the Mau Mau's oaths violent in form but their ceremonies consisted of a combination of both obscenity and bestiality. Those chieftains who did not agree were hacked to pieces with machetes. Dinan's visit to Kenya was postponed.

The murders of white settlers began in the autumn of 1952. On 3 October a European woman was stabbed to death on a farm outside Nairobi and a state of emergency was declared in Kenya. In January 1953 a farmer's wife died as her unborn child was ripped from her womb. Two months later, on a single night, ninety-seven inhabitants of an African village were butchered or burnt to death. Between excursions the Mau Mau retreated to the Aberdares, where they proved impervious to military assault.

That autumn, as Kenya disintegrated around Idina, her cancer tightened its grip. In December she was told that she needed a hysterectomy. But the Mau Mau had brought any income from the farm at Clouds to a standstill and, even at Kenyan prices, the operation was expensive. Buck, however, came to the rescue and offered to pay. Idina was admitted to the Princess Elizabeth Hospital in Nairobi and operated on immediately.

"My darling," she wrote to Dinan on 20 December,

I am progressing marvellously—record patient—but still feel very weak & tired so forgive this short scrawl to wish you a Happy Xmas & a lucky New Year—also to send you a miserable Xmas present—things are still such a muddle owing to Mau Mau I can't do more at the moment [the Christmas present was clearly a check] but there are one or two schemes on foot [sic] which pray God will materialize. Heaven to think Buckie is coming out on the 28th. Bless you my darlings—how I long to see you again.

Your devoted Mummie xxxx.

Buck arrived, and Idina rallied. The writer Errol Trzebinski was working as a student nurse on the ward in which Idina was a patient. "Her room," she remembers, "was filled with flowers, glamorous people visited her every day at all hours; merry laughter could be heard along the corridors. She was charming to care for and, of course, I had not the least clue that I was helping to fetch and carry as a probationer for a legend. . . ."[35] When Idina left the hospital she gave a case of champagne to the nursing staff. Trzebinski drank hers from a teacup: "And swore never to submit to that again . . . nor have I!"[36]

Idina moved back to her bungalow outside Mombasa with Jimmy Bird still by her side. Despite the hysterectomy, her cancer returned. "Poor Dina," wrote Elspeth Huxley's mother, Nellie Grant, as it was "a desperate cancer for a long time."[37] A year after Idina left the hospital, however, in January 1955, the Mau Mau emergency at last was coming to an end with the colonial government's invitation to the insurgents to surrender without punishment. Twelve thousand Kenyans had been murdered; of these not even a hundred were white. Each white death, however, had created a storm of publicity and within the small settler community everyone knew someone who had been killed. It was the beginning of the end of colonial rule.

For Idina, however, the end of the Mau Mau meant a chance to make another plan for Dinan to visit. But in January 1955, Dinan was pregnant with her third child. It would be born in July. The safari was therefore set for early the following year.

At the end of October Idina wrote to Dinan, giving her a list of clothes she and Iain would need to bring for the heat of the day and the cold of the night. But after a couple of pages her writing gave way to another hand. It was Jimmy's—after five divorces it was the man whom she didn't marry who stayed with her.

Jimmy finished the let-
ter and its safari instructions. Idina lay back on
her pillows, Euan still
gazing at her from the
photograph beside her
bed. She could relax. She
was now confident that
her daughter would know
exactly what to pack.

Five days later Idina
died. She left a dozen
silver-and-glass face-cream
and scent bottles, half
as many hairbrushes and
nail files, a silver glove
stretcher, a cocktail dress,
an evening gown, and a
large black taffeta bow.

Idina's brother, Buck

Idina had never wanted to be an old woman. By dying at just
sixty-two, she seems to have had her way. As Nancy Mitford puts
it in *The Pursuit of Love* when the Bolter visits her daughter
shortly after the birth of her first child, and when her wickedly
behaved niece Linda has just died giving birth to hers:

> The Bolter came to see me while I was still in the Oxford
> nursing home where my baby had been born and where
> Linda had died.
> "Poor Linda," she said, with feeling, "poor little thing.
> But, Fanny, don't you think it is perhaps just as well? The
> lives of women like Linda and me are not so much fun
> when one begins to grow older."[38]

Buck flew down to Kenya to bury his sister. He designed a
headstone: "In loving memory of a warm, generous and coura-
geous person." It gives only the date of her death, November 5,
1955—no birthday to age her by, leaving her forever young.

He laid her under the stone that she had raised for Gee. Where she still is.

FOUR DAYS AFTER IDINA'S DEATH Vita Sackville-West placed the following obituary in the *Times:*

No more succinct or better epitaph could be given to Idina Sackville than the following lines from the Chinese poet Wu-ti, 157–87 B.C., translated by Arthur Waley:

> *The sound of her silk skirt has stopped.*
> *On the marble pavement dust grows.*
> *Her empty room is cold and still.*
> *Fallen leaves are piled against the doors.*
> *Longing for that lovely lady*
> *How can I bring my aching heart to rest?*

V. S-W.[39]

Chapter 26

As a child, all I knew of this family, apart from my mother and her sister—David's two little daughters—was Barbie. And I clearly remember being just ten years old, and standing outside the front of a boarding school in Sussex, waiting for Barbie's butler, Claydon, to drive me to her house.

The house is square, pink, and has green window frames. We draw up at the back door, for the front is never used. Across the yard are two empty cottages, the glass falling from their windows. I walk into the house and I am led down the long passage to the breakfast room in which we are to eat an informal lunch. Informal means relaxed, yet I have never felt at ease with Barbie. I never will. I am not sure whether it is her height, the coolness of her blue eyes and gray hair, or that she is still imposingly beautiful. She is a survivor from that age when women were more glamorous, I was told, than I can imagine. Her best friend was the legendary beauty Diana Cooper. Barbie has spent her entire life among people who never had to dream of earning a living and dressed only in couture. When she married Euan Wallace she became one of them.

But I don't know this then. All I know is that she is very rich and lives a very different lifestyle from us. The year is 1980 and she still has a butler, a cook, and a lady's maid, Knightie, who started working for her when she married Euan, accompanying her on honeymoon, along with Euan's valet. Knightie's real name is Miss Something Knight, but the world has lost track of what that something might be as, being a lady's maid still, at eighty-odd herself, she is known only by Knight, the "ie" added as a sign of affection in exchange for long and faithful service. I adore Knightie. When my sister and I stay here alone, trembling with manners, Knightie looks after us. Whenever I am in the house and frightened or feeling lost it is to Knightie's room that I go.

This time it is just me, in the breakfast room, with Barbie and Herbert. Herbert Agar is Barbie's second husband. He is American, a Pulitzer Prize–winning journalist and concocter of lethal cocktails, which my father calls Herbert Specials. Barbie says very little to me. She doesn't do children, I'm told. Not since her sons all died young. Peter and Johnny followed Gee and David to their deaths in the Second World War. And even Billy, too young to fight, died childless of cancer at the age of forty-seven, leaving a widow, Liz.

After lunch I follow Barbie and Herbert down to the end of the passage and I look out of the windows of Barbie's drawing room and across its small lawn to the rolling lawn of the manor house beyond. Barbie's house is called Beechwood. It is the dower house for the main building, Lavington, which she bought with Euan in 1936.

When I am here with my sister we escape outside for as long as we can.

The garden is the one place here that we do not feel ill at ease. This is strange, as this is the house at which our mother was born, in the gardener's cottage, in the middle of the war. And, Liz aside, we, our baby brother, and my mother's sister's two children, are Barbie's only family.

IN 1981, BARBIE WALKED my mother around her rose garden and said that she had had "a lovely life." One evening soon after, as Claydon locked up, Barbie told him not to come to her in the night, whatever he might hear. When he came in with her tea the following morning she was lying in bed, her skin as white as her ermine bedspread, an empty bottle of sleeping pills on her dressing table.

Barbie did not leave my mother and her sister the pink house in her will, and it slipped from my view.

TWENTY-FIVE YEARS LATER, by one of those strange coincidences that people like to call fate, my sister and her husband have come to live and work at the boarding school. Their apartment consists of the grand first-floor rooms in the main house that, once upon a time, were Barbie's and Euan's bedrooms.

I walk with my sister's two sons to the chapel. It is a small, old chapel, built for a large household and servants rather than for a school. To the right of the altar the wall is covered in five stones bearing the same name, my mother's name, Wallace. A family wiped out, one by one.

My sister tells me that, since she has been at the school, she has heard of a rumor that the house is cursed. She shows me a large, leveled lawn fifty feet away from the main house. It is where the old, sixteenth-century house stood. The man who built it had made a fortune in piracy and had been just as unpleasant at home. He had raped a housemaid, making her pregnant. She died in childbirth. Her father stood at the gates of the house and cursed it with the wish that no male heir should ever live to inherit. Even though that house burnt down and this eighteenth-century building was raised on a different spot, in four hundred years no son, it is said, has inherited. When Barbie and Euan bought this house they had five sons between them. It occurs to me that Barbie may have heard this rumor as well, but too late. And this was why she did not leave her dower house to my mother and her sister, with a son apiece.

I FOUND IDINA IN HER KENYAN HOME, Clouds. I saw it five years ago, on its way to ruin. It had taken half a day of lumping and bumping uphill to reach it from Gilgil, still a frontier-town collection of low-built frames, some with corrugated-iron roofs and shops advertising themselves as barbers, tailors, and general stores. The mud road up was so deeply rutted that our Land

Rover shuddered and spluttered as I willed it around each turn. Solomon, our guide, sat in the front, hesitating at each unmarked junction before raising his long, thin fingers to indicate left or right. A couple of times we had to give up and turn back, find another way. How on earth, I ask, did Idina drive her Hispano-Suiza along here? The roads, I am told, were better back then. The graders, bulldozing machines that scrape the surface of the tracks flat, still came up here. But just after the rains, as we are now, even then the roads were not much better than this.

After a couple of hours of hesitations, and wheel-spinning turns and reversals, the road started running straight along the side of a hill coated in foliage and grass vibrantly green enough to be lit from the inside and rising out of thick, cloddy earth glowing a deep orange. Every now and again the bushes beside the road trembled and Solomon murmured an animal name. Eventually we reached a barbed-wire-surrounded compound. Inside was Clouds, now the home of several generations of a single Kenyan family. In we went, across the dusty courtyard, and into Idina's drawing room. The memory is still vivid.

THE FLOOR IS THICK WITH EARS of maize. I hop across the room from gap to gap, under the gaze of Peter, to whose family the crop belongs. He tells me that these main rooms are too large to feel comfortable living in, and so they are using them for storage. Instead each of his siblings has taken one of the six guest bedrooms around the courtyard of the single-story house, in which to live with their spouse and children. The room I am standing in is indeed not for sleeping in. It is one of three interconnecting spaces that stretch some eighty feet from the dining room on my far right to the end of the library on my left. But the ceilings are low, the walls wood-paneled, and the rooms have a homely feel, reminiscent of the farmhouses back where I live in England's Peak District.

I sit down on the wooden window seat in the maize-strewn room and feel curiously in place. I pull some photographs out of my pocket that show the room lightly furnished with high-armed Knole sofas and velvet curtains. They are no longer here but, apart from that, these rooms where my great-grandmother spent her days and evenings have not been touched since she left them fifty years ago. It is very much still Idina's house.

Leaning back on the seat I look down through the wooden archway at the far room and there I see something that makes my heart stop. I jump up and trip through the maize to the far end. I stand facing the wall opposite the window and run my fingers through the dust covering Idina's bookshelves. The photograph I am holding shows them packed and overflowing. Now they are bare but I can still feel the weight of her books upon them.

I walk on through, now going toward the back of the house, and find Idina's bathroom. A large bath sits along one wall, a lion's-head tap still ready to gush water hanging above it among the tiles. Next to it is a door that, were it not firmly locked, would take me discreetly into the adjoining bedroom. And then, along one wall, are Idina's cupboards. The hanging space stretches for twenty feet. I imagine it again full of her clothes.

I pull my jacket around me. We may be almost on the Equator but it is cold up here, at Clouds, and nobody has lit a fire in these rooms for decades. The floor is littered with dried leaves and dust, the furniture is gone. I am standing in the middle of the scene conjured up by Vita Sackville-West's obituary of Idina.

I close my eyes. Like silk, my feet rustle in the leaves on the floor. Standing here in this house that Idina built, loved, and lived in for two and a half decades, I feel that I have found her. It is the end of a long journey for me.

I open the French doors into the garden and walk out onto what was once a paved terrace and has been roughly, recently, cut back. Ahead of me stretches what was, in my photographs, a vast lawn. Now the lawn is where the maize and other vegetables are grown, thriving with the irrigation system and series of ponds Idina created here over half a century ago. We walk across the vast vegetable patch to the eucalyptus trees at the end. Here, Solomon tells me, as we stand surrounded by grass, flowers, even nettles, three times the size of their English cousins, we may see colobuses, the large, beautiful black-and-white monkeys that he is fighting to save from extinction. But beyond these trees lies the most startling sight. The ground gives way and I realize that this paradisical spot is truly precariously perched on a ledge of the looming, forested Kipipiri. Ahead of me stretches the great Rift Valley and, in sharp contrast to the lushness around me in the hills, the distant valley floor below is a dry yellow, clouded with the shadows of its diminishing herds.

I FELT MORE AT HOME at Clouds than I ever did in a couple of dozen visits to Barbie's. Yet as I think about Idina, my thoughts go immediately to my own children. I can't bring myself to say that Idina should have stayed in an unhappy marriage. But maybe, if she had been a little older, she could have seen a way to make it work. In one of Idina's letters to Dinan, written at the end of her life, I find an echo of just how hardhearted she had found Euan all those years before when she decided she had to leave him. She is writing to Dinan about Sir James Dunn; Jimmie Dunn, Idina calls him. He was the man who had commissioned Orpen to paint Idina, along with two or three other striking women of the day, back in 1915. At the time Idina wrote, in the late 1940s, Dunn had offered to give Dinan this portrait of her mother. "He is a sentimental old man," wrote Idina, "in spite of being a millionaire."[1] After Euan, Idina avoided rich men.

I never met Idina. She would have been seventy-five when I was born, but she had died thirteen years earlier. Nor did I meet, until I began to write this book, any of Dinan's four children, whose ages range from close to my mother's to my own. A few months after David's death, Buck invited Pru and the two- and three-year-old Davina and Laura to Fisher's Gate. It clearly meant a great deal to Idina that the family had met, as she wrote: "I am so glad Laura liked Dinan."[2]

But that was the end of it. Pru and the girls went to live in Greece and then Wales. None of them saw Dinan until Davina, aged eighteen, met her at a Highland Ball in Scotland. The two of them were introduced and stood there, neither knowing what to say—then the flow of dancers and music swept them away from each other.

Idina

And thus, with Idina dead, her family remained separated. Her role as a grandmother was split between the two women whose actions several decades earlier seem to have torn apart her marriage to Euan Wallace—setting her life off on its "turbulent"[3] course. Dinan and her children visited Avie. David's widow, Pru, sent her daughters to stay with Barbie. At one stage Barbie and Avie had been best friends. Now neither mentioned the other. And both sets of Idina's grandchildren grew up believing they didn't have any cousins at all. We played games, my mother said to me, in which we would pretend we had cousins. "So," said Merlin Erroll when I first met him, "did we."

But now, of course, this book has in a way brought Idina back to life. And with her long, manicured fingernails resting on my forearm, her family is finally coming together. Maybe, one day, we will all go on that Kenyan safari Idina so longed to arrange.

On that note I shall end. Sitting here at my desk in my hillside farmhouse overlooking the vast stretch of the Cheshire Plain, I can hear my two small children scampering back indoors. It is time I stopped writing and went to them.

Notes

CLARIDGE'S HOTEL, MAYFAIR, 1934

1. Wallace, David, personal diary, 1934.
2. Interviews with Davina Howell and Pru de Winton, David's daughter and wife (author's mother and grandmother).

CHAPTER I

1. Sunday *Times,* 7 November 1982.
2. Trzebinski, Errol, *The Life and Death of Lord Erroll* (Fourth Estate, London 2001), p. 76.
3. Fox, James, *White Mischief* (Penguin, London 1984), p. 31.
4. Sunday *Times,* 7 November 1982.
5. Wallace, Euan, personal diaries, 1917.
6. *New York Times,* 25 June 1929.
7. Interview with Frank Giles, Corfu, August 2007.
8. The *Times,* 10 November 1955.
9. Interview, 2004 (source wishes to remain anonymous).
10. In particular, Lady Eileen Scott, who also lived in Kenya.
11. Forbes, Rosita, *Appointment in the Sun* (Cassell & Co., London 1949), p. 274.
12. Ibid., p. 278.
13. Telephone interview, Ann McKay (née Soltau), July 2008.
14. Forbes, Rosita, *Appointment in the Sun* (Cassell & Co., London 1949), pp. 274–9.

15. Fox, James, *White Mischief* (Penguin, London 1984), p. 30.

16. Forbes, Rosita, *Appointment in the Sun* (Cassell & Co., London 1949), pp. 274, 275.

17. Mitford, Nancy, *Don't Tell Alfred* (Penguin Books, London 1963), p. 17.

18. Mitford, Nancy, *The Pursuit of Love* (Penguin Books, London 1945), p. 176.

19. Forbes, *Appointment in the Sun,* p. 278.

20. Interview with Ann Douglas, a later wife of Chris Langlands, London, 2004.

21. *A Woman of Affairs,* directed by Clarence Brown, 1928.

22. For example, *Nevada State Journal,* 18 April 1934.

23. Errol Trzebinski interview with David Fielden, Kilifi, Kenya, 1996.

24. Forbes, Rosita, *Appointment in the Sun.*

25. Philippa Neave to the author, 11 June 2008.

26. Ibid.

27. Interview, Nairobi, June 2004 (source wishes to remain anonymous).

28. Arlen, Michael, *The Green Hat* (Robin Clark, London 1991), p. 23.

29. Interview with Molly Hoare, Surrey, U.K., 2004.

30. Interview with Paul Spicer, London, 2005.

31. Interview with Patsy Chilton, London, 2004.

32. Interview, Kenya, 2004 (source wishes to remain anonymous).

33. Interview with Molly Hoare, Surrey, U.K., 2004.

34. Idina to Pru de Winton (then Mrs. David Wallace), 13 September 1944.

CHAPTER 2

1. Elliott, Geoffrey, *The Mystery of Overend and Gurney* (Methuen, London 2006), p. 186.

2. Brassey, Annie Allnut, *A Voyage in the "Sunbeam"* (Longmans, Green & Co., London 1878).

3. Republished November 2007 as *A Voyage in the Sunbeam* by Anna Brassey (Trotamundas Press Ltd., England 2007).

4. King George V, reigned 1910–36.

5. Royal Archives, Z449/80, Windsor Castle.

6. The *Times,* 20 March 1902.

7. Lansbury, George, *Looking Backwards and Forwards* (Blackie, London 1935).

8. Besant, Annie, *The Law of Population* (Freethought Publishing Co., London 1884).
9. Interview with Lady Kitty Giles, Corfu, August 2007.
10. Trzebinski, Errol, *The Life and Death of Lord Erroll* (Fourth Estate, London 2001), p. 52.
11. *Daily Express,* January 1929.
12. Trzebinski, *The Life and Death of Lord Erroll,* p. 52.
13. Errol Trzebinski interview with David Fielden, Kilifi, Kenya, 1996.
14. Pugh, Martin, "Conservative Recruits to Labour 1900–30," *English Historical Review,* Vol. 113, No. 450 (Feb. 1998), pp. 38–64.
15. The *Times,* 6 January 1911.
16. The *Times,* 29 April 1911.
17. Letter, David Wallace to his wife, Pru, 1942.
18. *Oakland Tribune,* 16 February 1913.
19. Ibid.
20. *New York Times,* 6 September 1911.
21. Ibid.
22. *New York Times,* 27 April 1917.
23. *New York Times,* 24 December 1908.
24. According to *The New York Times,* 11 January 1991, this is 840 Madison Avenue, but in the edition of 23 December 1991 it is given as 850 Madison Avenue.
25. *New York Times,* 24 December 1908.
26. *New York Times,* 11 January 1911.
27. *New York Times,* 23 December 1911.
28. *Washington Post,* 26 March 1919.
29. Ibid.
30. *East Grinstead Observer,* 26 July 1913.

CHAPTER 3

1. Wallace, Euan, personal diaries, 1917.
2. *Murray's Handbook for Travellers in Scotland* (John Murray, London 1875).
3. "The younger generation [of Bairds] born in the purple, eschew trade." John Guthrie Smith and John Oswald Mitchell, *The Old Country Houses of the Old Glasgow Gentry* (James Maclehose, Glasgow 1878), Chapter 48.
4. Wallace, Euan, personal diaries, 1917.

5. Lansbury, George, *Looking Backwards and Forwards* (Blackie, London 1935).
6. The *Times,* 25 November 1913, the day before the wedding.
7. Ibid.
8. Ibid.
9. The bra had been invented in 1910, by a New York socialite, Mary Phelps Jacob (she would later become Peabody, then Crosby, by marriage). Jacob had used a pair of handkerchiefs and later made brassieres for her friends. Eventually somebody paid her for one and she decided to patent it in 1914. Idina would almost certainly have met Mary in New York and, given her fascination with fashion, might have been a wearer of one of these early makeshift bras.
10. The *Times,* 11 February 1908.
11. Interview with Errol Trzebinski, Kilifi, Kenya, June 2004.
12. Having absented himself from his children's childhood, Gilbert Sackville joined the Navy at the outbreak of the Great War and died of fever at Messina in Sicily at the end of 1915.
13. Interview with Mr. Young, Barrhill, U.K., June 2007.

CHAPTER 4

1. Diana Manners would later marry Duff Cooper and is better known as Diana Cooper, under which name she wrote her autobiography, *The Rainbow Comes and Goes* (Penguin, London 1961).
2. Holmes, Richard, *Tommy* (HarperCollins, London 2004), p. 438.
3. Interview with John Julius Norwich, Hay-on-Wye, U.K., May 2006.
4. Roynon, Gavin, *Massacre of the Innocents: The Crofton Diaries, Ypres 1914–1915* (Sutton Publishing, Stroud 2004), p. 22.

CHAPTER 5

1. Wallace, Euan, personal diaries, 1917.
2. "Here even motorcars look out of date." Apollinaire, Guillaume, "Zone," first published in *Alcools,* Paris 1913.
3. Wallace, Euan, personal diaries, 1917.
4. Idina's own words, written by her in Euan Wallace, personal diaries, 1917.
5. Ibid.

6. Ibid.
7. Baedeker, Karl, *Paris and Its Environs,* 1913.

CHAPTER 6

1. Wallace, Euan, personal diaries, 1917–18.
2. Now known as "bring-a-bottle parties."
3. Idina's own words, written by her in Euan Wallace, personal diaries, 1917.
4. Lutyens, Mary, *Edwin Lutyens* (John Murray, London 1980), p. 148.
5. *Illustrated London News,* 17 December 1917.

CHAPTER 7

1. Telephone interview with Sarah Graham, 2004, who was struck by Idina's dressing table when she saw it. When Idina died, these pots and jars would form the bulk of the possessions she left behind.
2. Wallace, Euan, personal diaries, 1918.
3. Ibid.
4. Interview with Pru de Winton, David Wallace's wife and author's grandmother.
5. Wallace, Euan, personal diaries, 1918.
6. A servant would have packed his bag for him, driven it to him, and taken him on to the station.
7. Lady Sackville was the mother of Vita Sackville-West and had married her cousin, Lionel, who was Lord Sackville. Both Lionel and Lady Sackville, whose first name was Victoria, were first cousins of Idina's father, Gilbert.
8. Wallace, Euan, personal diaries, 1918.

CHAPTER 8

1. Wallace, Euan, personal diaries, 1918.
2. Ibid.

CHAPTER 9

1. Wallace, Euan, personal diaries, 1918.
2. The *Times,* 8 May 1918.
3. Ibid.

CHAPTER 10

1. Wallace, Euan, personal diaries, 1918.
2. Ibid.
3. Ibid.

CHAPTER 11

1. Norwich, John Julius, *The Duff Cooper Diaries* (Weidenfeld & Nicolson, London 2005), p. 5.
2. Ibid.
3. Interviews with Marybelle Drummond, Charles Gordon's daughter from a later marriage, London, 2004–2007.
4. Ibid.
5. Ibid.
6. Frampton, Peggy, *Seven Candles for My Life* (Pentland Press, Durham 1994).
7. Fox, James, *White Mischief* (Penguin, London 1984), p. 30.
8. Interviews with Marybelle Drummond, Charles Gordon's daughter from a later marriage, London, 2004–2007.
9. Wallace, Euan, personal diaries, 1918.
10. And would continue to do so, dying with a photograph of him by her bed.

CHAPTER 12

1. Wallace, Euan, personal diaries, 1918–19.
2. The *Times,* 29 November 1918.
3. Wallace, Euan, personal diaries, 1918–19.
4. *Washington Post,* 26 March 1919.

CHAPTER 13

1. The *Times,* 10 November 1955.
2. "The Watchman," *Times Almanac,* 10 November 1955.
3. Interviews with Marybelle Drummond, Charles Gordon's daughter from a later marriage, London, 2004–2007.
4. Ibid.
5. Ibid.

6. Wallace, Euan, personal diaries, 1920.
7. Mary Lutyens in conversation with one of Idina's great-granddaughters, Sophy Skeet.
8. As later referred to in *Daily Express,* January 1929.
9. *New York Times,* 31 August 1922.
10. But only her first. The following year she became engaged to a South American polo player, Guillemo Delanda. However, despite plans for a swift wedding, the marriage never took place.
11. Idina to David Wallace, 1 August 1936.

CHAPTER 14

1. Idina to David Wallace, 1 August 1936.
2. Arlen, Michael, *The Green Hat* (Robin Clark, London 1991), p. 15.
3. Interview with Mary Fox, London, May 2004.
4. De Janzé, Frédéric, *Vertical Land* (Duckworth, London 1928), p. 128.
5. Arlen, *The Green Hat,* p. 66.
6. Telephone interview with Ann McKay (née Soltau), July 2008.
7. Arlen, *The Green Hat,* p. 98.
8. Ibid., p. 111.
9. Ibid., p. 34.
10. Ibid., p. 16.
11. Ibid., p. 31.
12. Ibid., p. 32.
13. Ibid., p. 35.
14. Ibid., p. 23.
15. Ibid., p. 13.
16. Sitwell, Georgia, personal diary.
17. Errol Trzebinski interview with Kath Biggs, Kimpton, U.K., August 1995.
18. Faulks, Sebastian, *The Fatal Englishman* (Vintage, London 1997), p. 13.
19. Interview with Patsy Chilton, London, June 2004.
20. Arlen, *The Green Hat,* p. 28.
21. Ibid., p. 28.
22. *A Woman of Affairs,* directed by Clarence Brown, 1928.
23. Arlen, *The Green Hat,* p. 215.
24. Ibid., p. 112.

CHAPTER 15

1. Interview with Lady Kitty Giles, London, 2005.
2. Trzebinski, Errol, *The Life and Death of Lord Erroll* (Fourth Estate, London 2001), p. 51.
3. De Janzé, Frédéric, poem giving the key to the romans à clef *Vertical Land* and *Tarred with the Same Brush.*
4. Trzebinski, *The Life and Death of Lord Erroll,* p. 51.
5. Idina to Lord and Lady Kilmarnock, 11 May 1926.
6. Errol Trzebinski interview with the late Bettine Anderson, Aldeburgh, U.K., 1996.
7. Ibid.
8. Ibid.
9. Ibid.
10. Ibid.
11. Ibid.
12. Ibid.
13. The *Tatler,* 12 September 1923.
14. The *Times,* 23 September 1923.
15. Idina to Lord and Lady Kilmarnock, 11 May 1926.
16. Errol Trzebinski interview with the late Bettine Anderson, Aldeburgh, U.K., 1996.
17. Ibid.
18. Ibid.
19. Josslyn Hay to Lady Kilmarnock, 11 June 1924.
20. Ibid.
21. Ibid.
22. Josslyn Hay to Lady Kilmarnock, 23 June 1924.
23. Interview, Nairobi, June 2004 (source wishes to remain anonymous).
24. Josslyn Hay to Lady Kilmarnock, 11 June 1924.
25. Ibid.: "to grade with Friesian bulls" means to breed with.
26. Trzebinski, *The Life and Death of Lord Erroll,* p. 72.
27. Arlen, *The Green Hat,* p. 98.
28. Frampton, Peggy, *Seven Candles for My Life* (Pentland Press, Durham 1994), p. 36.
29. Interview, Nairobi, June 2004 (source wishes to remain anonymous).
30. De Janzé, Frédéric, *Vertical Land* (Duckworth, London 1928).

31. Trzebinski, Errol, *The Life and Death of Lord Erroll* (Fourth Estate, London 2001), p. 75.
32. De Janzé, *Vertical Land,* pp. 141–2.
33. Trzebinski, *The Life and Death of Lord Erroll,* p. 74.

CHAPTER 16

1. Wheeler, Sara, *Too Close to the Sun* (Jonathan Cape, London 2006), p. 173.
2. Huxley, Elspeth, *Out in the Midday Sun* (Chatto & Windus, London 1987), p. 67.
3. Diary of Lady Eileen Scott.
4. Arlen, Michael, *The Green Hat* (Robin Clark, London 1991), p. 15.
5. Fox, James, *White Mischief* (Penguin, London 1984), p. 42.
6. Letter, Josslyn Hay to Lady Kilmarnock, 27 December 1925.
7. Dinesen, Isak, *Letters from Africa, 1914–1931* (University of Chicago Press, Chicago 1981), p. 300.
8. De Janzé, Frédéric, *Vertical Land* (Duckworth, London 1928), p. 155.
9. Ibid.
10. Letter, Idina to Lord and Lady Kilmarnock, 11 May 1926.
13. Ibid.
14. Ibid.
15. Ibid.
16. Ibid.
17. Ibid.

CHAPTER 17

1. Trzebinski, Errol, *The Life and Death of Lord Erroll* (Fourth Estate, London 2001), p. 89.
2. Interview, Nairobi, June 2004 (source wishes to remain anonymous).
3. Frampton, Peggy, *Seven Candles for My Life* (Pentland Press, Durham 1994), p. 36.
4. Huxley, Elspeth, *Out in the Midday Sun* (Penguin, London 1987), pp. 77–8.
5. Interview, London, June 2004 (source wishes to remain anonymous).

6. De Janzé, Frédéric, *Vertical Land* (Duckworth, London 1928), p. 148.
7. Hayes, Charles, *Oserian* (Rima Books, Nairobi 1997), p. 208.
8. Fox, James, *White Mischief* (Penguin, London 1984), p. 70.
9. De Janzé, Frédéric, *Tarred with the Same Brush* (Duckworth, London 1929), pp. 119–23.
10. Ibid.
11. Ibid.

CHAPTER 18

1. Hayes, Charles, *Oserian* (Rima Books, Nairobi 1997), pp. 199–200.
2. De Janzé, Frédéric, *Tarred with the Same Brush* (Duckworth, London 1929), p. 98.
3. Ibid.
4. Fox, James, *White Mischief* (Penguin, London 1984), p. 44.
5. Trzebinski, Errol, *The Life and Death of Lord Erroll* (Fourth Estate, London 2001), p. 86.
6. *New York Times,* 9 April 1927.
7. Ibid.
8. Ibid.
9. Ibid.
10. *New York Times,* 28 March 1927.
11. *New York Times,* 27 March 1927.
12. *New York Times,* 20 May 1927.
13. Ibid.
14. Hayes, *Oserian*, p. 203.
15. Ibid.
16. *New York Times,* 24 December 1927.
17. Ibid.
18. Ibid.
19. Ibid.
20. Dinesen, Isak, *Letters from Africa, 1914–1931* (University of Chicago Press, Chicago 1981), p. 300.
21. Ibid., pp. 343–4.
22. Ibid.
23. Hayes, *Oserian,* p. 208.
24. *New York Times,* 29 January 1929.
25. Hayes, *Oserian,* p. 208.

26. Trzebinski, *The Life and Death of Lord Erroll*, p. 90.
27. These events included, among others, the wedding of their old friend Michael Lafone in January.
28. Hayes, *Oserian*, p. 209.
29. Trzebinski, *The Life and Death of Lord Erroll*, p. 91.
30. Ibid.
31. Interview, Nairobi, June 2004 (source wishes to remain anonymous).

CHAPTER 19

1. Since Joss had become the Earl of Erroll, Idina had become the Countess of Erroll, known as Lady Erroll. Although separated, they were still married.
2. All quotations up to and including "went through all their stunts": Sitwell, Georgia, diary, unpublished.
3. *Daily Express,* January 1929.
4. Ibid.

CHAPTER 20

1. Idina to David Wallace, 28 February 1939.
2. Will of Muriel Brassey, September 1929.
3. *Nevada State Journal,* 29 December 1930, and others.
4. Forbes, Rosita, *Appointment in the Sun* (Cassell & Co., London 1949), p. 275.
5. Frampton, Peggy, *Seven Candles for My Life* (Pentland Press, Durham 1994), p. 36.
6. Ibid., p. 37.
7. Huxley, Elspeth, *Nellie: Letters from Africa* (Weidenfeld & Nicolson, London 1973), p. 101.
8. Ibid.
9. *Nevada State Journal,* Wednesday, 18 April 1934.
10. Pru de Winton, Idina's daughter-in-law and the author's grandmother.
11. Letter, Viscountess Ridley (née Ursula Lutyens) to Davina Howell, 28 October 1965, quoting her diary for 9–17 September 1922.
12. Wallace, David, personal diary, 1934.

CHAPTER 21

1. As Idina styled herself to her daughter.
2. The most junior scullery maid, so called because in Victorian times she slept between the underside of the stairs and the coal cellar.
3. Interviews with Pru de Winton, author's grandmother and David's wife.
4. Letter, Viscountess Ridley (née Ursula Lutyens) to Davina Howell, 28 October 1965, quoting her diary for 9–17 September 1922.
5. Ibid.
6. As David later told his wife, Pru de Winton, author's grandmother.
7. Wallace, David, personal diary, 1934, and Wallace, Euan, personal diaries, 1931–34.
8. This and following quotes from Wallace, Euan, personal diaries, 1931–34.
9. From Barbie's reply to a letter to him.
10. Letter from his former housemaster, also clearly in reply to an unhappy letter from David.
11. Wallace, David, personal diary, 1934.
12. This and following quotes from Wallace, David, personal diary, 1934.
13. Wallace, Euan, personal diaries, 1934.
14. Wallace, David, personal diary, 1934.

CHAPTER 22

1. Wallace, Euan, personal diaries, 1934.
2. This and following quotes from Wallace, David, personal diary, 1934.
3. She had just bought an extensive peach wardrobe for that spring, as detailed in *Nevada State Journal,* Wednesday, 18 April 1934.
4. Idina to David Wallace, 2 June 1934.

CHAPTER 23

1. This and following quotes from Wallace, David, personal diary, 1934.
2. Ibid., 9 July.
3. This and following quote from Wallace, Euan, personal diaries, 1934.

4. Wallace, David, personal diary, 1934.
5. As he later told his wife, now Ann Douglas.
6. Idina to David Wallace, 1 August 1936.
7. This and following quotes from Forbes, Rosita, *Appointment in the Sun* (Cassell & Co., London 1949), pp. 274–8.
8. Published by Cassell & Co., London 1949.
9. Interview with Raymond Carr, May 2007.
10. Telephone interview with Patrick Leigh Fermor, 2004.
11. As David told his wife, the author's grandmother.
12. Ibid.
13. Idina to David Wallace, 28 February 1939.
14. Dinan said this to her son, Merlin Erroll.
15. Idina to David Wallace, 3 May 1939.
16. Telephone interview with Ann McKay (née Soltau), July 2008.
17. Idina to David Wallace, 3 May 1939.
18. Telephone interview with Ann McKay (née Soltau), July 2008.

CHAPTER 24

1. Words of the senior government pathologist, Dr. Vint, as quoted in Trzebinski, Errol, *The Life and Death of Lord Erroll* (Fourth Estate, London 2001), p. 210.
2. Ibid.
3. Nor was it ever returned.
4. Interview, Nairobi, June 2004 (source wishes to remain anonymous).
5. Interview with Pru de Winton (then Mrs. David Wallace).
6. Ibid.
7. Ibid.
8. Despite a wide variety of theories since, nobody has ever been convicted.
9. Interview with Patsy Chilton, London, 2004.
10. Idina to David Wallace, 28 February 1934.
11. Letters, David Wallace to his wife, Pru, 1942–43.
12. Ibid.
13. Interview with Andrew Kennedy, Barrhill, June 2007.
14. Gee Wallace to David Wallace.
15. Ibid., and Pru de Winton.
16. Correspondence between Errol Trzebinski and Anthea Venning, September 1997.

17. Ibid.
18. Pru de Winton.
19. Correspondence between Errol Trzebinski and Anthea Venning, September 1997.
20. Ibid.
21. Ibid.

CHAPTER 25

1. Idina to a friend, who wishes to remain anonymous. Interview, Nairobi, June 2004.
2. Interview with Molly Hoare, Surrey, U.K., 2004.
3. Ibid. It is not clear whether this was a sexual relationship, but wartime affairs, when couples were separated for years at a stretch, were neither uncommon nor seen as particularly wrong. It was understood that the affair belonged only to that time and place and that both parties would return to their families.
4. Ibid.
5. Ibid.
6. David Wallace to his wife, Pru. December 1943.
7. Idina to Pru de Winton, 1944.
8. *British Reports on Greece,* 1943–44 (Museum Tusculanum Press, Copenhagen 1982).
9. Ibid.
10. Ranfurly, Hermione, *To War with Whitaker* (Arrow Books, London 1998), p. 205.
11. Letters, David Wallace to Pru de Winton.
12. Clipping in the author's possession from the *Times*.
13. Ibid.
14. Telephone interview with Ann McKay (née Soltau), July 2008.
15. Ibid.
16. The *Times,* 9 September 1944.
17. Clipping in the author's possession from *The Evening News,* London.
18. *Eleftheria,* EDES (the Greek Democratic National Army) paper in Corfu, 1 November 1944.
19. Pru de Winton.
20. Aldridge, James, *The Sea Eagle* (Michael Joseph, London 1944).
21. Idina to Pru de Winton, 31 May 1947.
22. In her letter to Pru of 27 February 1945.
23. Queen Elizabeth, the Queen Mother.

24. Source wishes to remain anonymous. Telephone interview, June 2007.
25. Idina's usual request for a drink at this time. Interview, Patsy Chilton, London, May 2004.
26. Idina to Dinan Erroll, 12 August 1950.
27. Idina, Avie, and Buck's old governess.
28. Idina to Dinan Erroll, 12 August 1950.
29. Ibid.
30. Ibid.
31. Peregrine David Euan Moncrieffe was told that he had been named after Euan.
32. He climbed into bed with the source, who wishes to remain anonymous. Interview, London, 2005.
33. Source wishes to remain anonymous. Interview, London, 2004.
34. Peregrine now has six children of his own, two of whom are named Euan and Idina.
35. Errol Trzebinski, correspondence with author, 21 April 2004.
36. Ibid.
37. Huxley, Elspeth, *Nellie: Letters from Africa* (Weidenfeld & Nicolson, London 1973), p. 215.
38. Mitford, Nancy, *The Pursuit of Love* (Penguin Books, London 1945), p. 192.
39. The *Times,* 9 November 1955.

CHAPTER 26

1. Idina to Dinan Erroll, August 1950.
2. Idina's letter to Pru de Winton in February 1945.
3. Idina's letter to Pru de Winton in September 1944.

Select Bibliography

GENERAL

Aldridge, James, *The Sea Eagle* (Michael Joseph, London 1944)

Arlen, Michael, *The Green Hat* (W. Collins Sons & Co., London 1924)

Baedeker, Karl, *Paris and Its Environs* (Baedeker, London 1913)

Beckett, Ian, *Home Front 1914–1918* (The National Archives, Kew 2006)

Best, Nicholas, *Happy Valley* (Secker & Warburg, London 1979)

Brittain, Vera, *Testament of Youth* (Victor Gollancz, London 1933)

Buffetaut, Yves, *The 1917 Spring Offensives* (Histoire & Collections, Paris 1997)

Cannadine, David, *The Decline and Fall of the British Aristocracy* (Penguin, London 2005)

Cave Brown, Anthony, *The Secret Servant: The Life of Sir Stewart Menzies, Churchill's Spymaster* (Michael Joseph, London 1988)

Channon, Henry, *"Chips": The Diaries of Sir Henry Channon* (Weidenfeld & Nicolson, London 1993)

Clark, Alan, *The Donkeys* (Hutchinson, London 1961)

Clifford, Colin, *The Asquiths* (John Murray, London 2002)

Cooper, Artemis, *Cairo in the War* (Hamish Hamilton, London 1989)

Cooper, Diana, *The Rainbow Comes and Goes* (Rupert Hart-Davis, London 1958)

Cornforth, John, *London Interiors* (Aurum Press, London 2000)

Cretney, Stephen, *Family Law in the Twentieth Century* (Oxford University Press 2003)

Cronin, Vincent, *Paris on the Eve* (Collins, London 1989)

de Courcy, Anne, *Society's Queen* (Phoenix, London 2004)

———, *The Viceroy's Daughters* (Weidenfeld & Nicolson, London 2000)

de Janzé, Frédéric, *Tarred with the Same Brush* (Duckworth, London 1929)

———, *Vertical Land* (Duckworth, London 1928)

Fairley, Alastair, *Bucking the Trend* (The Pavilion Trust, Bexhill-on-Sea 2001)

Flanders, Judith, *The Victorian House* (HarperCollins, London 2003)

Grigg, John, *Lloyd George: The People's Champion 1902–1911* (Eyre Methuen, London 1978)

———, *Lloyd George: War Leader 1916–1918* (Allen Lane, London 2002)

Guest, Revel, and John, Angela, *Lady Charlotte Guest* (Weidenfeld & Nicolson, London 1989)

Hall, Lesley, *Sex, Gender and Social Change in Britain Since 1880* (Macmillan, London 2000)

Hattersley, Roy, *The Edwardians* (Little, Brown, London 2004)

Holmes, Richard, *Tommy* (Harper Perennial, London 2005)

Horne, Alastair, *Seven Ages of Paris* (Macmillan, London 2002)

Israel, Lee, *Miss Tallulah Bankhead* (W. H. Allen, London 1972)

Jenkins, Roy, *Churchill* (Macmillan, London 2001)

Keegan, John, *The First World War* (Hutchinson, London 1998)

Lansbury, George, *Looking Backwards and Forwards* (Blackie, London 1935)

Leslie, Anita, *Edwardians in Love* (Hutchinson, London 1972)

Liddington, Jill, *Rebel Girls* (Virago, London 2006)

Lutyens, Mary, *Edwin Lutyens* (John Murray, London 1980)

Millar, John, *Thomas Brassey* (John Millar, 1976)

Mitford, Nancy, *Don't Tell Alfred* (Hamish Hamilton, London 1960)

———, *Love in a Cold Climate* (Hamish Hamilton, London 1949)

———, *The Pursuit of Love* (Hamish Hamilton, London 1945)

Mordaunt Crook, J., *The Rise of the Nouveaux Riches* (John Murray, London 1999)

Mosley, Nicholas, *Rules of the Game, Beyond the Pale* (Pimlico Press, London 1998)

Muirhead, F., *London and Its Environs* (Macmillan, London 1918)

Nicholls, Jonathan, *Cheerful Sacrifice: The Battle of Arras 1917* (Leo Cooper, London 1990)

Nicolson, Juliet, *The Perfect Summer* (John Murray, London 2006)

Norwich, John Julius, *The Duff Cooper Diaries* (Weidenfeld & Nicolson, London 2005)

Pelling, Henry, *A Short History of the Labour Party* (Macmillan, London 1961)

Phillips, Stephen, *Marpessa* (John Lane, London 1900)

Pugh, Martin, *The Pankhursts* (Allen Lane, London 2001)

———, *Women and the Women's Movement in Britain* (Macmillan, London 1992)

Purvis, June, *Women's History: Britain, 1850–1945* (UCL Press, London 1995)

Ranfurly, Hermione, *To War with Whitaker* (Heinemann, London 1994)

Roynon, Gavin, *Massacre of the Innocents: The Crofton Diaries, Ypres 1914–1915* (Sutton Publishing, Stroud 2004)

Sackville-West, Vita, *The Edwardians* (The Hogarth Press, London 1930)

Stevens, J. M., C. M. Woodhouse, and D. J. Wallace, *British Reports on Greece, 1943–44* (Museum Tusculanum Press, Copenhagen 1982)

Stevenson, David, *1914–1918: The History of the First World War* (Penguin, London 2005)

Stokes, Sewell, *Without Veils: The Intimate Biography of Gladys Cooper* (Peter Davies, London 1953)

Stone, Lawrence, *Road to Divorce: England 1530–1987* (Oxford University Press 1990)

Waugh, Alec, *The Loom of Youth* (Richards Press, London 1917)

Waugh, Evelyn, *Vile Bodies* (Chapman & Hall, London 1930)

Wojtezak, Helena, *Notable Women of Victorian Hastings* (The Hastings Press, Hastings 2002)

Ziegler, Philip, *Diana Cooper* (Hamish Hamilton, London 1981)

KENYA

Carberry, Juanita, with Tyrer, Nicola, *Child of Happy Valley* (Heinemann, London 1999)

Cavendish O'Neill, Pat, *A Lion in the Bedroom* (Park Street Press, Mascot, Australia 2004)

Dinesen, Isak (Karen Blixen), *Letters from Africa, 1914–1931* (University of Chicago Press, Chicago 1981)

———, *Out of Africa* [1937] (Penguin, London 1954)

Fox, James, *White Mischief* (Jonathan Cape, London 1982)

Frampton, Peggy, *Seven Candles for My Life* (Pentland Press, Durham 1994)

Hayes, Charles, *Oserian: Place of Peace* (Rima Books, Nairobi 1997)

Hemingway, Ernest, *Green Hills of Africa* (Jonathan Cape, London 1936)

Huxley, Elspeth, *Nellie: Letters from Africa* (Weidenfeld & Nicolson, London 1973)

———, *Out in the Midday Sun* (Chatto & Windus, London 1985)

Markham, Beryl, *West with the Night* [1942] (Penguin, London 1988)

Marshall MacPhee, A., *Kenya* (Ernest Benn Limited, London 1968)

Nicholls, C. S., *Elspeth Huxley* (HarperCollins, London 2002)

———, *Red Strangers: The White Tribe of Kenya* (Timewell Press, London 2005)

Rodwell, Edward, *The Mombasa Club* (The Mombasa Club, Mombasa 1988)

Trzebinski, Errol, *The Kenya Pioneers* (Norton, New York 1985)

———, *The Life and Death of Lord Erroll* (Fourth Estate, London 2001)

———, *The Lives of Beryl Markham* (Norton, New York 1995)

Wheeler, Sara, *Too Close to the Sun: The Life and Times of Denys Finch Hatton* (Jonathan Cape, London 2006)

UNPUBLISHED SOURCES

Georgia Sitwell, personal diary

Euan Wallace, personal diaries, 1917–41

David Wallace, personal diary, 1934

Arthur Wolseley-Lewis, "Empire to Dust," unpublished personal reminiscences

Letters from the Wallace and Erroll families

"Reminiscences of Kildonan House, Barrhill," *Ayrshire Notes 25,* Autumn 2003

Acknowledgments

I am far from alone in having long been fascinated by Idina. Luckily so, for this book could not have been written without the enthusiasm and memories of many others. First and foremost among these is my inspirational fellow writer Errol Trzebinski, whose compelling biography of Joss Erroll led me to her. Errol opened both her door and her copious research to me, displaying an outstanding generosity of both time and spirit. Most important, she shared her belief that not only was there a book in Idina, but it was one that ought to be written. She found me a Kenyan guide, the unflappable Tina Behrens, and places to stay. She took me to meet those who remembered Idina. And she went back to some of the sources she had spoken to, and asked them for more information. She set a great example of how experienced writers can help those just starting on their career. I shall be not only eternally grateful but bound, years hence, if I am ever able, to do the same for the next generation.

Other Kenyans who helped me along the way out there were Robin Long (Boy and Genesta Long's son), and his friend Cynthia Ravenscroft, for her memories of Idina in the Gilgil club; Nan Barratt, Fergus and Rachel Robley, who had me to stay on their Kenyan farms; Juliet Barnes and Solomon, for guiding me up the dirt tracks of the Wanjohi Valley; Peter Nuthu Mughiri and his family for showing me around Clouds, which is now their home; the Earl and Countess of Enniskillen for allowing me to wander around the heavenly Mundui and imagine Idina and Kiki Preston whiling away afternoons on the veranda on the shores of Lake Naivasha; and Mr. and Mrs. Arthur

Wolseley-Lewis and Maureen Delap for their reminiscences of Idina. More Kenya hands were to be found back here in England, providing ebullient conversation packed with abundant information. Among them were Patsy Chilton, Lord and Lady Delamere, Mary Fox, Sarah Graham, Joan Hecktermann, Molly and Arthur Hoare, Paul Spicer, and Anne Wadley.

I scooted up to Scotland, lolled on Kildonan's lawns, and was shown around by Colin the caretaker, who was a mine of information about my family's history in the house. Elizabeth Hughes of Blair Farm tracked down a local history from Duncan Barr. The centenarian Mr. Young of Duisk Lodge racked his razor-sharp recollections, as did Andy Kennedy of Wallace Terrace, who for many years worked at Kildonan. Mr. and Mrs. Hall of the old Kildonan stable block offered me delicious coffee and further pages of information.

Elsewhere I found many helping hands: some writers, some observers, some sources of vital facts. There are too many to list in full, but: Norah Angelbeck, Mabel Derry, Tom and Su de Trafford, Ann Douglas, Marybelle Drummond, James Fox (who took me to Idina in the first place with *White Mischief*), Odile Fraigneau of Lanvin, Annabel Freyberg, Justine Hardy, Lucy Heathcoat-Amory, Alexandra Ignatieff, Ffion Jenkins, Jeremy Langlands, Patrick Leigh Fermor, Chris Lockwood and Venetia Butterfield, Louise Miller Frost, Christine Nicholls, Viscount Norwich, Andrew Roberts, Jane Robertson, Xan Smiley, Pat Thane, Veronica Wadley, Justin Warshaw, Sara Wheeler, and Patricia O'Neill, who wrote from South Africa, were all kind and informative. Here also I should thank Liza Filby, who helped me with some of the research. Her dexterity with databases proved invaluable. And thank you, too, to all those at the Victoria and Albert Museum, the National Army Museum, the Household Cavalry Museum, the Vintage Motorcycle Club Limited, and Coys of South Kensington.

Then there is the family: Idina's children, nieces, and nephews, and their descendants. They have been, as is clear, a huge resource in this resurrection of Idina. I started this book with only the remains of the Wallaces: my grandmother Pru; my mother, Davina; and her sister, Laura; and their five children and (now) ten grandchildren. In particular, my sister, Kate Bain, and my cousin Sophy Skeet have dug up both photographs and keen memories of what Barbie and her sisters told them about who said what to whom when. I have had immense fun getting to know the rest, and some uncanny moments realizing how similar some of us look—Idina's blood runs thick. Dinan's children—

Merlin Erroll, Peregrine Moncreiffe, Alexandra Connell, and Jocelyn Carnegie—have all been a font of pictures and information, as have Buck's daughter, Lady Kitty Giles, and her husband, Frank. The Earl and Countess De La Warr and the Dowager Countess De La Warr have shared their traces of Idina and the Sackvilles with enthusiasm. Rowena Fielding has shown the way to all things Brassey. My father's sister, Jane Townsend, who is no relation to Idina but a long-standing fan of the legend, has helped me find out more. And thank you to Ali Hope, an old friend and, coincidentally, a step-great-something of Idina, who brought some of the family back together. Finally, a warm and grateful welcome to Ann McKay (née Soltau), Idina's beloved stepdaughter.

But research is only a part of the creation of a book. And, were it not for the unflinching faith of my outstanding agent, Gill Coleridge, helped by her assistant, Cara Jones, Idina would have dissolved back into the dust from which I have sought to resurrect her. Gill has been a heaven-sent guiding hand for an author in that well-known state of Struggling with the Second Book, nursing Idina through various metamorphoses and choosing just the right moment to steer me on to my wonderful new British editor, Lennie Goodings, and her team at Virago. Lennie's faint pencil marks shifted the scales from my eyes. It has been a joy to work with her and with my wise American editor, Vicky Wilson, at Knopf, who teased yet more of Idina's story from me, and taught me much. A huge debt of thanks is owed to her assistant, Carmen Johnson, who, among many other tasks, painstakingly put together the dozens of photographs in this book. I should also like to thank the copy editor, Kate Norris. And, of course, my fantastic American agent, Melanie Jackson, who put *The Bolter* into Vicky's hands. Already, the next book is under way. . . .

Finally, I have my close family to thank: my mother, for being there for me and the children at all those crucial moments of both industry and inquiry; Luke and Liberty themselves, for patiently waiting for me to finish the book; Suzie, for keeping the children and fridge full of food when I was absorbed in writing; George, for putting up with me then, now, and all those years past and yet to come.

London, October 2008

Index

Note: Page numbers in *italics* refer to illustrations and information in captions.

Aberdare Hills, Kenya, 138, 165
adultery, attitudes toward, 28–9,
    113, 206, 210
Agar, Herbert, 296
Albert Hall, 125
Alington, 3rd Baron, 155
Appointment in the Sun (Forbes), 253
Aquitania, 213
Arlen, Michael, 14, 15, 150,
    152–4, 155
Asquith, Henry Herbert, 40, 67

Bain, Kate (née Howell) (sister of
    author), 8, 296
Bain, Paul, 296
Baird, Alexander, 47
Baker, Edith, 211, 212
Ballets Russes, 249
Balliol College, 228
Bankhead, Tallulah, 154–5
Barrachin, Madame, 78
Barrès, Maurice, 158

Beale & Inman, 243
Beaton, Cecil, 14, 211, 212, 213,
    230, 301
Beecham, Dr. William, 93, 94
Beechwood (dower house for
    Lavington Park), 296–7
Belgian Congo, 253–4
Belper, Eva, 96–7, 123
Berkeley Hotel, 94
Besant, Annie, 32–4, 51
Bethell, Sir Hugh Keppel, 129
Bevan, Aneurin, 237
Bing Boys, 80
Bing Girls, 80
Bird, James or Jimmy, 287, 289,
    290, 292
Birkbeck, Ben, 184
Birkbeck, Cockie, 184–5, 226
birth control, 33
Blackburn, Lord, 128
Black Gang, *100, 102*–6
Blavatsky, Madame, 33

Blin Stoyle, Dorothy, 278
Blin Stoyle, Herbert, 278
Blin Stoyle, Molly, 278
Blixen, Bror, 184, 226
　affair with Cockie Birkbeck,
　　184–5
　divorce from Karen Blixen,
　　184–5
Blixen, Karen (Tania) (Isak
　Dinesen), 170–1
　Denys Finch Hatton and, 170–1,
　　184, 185
　the Gordons and, 185
　Joss Hay and, 206
Blue Bird Flying Circus, 250
Blue Goose, 251
Bocardo, Mademoiselle Ida
　"Zellée," 257, 286
Boots (pharmacy chain), 191
Boucher, Jean-Honoré, 190
Boy, The, 96
Brassey, Lady, Annie (née Allnut)
　(maternal grandmother),
　　23–5, 23, 30, 49–50, 250
　travels of, 23–5, 120, 151
Brassey, Lady Helen (aunt), 30
Brassey, Lady Mabelle, see Egerton,
　Mabelle (née Brassey)
　(aunt)
Brassey, Lady Marie, Marchioness
　of Willingdon (aunt), 24,
　　25, 30
　son Gerard, 30, 61
Brassey, Lady Muriel, Countess
　De La Warr, see Sackville,
　Lady Muriel, Countess
　De La Warr (née Brassey)
　(mother)
Brassey, Thomas (great-
　grandfather), 22–3, 22

Brassey, Thomas (Sir Thomas
　Brassey, later Lord Brassey,
　later 1st Earl Brassey)
　(maternal grandfather), 23,
　　23, 24, 25–6, 50, 77, 159
　second marriage, 30
Brassey, Tom (2nd Earl Brassey)
　(uncle), 26, 70
British East Africa protectorate
　becomes Crown Colony of
　　Kenya, 144
　boundaries of, 150
　British gentry seeking new life
　　in, 137–8
　lottery to distribute farms in,
　　137
　Sackville-Gordon farm, 138–42
　scramble for Africa and, 150
　see also Kenya (formerly British
　　East Africa)
British Expeditionary Force, 61
British Residence, Koblenz,
　Germany, 161, 164
British Special Operations
　Executive (SOE), 274,
　　279–80
British Theosophical Society, 33–4
Brotherhood of the Holy Cross,
　245
Bryant and May, 32–3
Bubbly, 80
Burton, Ralph, 102

Café de Flore, Paris, 72
Café de Paris, 76–7, 85, 147
Cairo, Egypt, during World
　War II, 270–1, 274–5
Calcott, gas-powered automobile,
　87, 88–9, 88, 91
Callot Soeurs, Paris, 75, 86

Cambridge University, 91, 94, 97,
        105
Campbell, Mrs. Patrick, 45
Carey, Philip, 162
Carlisle, Mr. (of Harland &
        Wolff), 41
Carlton, London, 58, 81
Carmen, 95
Carnegie, Jocelyn, 300
Cavendish, Alix, 143
Chapel Royal at the Savoy, 94
Cholmondeley, Tom, 200
Churchill, Pamela, 283
Churchill, Winston, 129, 283
Churchill, Winston (son of
        Pamela), 283
Ciro's, 147
Claridge's Hotel, 58, 93–4, 112
    reunion of Idina with son David
        at, 3–4, 239–42, 240
Clouds (Kenyan farm), 14–15,
        220, 225–6, 241, 272, 279,
        288
    author's visit to, 297–300
    birds at, 219–20
    dairy farming at, 14, 219,
        265
    described, 218–22
    furnishings at, 221
    guests and entertaining at, 222,
        223
    Idina leaves, due to health
        problems, 284
    kitchen staff at, 222–3
    Chris Langlands at, 250–1
    location of, 14, 218, 219
    Marie, housekeeper at, 222–3,
        250
    Mau Mau uprising and, 182,
        291

Soltau children at, 264–5, 279,
        283, 287
Cole, Berkeley, 170, 175
Cole, Galbraith, 175
Congo, 253–4
Connaught Place, 124, 126, 144
    entertaining at, 57, 58, 83–4,
        105
    Euan moves out of, 127
    selection of, 52–3
    during World War I, 68, 83,
        88–9, 94, 97, 105, 112
Cooper, Lady Diana (née Manners),
        60, 238, 295
Cooper, Duff, 238
Cooper, Gladys, 149
Colvile, Gilbert, 175
Cranwell training academy, 228
Curzon, Cimmie, *see* Mosley,
        Cimmie (Lady Mosley)
        (née Cimmie Curzon)
Curzon, Irene, 98, 211
Cushings, 142

Daily Express, 36, 213
    Idina sues, 213
Daily Herald, 31
Dancers, The, 154–5
Dartmouth House, 83
Daughter of the Gods, A, 80
Davison, Emily Wilding, 44
Dawson, Charlie, 258–9
Debussy, Claude, 72
Defence of the Realm Act, 60
de Janzé, Alice (née Silverthorne,
        later de Trafford), *183*,
        188
    affair with and shooting of
        Raymond de Trafford, 200,
        201, 201–4, 207

de Janzé, Alice (continued)
  marriage and separation, 223,
    251
  the trial, 205
  affair with Joss Hay, 158, 182–3,
    186, 195, 199, 200, 206
  Joss's murder and subsequent
    trial, 269, 271, 272
  annual Happy Valley party,
    186–8
  deportation from Kenya, 207
  described, 158
  drug habit, 251–2
  as guest at Slains, 182–3, 186,
    187
  marriage to Frédéric, 158
  return to Kenya after murder
    trial, 205–7
  on safari, 185–6
  suicidal, 269, 272
  Wanjohi Farm, 188, 194–5
de Janzé, Frédéric, 200
  alphabetical poem of Kenyan
    characters, 15
  annual Happy Valley party,
    186–8
  divorce from Alice, 202, 204
  as guest at Slains, 182–3, 186,
    194–5
  marriage to Alice, 158
  on safari, 185–6
  Vertical Land—for Horizontal
    People, 150, 176–7, 195
  Wanjohi Farm, 188, 194–5
de la Barondière, Madame, 90
Delamere, Lady, 175, 200
Delamere, Lord, 170–1, 175, 194,
    200
Delves Broughton, Diana, 266–7,
    268

Delves Broughton, Sir Jock,
    266–7, 270
  trial of, 271, 272
de Noailles, Charles, 130
Derby, 15th Earl of, 23
d'Erlanger, Pop, 211, 212
de Trafford, Alice, see de Janzé,
    Alice (née Silverthorne,
    later de Trafford)
de Trafford, Raymond, 183, 200
  affair with Alice de Janzé, 200,
    201, 202–4
  Alice's trial for attempted
    murder, 205
  marriage and separation, 223
Deux Magots, Paris, 72
divorce
  after World War I, 113, 149–50
  changes in divorce law, 153–4
  as common in 1928, 210
  in early 1900s, 28, 29–30
Dodge, Mary, 41, 215
Dodges (American railroad
    family), 31
Don't Tell Alfred (Mitford), 12–13
Dorchester House, 95, 124
Dufferin, Brenda, 162
Dukes, 142
Dunkeld, 99
Dunlop Tyres, 52
Dunn, Sir James, 64–5, 289, 300
Durbar Hall, 26

East Grinstead Observer, 44
East Grinstead Women's Suffrage
    Society, 40, 44
Eden, Anthony, 280–1, 282, 284,
    285
Ednam, Viscount, Eric, 97–8,
    103

Edwardian age
  divorce in, 28, 29–30
  female independence, 37
  sexual behavior in, 37, 113
Edward VII, King, 28, 29–30, 50
Egerton, Jack, 30
Egerton, Mabelle (née Brassey)
  (aunt), 24, 30, 38
Egypt, 134
  Cairo during World War II,
    270–1, 274–5
Elizabeth, Princess, 16, 286
Elizabeth, Queen (the Queen
  Mother), 286
Embassy club, 147
Emmanuele (companion on drive
  through the Sahara),
  13–14, 258–9
Equality (Tawney), 236
Erroll, Diana Denyse "Dinan,"
  23rd Countess of, see Hay,
  Diana Denyse "Dinan"
Erroll, Lady Idina, Countess of, see
  Sackville, Lady Idina
Erroll, Josslyn "Joss," 22nd Earl of,
  see Hay, Josslyn
Erroll, Mary "Molly," Countess of,
  see Ramsay-Hill, Mary
  "Molly," later Countess of
  Erroll (née Maude)
Erroll, Merlin, 24th Earl of, see
  Hay, Merlin
Eton, 62, 104, 159, 217, 228,
  234, 235

Fair and Warmer, 112
Fenhall, Miss, 249
Ferguson, Lieutenant Colonel
  Algernon, 51, 69
Filmer, Phyllis, 266, 272

Finch Hatton, Denys, 170–1,
  184
  Karen Blixen and, 170–1, 184,
    185
Fisher, Derek, 196, 252
Fisher, Pat, 196
Fisher's Gate, 203, 213, 226, 257,
  287, 300
Folies Bergère, 77, 90
Forbes, Rosita, 119, 258
  at Clouds, 220, 252
  description of Idina, 11, 14, 19
  divorce from first husband, 108,
    149
  friendship with Idina, 124, 130,
    253–6
  travels and sense of adventure,
    119–20, 253–6
Fox, James, 8
Fragonard, François, 190
Frampton, Peggy, 223

Garbo, Greta, 14, 155
Gartsherrie ironworks, 47
Gellibrand, Paula, 222
George, Prince (of Russia), 162
George V, King, 44
Germany
  scramble for Africa and, 134
  World War I and, 70, 72,
    78, 92
Gibbs, Lionel, 103
Gide, André, 72
Gielgud, John, 259
Giles, Lady Kitty (née Sackville),
  204, 225, 257, 285
Gilgil Club, 14, 19
Gladstone, William, British Prime
  Minister, 25–6
Gloucester, Duke of, 251

Gordon, Charles (second husband),
    116–20, *136*
  affair with Idina, 116–20, 123
  described, 117–18, 141
  finances of, 117, 120
  marriage to Honor, 185
  marriage to Idina, *see* Gordon-
    Sackville marriage (second
    marriage)
Gordon, Honor, 185
Gordon, Lady Idina, *see* Sackville,
    Lady Idina
Gordon, Jack, 117
Gordon, Lukyn, 185
Gordon-Sackville marriage (second
    marriage), 133–42, 144–5
  divorce, 150, 156
  early problems in, 141
  farm lottery and, 137
  Gilgil farm, 138–42, 145
  on safari, 140
  travel to Nairobi in search of a
    farm *(shamba)*, 130, 133–7
  wedding, 130
Gore Brown, Mr., 105–6
gorilla watching, 253
Grand Guignol ("The Big Puppet
    Show"), 77
Grant, Jos, 175
Grant, Nellie, 175, 226, 292
Great Depression, 214, 219, 223,
    234–5
Greece, 249, 254, 256–7
  during World War II, 274,
    279–81, 285
Green Hat, The (Arlen), 14, 150,
    152–4, 155
Grigg, Sir Edward, 207
Grigg, Lady, 207
Grigsby, Emilie, 41

Haldeman, Donald (fourth
    husband), 13, 216–18,
    217, 218
Haldeman, Lady Idina, *see*
    Sackville, Lady Idina
Haldeman-Sackville marriage
    (fourth marriage), 216–18,
    250
  Donald's violent jealousy, 13,
    223–5, 226, 251
  end of, 224–6
  Idina's affairs during, 223–4,
    251
  wedding, 216, *217, 218*
Hall's History of the Near East, 249
Hamilton, Lord Claud, 194
Happy Valley crowd, *see* Kenya
    (formerly British East
    Africa), Happy Valley
    crowd
Harrow, 48
Hay, Diana Denyse "Dinan," 23rd
    Countess of Erroll
    (daughter), 15, 270,
    285–7, 300–1
  birth of, 184
  brother David and, 258
  childhood and teenage years,
    187, 201, 208, 224, 250,
    258, 270, 286–7
  at Fisher's Gate with Buck and
    Diana, 13, 203–4, 209,
    213, 225–6, 257–8, 285
  raised by Avie, 257, 270,
    286
  marriage of, 286
  naming of, 184
  nannies, 187, 201
  reunited with Idina, 287–92,
    300

trust money from grandmother
Muriel, 216, 225, 287
Hay, Lady Idina, *see* Sackville, Lady
Idina
Hay, Ivan, 210
Hay, Josslyn, 22nd Earl of Erroll
(third husband), 7–8, *176,
183, 193*
Alice de Janzé and, *see* de Janzé,
Alice (née Silverthorne,
later de Trafford), affair
with Joss Hay
ancestry of, 159
appearance of, 155–6, 159
career
in the Foreign Office, 155–6,
159
in Kenyan Legislative Council,
266
finances of, 159, 182, 187,
191–2
inheritance, 204
friendship with Idina after their
marriage, 266, 268–9
malaria, 186–8
marriages
to Idina, *see* Hay-Sackville
marriage (third marriage)
to Molly (formerly Ramsay-
Hill), 215, 251–2, 266
murder of, 7, 267–9, *268,* 270,
286
during World War II, 266
Hay, Merlin, 24th Earl of Erroll
(grandson), 185, 289, 300,
301
Hay-Sackville marriage (third
marriage), 7–8, 155–8,
176, 164–89, 177
age gap, 155, 158, 161

divorce, 214
Joss abandons Idina, 207–8
Joss's affair with Alice de Janzé,
see de Janzé, Alice (née
Silverthorne, *later* de
Trafford), affair with Joss
Hay
Joss's bout with malaria, 186–8
Kenyan farm, *see* Lion Island
(Sackville-Hay farm)
Kenyan home, *see* Slains
as open marriage, 157–8, 164–5,
170–8, 182–3, 194–5,
199–200, 206
Idina's affair with Caswell
"Boy" Long, 193–4
Joss's affair with Molly
Ramsay-Hill, *see* Ramsay-
Hill, Mary "Molly," *later*
Countess of Erroll (née
Maude), affair with Joss Hay
safaris, 185–6
wedding, 161–3, *162*
Hello Boys, 87
Hispano-Suiza, 151, 165, *171,
171,* 298
Holford, Sir George, 95
Howell, (Cary) Davina (née
Wallace) (author's mother,
Idina's granddaughter), 13,
16–18, 19, *274, 278, 282,*
284, 285–6, 296, 297, 300
Howell, Toby (brother of author),
296
Hughes, Guy, 190–1
Huxley, Elspeth, 168, 180–1, 193

Illustrated London News, 88
Imperial British East Africa
Company (IBEAC), 134

Inter-Allied Rhineland High
    Commission, 159

Jaipur, Maharajah of, 253
Jamestown colonists, 22
Jeffreys, Miss (governess), 129,
    231
Joyce, James, 158

Kennard, Sir Coleridge, 108, 150
Kennard, Lady, Dorothy "Dorry,"
    108, 109, 119
Kenya (formerly British East
    Africa)
  Aberdare Hills, 138, 165
  becomes Crown Colony, 144
  Clouds, see Clouds (Kenyan farm)
  colonial administration, 180,
    196, 292
    horsewhipping of Joss Hay
      and, 208
  Happy Valley crowd, 8, 11,
    251–2, 272
    hosting of annual parties,
      195–8
    Oserian parties, 205
    rechristening of Wanjohi
      Valley as Happy Valley,
      196
    reputation of, 195–6, 200
  Idina's love of, 140
  Kipipiri area, 218, 300
  Lion Island, see Lion Island
    (Sackville-Hay farm)
  livestock auction days, 172
  Mau Mau uprising, see Mau Mau
    uprising
  Race Weeks, 172–4, 194
  Sackville-Gordon farm in Gilgil,
    138–42,145

Slains, see Slains
Soldier Settlement Scheme,
    266
White Highlands, 171
wildlife, 139, 140, 219–20
see also British East Africa
    protectorate
Kidnapped (Stevenson), 47
Kikuyu tribesmen, 138, 168–9,
    218
  Mau Mau uprising and, 291
Kildonan House, 163, 247, 248
  as Barbie and Euan Wallace's
    home, 144, 232, 248–9,
    274
  David and Gerard Wallace at,
    232–4, 247, 249
  grouse season at, 248–9
  planning of, by Idina and Euan
    Wallace, 53–7, 56, 58, 64,
    65 232
Kilimanjaro, Mount, 135
Kilmarnock, Lord, Victor (father-
    in law, third marriage),
    159, 161, 164, 204
  death of, 207
  wife of, 164, 167, 204, 207
King Alfred School, 83
King's Household Cavalry, 46
  2nd Life Guards, 46, 48, 50–1,
    59, 63, 67, 125–6
Kirkwood, Dr., 249
Kitchener, Lord, 59–60, 61
Knight, Miss (Barbie's lady's
    maid), 232, 295–6
Koch de Gooreynd, Gerard, 280
Krishnamurti, 34–5, 36, 82

Labour Party, 31, 209, 215
Ladies' Automobile Club, 52

Lafone, Michael, 186, 196
Lake Victoria, 134
Lambton, Ralph, 77
Langlands, Chris, 250–1
Langmead, "Precious," 252,
    253–4, 274
Lansbury, George, 31, 32, 39, 40,
    45, 164, 192
Lanvin, Jeanne, 76
Lanvin, Paris, 75–6, 75
Lavington Park, 274, 291, 296
Law of Population, The
    (Besant), 33
Lawrence, Captain, 169
Leadbeater, Charles, 33, 34
le Carré, John, 50
Legacy of Greece, The, 249
Leigh Fermor, Patrick, 256
Leiters, Mr. and Mrs. Joe, 142
Leviathan, 213
Lion Island (Sackville-Hay farm),
    165
  dairy farming at, 165, 167–8
  house on, see Slains
  sheep at, 168
  see also Slains
Lloyd George, David, 39, 44, 67
Loeffler, Mrs., 109
Loews, 142
London, England
  in 1921, 147–9
  pre–World War I strikes, 38–9,
    40
  during World War I, 60–1,
    79–82, 92, 93
Long, Caswell "Boy," 193–4, 196,
    222
Long, Dan, 223
Long, Genesta, 193–4, 196
Long, Robin, 225

Love in a Cold Climate (Mitford),
    12–13
Lutyens, Barbie, see Wallace,
    Barbie (née Lutyens)
Lutyens, Sir Edwin, 16, 34, 82–3,
    96
Lutyens, Lady Emily, 34, 82, 96
Lutyens, Mary, 83
Lutyens, Ursula, 163, 227
Lynn, Olga "Oggie" (née
    Löwenthal), 116, 158
  Catherine Street house, the
    crowd at, 143, 147, 148,
    154–5, 157–8, 178
  Idina meets Charles Gordon
    at, 116, 141
  Glebe Place, Idina stays at, 209,
    213
  travels of, 151, 162–3, 258

MacDonald, Ramsay, 33, 164, 234
MacDowell (Kildonan
    groundsman), 232
Macmillan, Lady Dorothy (née
    Cavendish), 143
Macmillan, Harold, 143
Magor, Joan Prudence "Pru," see
    Wallace, Joan Prudence
    "Pru" (née Magor)
    (daughter-in-law)
Maidenhead Boat Club, 81, 84,
    103–4, 105
Maid of the Mountains, The, 80, 81
malaria, 186–8
Manners, Lady Diana, see Cooper,
    Lady Diana (née Manners)
Margaret, Princess, 16, 286
Markham, Beryl (formerly Purves),
    170, 186, 187
Marlborough House Set, 28

Marxism, 32

Masai tribesmen, 135, 138

Mau Mau uprising, 291–2
  Clouds and, 182, 291

Maxwell, Ian, 108

Mayol, Paris, 77

McGrath, Arthur, 252–4

Menina, Greece, 279–81

Menzies, Lady Avice "Avie," *see*
  Sackville, Lady Avice
  "Avie" (sister)

Menzies, Stewart, 85, 129
  background of, 50–1
  British Intelligence and, 50, 69
  end of Idina's marriage to Euan
    and, 127
  friendship with Euan Wallace,
    50, 51, 77, 85, 86, 112,
    125
  marriage to Avie, 115, 120, 121,
    125–7, 163
  2nd Life Guards and, 50–1

Milbanke, Sir John "Buffles,"
  227

Milbanke, Sheila, 3, 227, 228,
  238

Milford Haven, Lady, 254

Miller, James, 54–5, 65

Minto, Earl of, Viceroy of India,
  181

Miss Wolff's finishing school, 83

Mitford, Nancy, 12–13, *12*, 293

Molyneux, Captain Edward, 14,
  153, 155, 213, 226

Mombasa, Kenya, 133–5, 137
  railway to Lake Victoria from,
    134–5

Mombasa Club, 133–4, 261

Moncreiffe, Lady Alexandra
  (granddaughter), 292, 300

Moncreiffe, Iain (son-in-law), 286,
  289

Moncreiffe, Peregrine David Euan
  (grandson), 15, 289, 290,
  300

Moore, George, 81

Moore, Kathleen, Countess of
  Drogheda, 145–6

Morgan, J. P., 41

Morgan, Sarah Spencer, 43

Morland, Laura (née Wallace)
  (granddaughter), 13, 274,
  278, 282, 284, 285, 297,
  300

Mosley, Cimmie (Lady Mosley)
  (née Curzon), 98, 113,
  162–3, 209–10, 212

Mosley, Tom (Sir Oswald), 162–3,
  209–12
  affair with Idina, 209–12
  as Labour MP, 209–10
  wealth of, 209

Motion, Vernon, 266–7

Mountbatten, Edwina (Lady
  Louis), 254

Mundui, 219

Muthaiga Country Club, Nairobi,
  135–6, 137, 165, 170, 183,
  265–6
  described, 135–6
  Race Weeks, 172–4, 194

Myers, Brigadier, 279

Nairobi, Kenya, 135, 137
  Race Weeks, 172–4, 194

New York Times, The, 11, 145–6,
  203

Nicholson, Harold, 289

Nile River, 134

Norfolk Hotel, Nairobi, 136

Normanhurst Court, 26
Nothing but the Truth, 94
NUWSS (National Union of
    Women's Suffrage
    Societies), 44

Oakland Tribune, 40
O'Dell, Miss, 263
Old Glassingall estate, 47–8
Old Lodge (Muriel Brassey's
    home), 31, 35, 36, 40, 126,
    128, *128,* 168, 215
Old Vic, London, 249
Olivier, Laurence, 249
Olympic, 40–1
Orpen, Sir William, *10,* 11, 14,
    64–5, 289, 300
Osborn, Aileen, 42–3
Osborn, Alice (née Dodge), 41
Osborn, Henry Fairfield, 41
Osborn, Josephine, 41–2
Osborn, Lucretia, 41–3
Osborn, William Church, 41
Osborn, William Henry, 41
Osborne, Frances (author), 8–9,
    16–20, 295–302
Osborns (American railroad
    family), 31, 41
Oserian, *191,* 204, 215, 219,
    266
    described, 189–90
    furnishing of, 190
    naming of, 190
    parties for Happy Valley crowd
        at, 205
    setting of, 190
    transfer of half share to Molly,
        205, 221–2
Out of Africa (Dinesen), 170–1,
    184

Oxford University, 228, 235–7,
    242, 254–6

Palazzo Barzizza, Venice, 161
Pankhurst family suffragettes, 31
Paris, France, 226
    during World War I, 70–78,
        84, 90
Pearson, Mary Mond, 148
Pembroke House (boarding
    school), 284
Phillips, Buns, 254
photographic camera, 23
Picasso, Pablo, 72
Pidcock, Mr., 169
Poiret, Paul, 72
Portal, General, 69
Preston, Gerry, 192, 193, *193,*
    196
Preston, Kiki, 192–3, *193,* 196
    morphine addict, 192, 195,
        251–2
Princess Elizabeth Hospital,
    Nairobi, 291, 292
Proust, Marcel, 72, 158
Pursuit of Love, The (Mitford), 12,
    293
Purves, Beryl, *see* Markham, Beryl
    (*formerly* Purves)

Railhead Club, 135
Ramsay-Hill, Cyril, 189–90, 196,
    199, 201, 204–5
    divorces Molly, 212–13
    horsewhipping of Joss Hay, 13,
        207–8, 209
    Kenyan home, *see* Oserian
Ramsay-Hill, Mary "Molly," *later*
    Countess of Erroll (née
    Maude), 190, 196, 198

Ramsay-Hill, Mary (*continued*)
  affair with Joss Hay, 189, 195,
      199, 201, 203, 204–6,
      212–13
    horsewhipping of Joss by Cyril
        Ramsay-Hill, 13, 207–8,
        209
  appearance of, 191
  death of, 251–2, 266
  finances of, 191
  marriages
    first marriage, 190–1
    second marriage to Cyril
        Ramsay-Hill, 191
    third marriage to Joss Hay,
        215, 251–2, 266
Ramsden, Sir John "Chops," 167,
    196, 218
Reading, Lord, 129
Rift Valley, 135, 138, 218, 300
Rigden, Mrs., 97, 98
Ritz, London, 38, 58, 94, 95–6,
    125, 126
Ritz, Paris, 71, 73–4, 75–6, 77,
    84–5, 90
Roedean boarding school, 246
Roosevelt, Ethel, 42
Roosevelt, Franklin, 142
Roosevelt, Kermit, 42
Roosevelt, Theodore, 142
Rowden, Miss (governess), 35
Royal Geographic Society, 253
Royal Military College at
    Sandhurst, 46
Ryan, Nin, 249

Sackville, Lady Avice "Avie"
    (sister), 57, 58, *100, 101,*
    221, 231, 244, 301
  affairs, 162

birth of, 21, 27
childhood, *34, 35*
described, 82
Dinan raised by, 257, 270, 286
friendship with Barbie, 82–4,
    88–9, 257, 301
marriage to Frank Spicer, 216,
    257
marriage to Stewart Menzies,
    115, 120, 121, 125–7, 163
divorce, 216
during World War I, 82–4,
    95–8, 99–106, 110,
    111–12
Sackville, Diana, Countess De La
    Warr (wife of Herbrand
    "Buck," 9th Earl), 162,
    203, 244
cares for Idina's daughter at
    Fisher's Gate, 203–4, 225–6
Idina's daughter named after, 184
Sackville, Gilbert, 8th Earl De La
    Warr (father), 27, 27
abandons his family, 21, 27
divorce, 27–8, 30–1, 130
family ancestry, 21–2, 26–7
marriage to Muriel, 21–2
second and third marriages, 31
Sackville, Gilbert, 7th Earl De La
    Warr (grandfather), 26, 52,
    53
Sackville, Herbrand "Buck," 9th
    Earl De La Warr (brother),
    13, 57, 62, 104, 126, 162,
    168, 203, 216, 221, 244,
    289, 291, 292, 293, 300
birth of, 27
burial of Idina, 293
cares for Dinan at Fisher's Gate,
    13, 225–6, 257–8

childhood, *34, 35*
Fisher's Gate, *see* Fisher's Gate
paternity of, 32
political career, 257
  as member of Parliament,
    209–10
  as minister in MacDonald's
    government, 32, 164
  reuniting of Idina and Dinan,
    289
  Theosophy and, 33–4
Sackville, Lady Idina
  appearance of, 7, 9, 19, 36–7,
    161, 214, 256, 289
  birth of, 26–7
  Clouds (Kenyan farm), *see* Clouds
    (Kenyan farm)
  death of, 15, 293–4, 300
  as debutante, 38, 39–40,
    42, 43
  dress and sense of style, 7, 9–11,
    13, 36, 39, 153, 226
  Daily Express story and
    lawsuit, 213
  education of, 36
  finances, personal, 122, 141,
    159, 199, 287
    allowance from her brother,
      159, 182
    Brassey family trust, 216
    Wall Street crash of 1929 and,
      214
    wedding gift from Muriel,
      120, 151, 159, 216
  first name (Myra), 26–7
  health problems
    after death of her sons, 283–4,
      285–6
    cancer of the womb, 287, 291,
      292

    during marriage to Euan, 90,
      91–5, 97, 99
  Lion Island farm in Kenya, *see*
    Lion Island (Sackville-Hay
    farm)
  marriages, 11–12
    chart, viii
    first marriage, *see* Wallace-
      Sackville marriage (first
      marriage)
    second marriage, *see* Gordon-
      Sackville marriage (second
      marriage)
    third marriage, *see* Hay-
      Sackville marriage (third
      marriage)
    fourth marriage, *see*
      Haldeman-Sackville
      marriage (fourth marriage)
    fifth marriage, *see* Soltau-
      Sackville marriage (fifth
      marriage)
  as mother to David and Gerard
    "Gee," 261
    abandons sons to obtain
      divorce, 4, 18, 122–3
    David's death, 281–2, 285
    Gerard's death, 277–9
    prior to divorce from Euan,
      68, 69, 104–5, 122–3
    reunited with David, 3–4,
      227, 228, 238–44, 256–7
    reunited with Gerard, 274–6
    visits David in Greece, 256–7
  as mother to Dinan, 183–84,
    201, 213, 224, 224–5, 258,
    286–92, 300
    see also Hay, Diana Denyse
      "Dinan," 23rd Countess of
      Erroll (daughter)

Sackville, Lady Idina (*continued*)
  nudity and, 148, 151
  parents' divorce, impact of, 28,
    36, 37, 45, 65
  pearl ring given to her by Euan,
    19, 86, 146, 153, 154
  photographs and portraits of, *ii*,
    9, *10*, 11, *34, 35,* 49, 64–5,
    149, 160, 177, 183, 197,
    217, 218, 222, 224, 261,
    288, 289, 290, 301
  pregnancies, 52, 60, 64, 178–9,
    182–3
  reading habits, 175–6
  safaris, 140, 145–6, 185–6, 250
  sex appeal, 40
  sexuality and affairs, 51–2, 65,
    141
    between husbands, 151, 153,
      209–12, 250–1, 259
    see also under individual
      marriages
  Slains home in Kenya, *see* Slains
  as stepmother to Ann and Tom,
    see Soltau, Ann; Soltau,
    Tom
Sackville, Lady Kitty (niece), *see*
  Giles, Lady Kitty (née
  Sackville)
Sackville, Lady Margaret (aunt), 32
Sackville, Lady Muriel, Countess
  De La Warr (née Brassey)
  (mother), 125, 231
  childhood of, 24–6, 25
  death of, 215
  divorces Gilbert, 27–8, 30–1,
    130
  family wealth, 22
  marriage of, 21
  motoring and, 52

political and social causes, 31–2,
  39, 40, 41, 122, 151, 164,
  192, 215, 250
Theosophy and, 33–5, 122,
  192
will of, 216
during World War I, 70,
  71, 77
Sackville, Lady, Victoria (cousin),
  82, 96
Sackville-West, Vita (cousin), 12,
  289, 294
Ste. Allegonde, Madame, 77
St. John's Wood, 95
Saint-Lazare Prison, 203
St. Martin-in-the-Fields, 125–6
St. Maur, Gemma, 225
St. Patrick's golf club, 107
Salvation Army, 246
Samson (lion cub), 197–8
Satan (pet dog), 9, 40, 65
Savehay Farm, 209
Savoy, London, 94, 147, 162
Scott, Alice, 251
Scott, Lady Eileen, 180–1
Scott, Lord Francis, 181
Sea Eagle, The, 283, 285
Shapley, Walter, 205
Sharp, Arnold, 274, 283
Shepheard's Hotel, Cairo, 270
Sitwell, Edith, 210, 211, 212
Sitwell, Georgia, 210
Sitwell, Osbert, 210
Sitwell, Sacheverell, 210
Slains, *169, 201, 208*
  building of, 165–6
  farm accounts, 187
  foreclosed on, by Idina's bankers,
    213
  furnishing of, 167

guests and house parties at,
173–8, 174, 182–3, 186,
192, 194–6
Idina's attire at, disapproval of,
180–1
Marie, housekeeper at, 169, 175
sexual games and partner
swapping at, 8, 176–8,
179, 183
reaction of middle-class settler
farmers to, 179–80, 196
treatment of servants at,
181–2
see also Lion Island (Sackville-
Hay farm)
Slains Castle, 159, 166
Sleath, Nanny, 231–2, 233, 237
Soames, Jack, 196
Soltau, Ann, 260–6, 268–9, 274,
279, 283, 284, 287
Soltau, Grace (née Sleddon), 287
Soltau, Lady Idina, see Sackville,
Lady Idina
Soltau, Tom, 260–6, 268–9, 274,
279, 283, 284, 287
Soltau, Vincent "Lynx" (fifth
husband), 13, 279, 285,
287
during World War II, 265, 271,
273, 274, 281
Soltau-Sackville marriage (fifth
marriage), 13, 260–2, 261,
265–6, 270
end of, 284
Idina's affairs during, 265–6,
273–4
Spanish flu, 129
Speke, John Hanning, 134
Spender, Stephen, 212
Spicer, Frank, 216, 257, 270

Stein, Gertrude, 158
Stevenson, Robert Louis, 47
"Stormy Weather," 264
strikes of 1911, 38–9, 40
Strutt, Algernon, 96–7
Sturges, Jonathan, 41
Suez Canal, 134
suffragettes, see women's suffrage
Sunbeam (Annie Brassey's yacht),
23–4
Sunday Times (London), 7

Tatler, 162
Tawney, R. H., 236
Theatre Royal, Nairobi, 138
Theosophy, 33–5, 82, 122
"There's a Small Hotel," 264
Tillett, Ben, 38–9
Times (London), 11, 33, 38, 52,
282, 294
Titanic, 41
Titchfield, Lord, 238
Topsy Turvy, 80
Trades Union Congress, 31
Trent, Joan, 221, 223
Trzebinski, Errol, 292
tsetse fly, 134

Uganda Railway (Iron Snake),
134–5
farming along tracks of,
136–7

Valentino, Rudolph, 192
Vanderbilts, 142
Vertical Land—for Horizontal People
(de Janzé), 150, 176–7,
195
Viceroy's Palace, Delhi, 82
Victoria, Queen, 28, 29–30

Victorian attitudes toward
        sex, 33
Voyage in the "Sunbeam," A
        (Brassey), 24–5

Wales, Prince of, 143, 184, 192,
        225
Wallace, Barbie (née Lutyens),
        100, 101, 271, 295–7
    described, 82–3, 99
    education of, 83
    end of Idina's marriage to Euan
        and, 127–8
    honeymoon, 232
    during Idina's marriage to Euan,
        82, 88–9, 94–106, *100,*
        101, 111–12, 113
    Kildonan House and, 144, 232,
        248–9, 274
    Lavington Park and, 274, 291,
        296
    marriage to Euan, 16, 143, *145,*
        231–2
    as "mother" to David Wallace,
        17, 144, 227, 228, 229–32,
        235–6, 237, 243–4,
        245–6, 247–9, 296
    as "mother" to Gerard "Gee"
        Wallace, 17, 144, 227,
        231–2, 257, 296
    as mother to Johnny, Peter, and
        Billy (children with Euan),
        234, 236, 296
    second marriage, 296
Wallace, Billy (son of Euan and
        Barbie), 16, 17, 234, 296
Wallace, (David) Euan (first
        husband), 20, *48, 100, 101*
    appearance of, 17, 46
    death of, 16, 269

diaries of, 20, 66–7, 68, 73, 74,
        81, 84, 86, 107, 108, 145,
        234–5
education of, 46
as father to David and Gerard
        "Gee," 231, 234, 235,
        237–8, 247
    while married to Idina, 61, 84,
        104–5, 106, 109, 122, 126,
        128, 129
health problems, 128–9
Life Guards (King's Royal
        Cavalry) and service in
        World War I, 46, 48, 50,
        60, 61–4, 67, 89–90, 91,
        106, 110, 113–5
marriage to Barbie Lutyens, 16,
        143, *145,* 231–2
marriage to Idina, *see* Wallace-
        Sackville marriage (first
        marriage)
political career, 228, 234, 235,
        257
Scottish estates, 53, 68–9
wealth of, 46–7
    Great Depression and, 234–5
year abroad after divorce from
        Idina, 142–3
Wallace, David John (son), 16, 17,
        236, 237
    abandoned by Idina, 4, 18,
        122–3
    appearance of, 4, 239–40, 256
    arrest at Oxford, 255–6
    Barbie as mother to, 17, 144,
        227, 228, 229–32, 235–6,
        237, 243–4, 245–6,
        247–9, 296
    birth of, 61
    childhood of, 18, *18,* 68, 69, *69,*

84, 89, 93, 94, 104–5, 109, 122, 126, *128,* 129, 231
death of, 16, 17, 281–3, 296
education of, 228, 233, 234, 235–6
    fellowship in Greece, 256, 258
    graduation from Oxford, 256
Gerard's death and, 280–1
Greek culture, passion for, 249, 254, 256–7
marriage of, 259–60, *260*
personality of, 227
political beliefs, 228, 230, 234, 235, 255–6
priesthood, considers entering, 228, 237, 241–2, 244, 245
reunited with Idina
    in 1934, 3–4, 227, 228, 238–44
    trip to Greece, 256–7
scabies sores, 247–9
sister Dinan and, 258
as tramp, 246–7
during World War II, 16, 271, *273,* 274–5, 280–1, 296
Wallace, Davina, *see* Howell, (Cary) Davina (née Wallace) (author's mother, Idina's granddaughter)
Wallace, Elizabeth (*formerly* Koch de Gooreynd) (daughter-in-law), 274–5, *280,* 285
Wallace, Gerard Euan "Gee" (son), 16, 17, 235, 247
    abandoned by Idina, 4, 18, *122–3*
    appearance of, 275
    Barbie as mother to, 17, 144, 227, 231–2, 257, 296
    childhood of, 18, *18,* 68, 69, *69,*

84, 89, 93, 94, 104–5, 122, 126, 128, *129,* 231
death of, 16, 277–81, 296
education of, 228, 233
marriage of, 274–5, 280
namesake, 62
personality of, 227, 275–6
reunited with Idina, 274–6
visits brother at Oxford, 237
during World War II, 275, 277–81, 296
Wallace, Lady Idina, *see* Sackville, Lady Idina
Wallace, Jean (sister-in-law, first marriage), 231
Wallace, Joan Prudence "Pru" (née Magor) (daughter-in-law), 271–2, 274, 275, *278,* 300
    as actress, 259
    Barbie Wallace and, 271, 274, 285–6
    husband David's death and, 282–3
    letters exchanged with Idina after David's death, 282–3, 284–5
    second marriage, 286
Wallace, John "Jack" (father of Euan), 47–8, 92
Wallace, Johnny (son of Euan and Barbie), 16, 17, 234, 237, 296
Wallace, Laura (granddaughter), *see* Morland, Laura (née Wallace) (granddaughter)
Wallace, Liz, 16
Wallace, Minnie (Euan's mother, Idina's mother-in-law, first marriage), 92–3, 112, 243, 249

Wallace, Peter (son of Euan and
    Barbie), 17, 234, 237, 296
Wallace Cuninghame, Mr., 78
Wallace-Sackville marriage (first
    marriage), 10–11, 50–8,
    279
  differences in approaches to life,
    49–50
  divorce, 15, 120–4, 125, 126–7,
    129–30, 142
  engagement, 45–6, 48
  during Euan's leaves from the
    Cavalry, 70–1, 74–9,
    81–90
  honeymoon, 51–2
  Kildonan House, planning of,
    53–7, 56, 58, 64, 65
  London home, see Connaught
    Place
  marriage contract, 50, 121
  motoring and, 52, 88–9
  other lovers and relationships
    and, 64, 73, 82, 83–4,
    88–9, 95–106, 110,
    116–21
  wedding, 50, 51
  during World War I, 69–119
Wanjohi Farm
  life of the de Janzés at, 194–5
  purchased by the de Janzés, 188
Ward, Lady Morvyth "Dickie,"
    98–106, 100, 101,
    111–12, 113–14, 125,
    126, 127
Washington Post, 43, 129
Watteau, Jean-Antoine, 190

Waweru (Joss Hay's Kenyan valet),
    189
Webb, Beatrice, 31
Webb, Sidney, 31
Weir, William, 64–5, 69
Whigs, 27
Whistler, Rex, 243
White Mischief (Fox), 7–8
White's, gentlemen's club, 127
William Baird & Co., 47, 64
Williams and James (attorneys),
    124
William the Conqueror, 21
Wilson, Edith, 142
Witley Court, 99, 106, 110, 111
Wodehouse, P. G., 142
Woman of Affairs, A, 14
women's suffrage, 24, 26, 31, 37,
    40, 43–4, 151
Wood, Rosa, 130
Wooster (valet), 232
World War I, 59–64, 68–70,
    79–82, 113–14
  end of, 114, 120
  First Battle of Ypres, 63
  rationing during, 92
  sexual mores during, 80–1, 99,
    113
  start of, 58, 59–61
  trench warfare, 67, 79, 89
World War II, 16, 262–3, 270–1,
    275, 296
  Greece during, 274, 279–81,
    285

Ziegfeld Midnight Frolic, 142

PARK LANE

When eighteen-year-old Grace Campbell arrives in London in 1914, she's unable to fulfill her family's ambitions and find a position as an office secretary. Lying to her parents and her brother, Michael, she takes a job as a housemaid at Number Thirty-Five Park Lane, where she is quickly caught up in lives of its inhabitants—in particular, those of its privileged son, Edward, and daughter, Beatrice, who is recovering from a failed relationship that would have taken her away from an increasingly stifling life. Desperate to find a new purpose, Beatrice joins a group of radical suffragettes and strikes up an intriguing romance with an impassioned young lawyer. Unbeknownst to each of the young women, the choices they make amid the rapidly changing world of World War I will connect their chances at future happiness in dramatic and inevitable ways.

Fiction

Meet with Interesting People
Enjoy Stimulating Conversation
Discover Wonderful Books